DESIGN AS POLITICS

DESIGN AS POLITICS

Tony Fry

Oxford • New York

English edition
First published in 2011 by
Berg
Editorial offices:
First Floor, Angel Court, 81 St Clements Street, Oxford OX4 1AW, UK
175 Fifth Avenue, New York, NY 10010, USA

Berg is the imprint of Oxford International Publishers Ltd.

Library of Congress Cataloging-in-Publication Data

Fry, Tony.
    Design as politics / Tony Fry. — English ed.
       p. cm.
    Includes bibliographical references and index.
    ISBN 978-1-84788-567-8 (pbk.) — ISBN 978-1-84788-568-5 (cloth)
 1. Design—Political aspects. 2. Sustainability. I. Title.
    NK1520.F78 2010
    745.2—dc22

                                                        2010036952

British Library Cataloguing-in-Publication Data

A catalogue record for this book is available from the British Library.

ISBN 978 1 84788 568 5 (Cloth)
        978 1 84788 567 8 (Paper)

Typeset by JS Typesetting Ltd, Porthcawl, Mid Glamorgan
Printed in the UK by the MPG Books Group

www.bergpublishers.com

Contents

Preface   vii

Introduction   1

Part I Design, Politics and Defuturing
1   Facing Finitude   21
2   Inadequate Solutions of Now   47
3   Redirection, Design and Things   75

Part II Re-framing the Political
4   The Political, Sovereignty and Design   101
5   In the Shadow of Carl Schmitt's Politics   115
6   Pluralism Is a Political Problem   143
7   Remaking Sovereignty   169

Part III Design Futuring as Making Time
8   *Neu Bildung* for a New World   187
9   On Freedom by Design   209
10   Design Beyond the Limits   237

Notes   253
Select Bibliography   283
Index   289

Preface

Whatever we write is always, unavoidably, from a perspective. This book comes from a Western sensibility that fully acknowledges the significance of its other but can never speak as or for it. Likewise, its engagement with design and the political comes from a longstanding attachment to thinking about and acting within both domains. Out of the sediment of this history the book offers original thinking. Such a claim begs being tempered by a remark of Martin Heidegger's: 'the more original the thinking, the richer will be what is unthought in it. The unthought is the greatest gift that thinking can bestow.'[1] By implication, the reader is faced with the challenge of judging what is said and discovering what is not.

Unapologetically, this is predominantly a work of theory but with an overriding practical aim: to bring into presence thinking that can be acted upon in situated contexts. So while there are examples of action they are merely illustrative of this intent.

There is a simple and vital question that needs to be posed immediately: in the face of the unsustainable state of the world, what can political activists and designers (including myriad other professionals who, knowingly or unknowingly, make design decisions) do? In the shadow of this question, and prior to answering it, there are a few things that need to be understood.

We all confront an unavoidable choice: we either support the status quo (a choice so often made unknowingly) or we choose a path of change (which few do). Change only occurs in two ways: by accident or by prefigured intent (which is *de facto* design). To choose change means knowing how to identify, create and become an agent of change who is able to mobilize design to this end. For non-designers and designers, the potential (rather than the actual) capability of design as an instrument of change needs to be grasped. Specifically, to design against the unsustainable requires the nature of design itself to be transformed. It needs to become (as was argued in my *Design Futuring*) a redirective practice.

Now to answer the question. What all agents of change need to do is to learn how to move design out of its economic function and into a political frame. But for this to be possible the current nature of that frame needs to be understood. For people outside design practice, the potential of design transformed requires exposure, as does the current designing nature of the political. So contextualized, the entire project of the book can be summed up as the transformation of design and of politics combining, for all agents of change, to become the means by which the moment and process of Sustainment (the overcoming of the unsustainable) is attained. For this to be realized design, designing and politics need to be thought about in a new way. This book is about such thinking, and it's not easy. How could it be when the challenge is so enormous?

Certainly, the tone and content is very different from 'good news' sustainability narratives that try to give the impression that critique is negative and disabling and that the real task is to pragmatically get stuck into 'positive' projects. Of course positive projects are needed but they have to be based on a well-developed grasp of the nature of the unsustainable and of a significant scale to make a real difference. This implies confronting the problem, no matter how daunting, while rejecting all gestural activity that plays into the hands of 'green-washers'. Clearly how problems are brought to light is absolutely critical. They cannot simply be taken as given: to be solved they have to be understood and engaged at a level of foundational causality. So much of what is taken to be 'the problem' (not least in the environmental area) is actually symptomatic of something far more deeply entrenched. This is not acknowledged. So, while environmental impacts have to be dealt with, 'the problem' will not be solved unless their economic and cultural causes are confronted and resolved.

A foundational engagement with causes so often requires one to learn to think and act in another way, and therefore to participate in a process of unlearning. This is hard to do – attachments to habitual ways of thinking are especially difficult to break. More than this, that which is familiar and taken-for-granted fades into the background. We simply do not see, feel or think about what has become embedded in our mode of being. For instance, we make judgements about so many things every day, and while we are aware of those that are obvious, mostly we do not even notice.

Yet many of the actions that follow from these judgements have significant consequence for our health, the wellbeing of others, the material environment and so on. Likewise, within the frame of reference of Sustainment, which was never present in our upbringing – or if it was, only in a very underdeveloped way – what we fail to realize is that we were educated in error. To grasp this is to face the challenge of confronting what we have learned, which means finding ways to drag it out of the familiar, unlearning it and learning anew.

It is not hard to comprehend how the different worlds within the world we human beings make arrive via artifice as physical constructs. What is harder to recognize and work with is the reality of our world-making as culturally directed. Essentially, we see and make a world through the prism of our culture, but mostly it exists as an unconsidered condition of normality. Here, then, is another dimension of the predominantly taken-for-granted, but in this case our inner experience and our external world of meaning fuse. There is simply no clear dividing line between the culture we dwell in and the dwelling of the culture within us.

The implication in relation to Sustainment is obvious. Foundationally and indivisibly, we are simultaneously 'bare life,' inculcated knowing beings and 'beings-in-culture'. For a culture of sustainment to become possible both our culture and ourselves require to change via directed cultural transformation (culture changes all the time, but not in any specifically directed manner).

The only way that the nature of culture is directionally changed toward a specific direction is by some form of cultural politics.

To emphasize: one can say that in making 'one's self', that self is also being made in the material and cultural environment we call world (the *de facto* world within the world). In so doing, 'we' are created in/as 'a world' of difference. However, this formation is contradicted by our collective classification as 'humanity'.

'Humanity' is a tricky term. It is invoked continuously, yet the bonds of commonality it trades on are weak. Yes, we all need the essentials of 'bare life' but from this point on difference proliferates (language, social mores, ways of life, diet and so on). At the same time, the history of modernity and globalization negate this difference. Sadly, the dominant commonality has become the unsustainable (including the attempt to create monocultures in all domains).

Sustainment and sustain-able action cuts into, and across, this 'developmental' pattern. As a project, its foundation is 'commonality in difference' wherein what is named as 'humanity' is broken away from humanism as a specific cultural locus. Commonality here is not claimed as a pre-existing condition but as a futural necessity.

'We' simply cannot continue to be and be as we are: we are literally taking 'our' future away. What this means is that a commonality of human being has to be created rather than appealed to tokenistically (and often ethnocentrically).

A needed politics of commonality is not present in currently available institutional politics anywhere. If commonality in difference is as vital as it will be shown to be, it follows that this politics has to be created as a new form of the political. Not only can such a creation only arrive by design, but design has to be elemental to it. Unambiguously, this means that the political as it is currently, has to be critically reviewed and thereafter remade. As we shall see, this will imply rethinking political subjectivity, reconsidering the locus of the political outside the sphere of institutionalized politics, fundamentally reconfiguring sovereignty, understanding the significance of cultural difference, identifying a political ideology beyond democracy. Rather than design being marginal to these weighty considerations, it will weave its way through them as a vital political agent.

This book has been a long time in coming. Some of its content pre-dated the two books before it – *A New Design Philosophy: An Introduction to Defuturing* (1999) and *Design Futuring: Sustainability, Ethics and New Practice* (2009). Unsurprisingly, both of these books signalled its project. For many readers, what it says, and how it says it, will be challenging. It will take many into uncharted territory. There is complexity to navigate, but it is the nature and scale of the challenge put forward that will most disrupt comfort zones. To get all that the book offers will take work, but from what I have been told by the few colleagues who have read it, effort is rewarded. It is explicitly written for those people who want things to be other than they are – people who want a future with a future worth having. It is also important to grasp that like no other critical moment before, there are going to be unprecedented opportunities in coming decades as the world of human habitation is transformed. This is the opportunity of crisis. However, it is always ambiguous. Loss and breakdown will certainly occur and the new will come at a price, but what is certain is that design transformed will have a central role to play in the creation of any futuring process.

Transformation is not, of course, confined to design as elevated to the overtly political and made sovereign. It equally embraces a break with the Enlightenment tradition and the opening into a new one – the Sustainment. As will be seen, what this names is not an extension of the modern world, or an utopian return to a fictionalized idyllic past, but a project that confronts the destruction of productivism, the unsustainability of 'our' anthropocentric 'nature' and the need to deal with what it has brought into being. Sustainment affirms that now, to have time, to have a future, it has to be made, not assumed as given.

In some ways, it is hard to know whose support should be acknowledged in bringing this book into being. It could be said partly to be the product of many conversations with friends, colleagues and students over the years. In this respect, two people stand out, Abby Lopes, who gave valued encouragement and useful feedback on the final draft and my partner Anne-Marie Willis – my greatest critic, my most supportive editor and my best friend. I would like to thank my reviewers Lisa Norton, Clive Dilnot and Duncan Fairfax for incisive comments and also give special thanks to Tristan Palmer at Berg.

Introduction

Martin Heidegger, as one of the most influential philosophers of the twentieth century, was an insightful, extremely scholarly and somewhat idiosyncratic reader of Friedrich Nietzsche. He drew out and pulled together observations that exposed the extraordinary reach of the nature of Nietzsche's prophetic vision.

As Nietzsche well understood, human beings have always had a propensity toward destruction. The more we made, the more we destroyed. In making our world within the world we failed to understand what of the former was being destroyed. Once we reached sufficient numbers and gained sufficient technological muscle, destruction became devastation – which we render in both horrific material and aestheticized forms. Prosaically, technocratically, this situation may now be called structural unsustainability.

Nietzsche saw this moment coming and named it in a very particular way around 1883–5 when he was writing *Thus Spoke Zarathustra*. He wrote of the last man, the overman, the superman and of the wasteland growing. He issued the warning: 'woe to him who harbours wastelands within.' The wastelands are of course the product of devastation.

What he meant by 'the last man' was a subjective and anthropocentric being fated unless able to change. In facing this finitudinal circumstance 'we' collectively either rise above ourselves or fall. Nietzsche names what we need to become: 'superman'. It's become an unfortunate term, partly because of its crude and misplaced appropriation by the Nazis in Germany in the 1920s, and partly because of its science fiction connotations. I am going to use Heidegger's reading of the term to radically recast what it usually means. Heidegger said:

> The 'superman' does not simply carry the accustomed drives and strivings of the customary type of man beyond all measure and bounds. Superman is a qualitatively, not quantitatively, different form of existing man. The thing that the superman discards is precisely our boundless, purely quantitative non-stop progress. The superman is poorer, simpler, tenderer and tougher, quieter and more self-sacrificing and slow of decision and more economical of speech.[1]

From a Western culture of excess, from the wasteland, if we want a future, we unreservedly need to become supermen and superwomen.

It could well be that in the next few decades the way that human beings occupy the planet will radically change. It is becoming clear that humanity is on the edge of its third epoch of worldly occupation – which here we will call the age of unsettlement. The first age, which extended for 100,000 years or more, was a nomadic age of non-settlement. The second, which commenced around 12,000 years ago and delivered the urban reality with which we are familiar, was the age of settlement. Now 'security of place' looks to be increasingly challenged by the socio-environmental impacts of climate change. Potentially hundreds of millions of people will be displaced and so unsettled. How place, economy, the present and future are all perceived will change. Unsettlement will produce a change in human psychology itself.

As with massive changes of the past, responses to this situation will be from necessity rather than by choice. The combination of the still deepening propensity toward structural unsustainability and still growing global population will certainly overwhelm current feeble efforts to reduce the environmental impacts of human actions. While the form of this future is still unclear, some things are discernable. Unsettlement will give rise to a new mode of dwelling, which itself will require a huge design effort (as the alternative to chaos), combined with an enormous transformation of the political. It is with this prospect in mind that the proposition of 'design as politics' will be explored.

Many of problems before us are not new. Human beings were mistreating the planet long before the Industrial Revolution. But what is new is the scale and the technologically amplified momentum of destruction. The damage to so many ecologies now exceeds their ability to recover. As has been increasingly recognized over the past five decades, the creative impetus of industrial society has turned on itself and become a defuturing force. Current social, political, economic and technological responses are meagre when measured against the growth and speed of this problem of human creation. From loss of biodiversity to the melting of polar ice and the acidification of oceans, symptomatic appearances of defuturing are now well known. Yet their fundamental cause, as it reduces to the anthropocentric mode of being-in-the-world, is still mostly unrecognized.[2] *De facto* 'we' live a 'crisis of crisis' wherein the absolutely critical is not addressed – we are terminal beings so long as we continue to terminate so much that living beings (including our selves) depend upon. Techno-scientific understandings of 'environmental problems' come nowhere near understanding this situation.

We have passed a point whereby much that has been put in process can be reversed – irreparable damage has already been done. Evidence of dramatic changes in the planet's climate in the distant past is beside the point. The fact is that unless we fundamentally change how *en masse* we dwell within ourselves, the worlds within the world we have created, and the world at large, we will have no future worth having. Our commodity-infused dreams, desires and current ways of life have to die for us to live.

Let's be clear from the outset: action focused on design, politics and the political does not imply exclusivity – clearly there are other fields of human conduct that should be viewed as contributors to those transformations so desperately needed – but design-led change is tremendously important, and will become ever more so – as a means to essential change.

Unquestionably, as writers and readers, the challenge to be unfolded is huge. What is to be thought and attempted to be communicated will cross many conceptual boundaries. The task of dragging design away from its current place of belonging and into another domain is difficult, as is breaking down the exclusivity of the discourse of politics. A good deal of what will be presented will be heterodoxical. At the same time, one can claim a rich reward from meeting the challenge posed.

The Argument

The central argument of the book is that democracy is unable to deliver Sustainment (the post-Enlightenment project beyond 'sustainability'). Why this is the case, and the implications of the statement, will direct the book's narrative, as will the need for a shift from institutionalized politics as we know it to action in the realm of the political – the difference between the two will be made clear. Basically five modes of exposition will be woven together: analysis, critique, design-linked proposals, explorations (offered to provoke thought) and case studies.

Supporting the central argument are two propositions. The first is that a future worth having requires a political transformation of existing social and economic life, underpinned by a praxis more capable of enabling, directing and maintaining affirmative change than existing institutions of democracy (for they lack the appropriate *nous* and *techne*). The second is that the needed change cannot arrive via the existing political discourse (as it enfolds political practice, political commentary, political science and political philosophy). The kinds of changes that are so vital require another kind of politics united with a dynamic transformative agency (exposited as design remade). Change cannot and should not be reduced to instrumental actions. Moreover, the political transformation to be elaborated folds into an even larger project: the creation of Sustainment.

As opposed to the idealism that underpinned so much of the Enlightenment, the Sustainment (as project and process) is defined as the counter force to *defuturing* – a product of the world of modernity that the Enlightenment brought into being. Obviously, a task of such a magnitude requires many thinkers, a great deal of rethinking, new thinking and a large amount of focused conversation within and between the fields of politics and design. This book aims to prompt such activities.

Three presumptions underpin the critique of democracy, two of which are very basic. The first is that democracy does not receive enough or sufficiently vigorous criticism. The second is that to criticize democracy is not to suggest that it can be reduced to a simple singularity and that there are not other modes of politics that equally demand critical scrutiny. Presumption three stands on more challenging ground and states that democracy as an operative political system must not be viewed as the most advanced possible form of political practice. Rather it must be exceeded and replaced by a superior form of politics. To gain a measure of this last presumption we need to acknowledge that democratic (liberal) politics does not equate with actual (popular) democratic practice. The question of the character of democratic practice thus needs to be kept open.

Design, the Political and Politics

Human beings have turned the very ground of being into design, the designed, decision and direction – this not least by how 'we' live and act upon our world and the worlds of others. 'We' live in a world where 'everything "is made" and can "be made"'.[3] This means that everything actually or metaphorically, touched by human hands has, by degree, a determinant consequence on the form of the future. Effectively, artifice does not arrive without design and design and artifice combine to render 'the world of our dwelling' political, and thus contestable. In any real sense, as said, politics does not grasp this. In fact institutional politics actually lacks cognisance of the enormous ontological shifts taking place on the very ground of 'human being' via designed hegemonic technology and the world made unsustainable.

The difference between politics and the political will be examined in detail later, but for the moment we need to briefly differentiate the one from the other. Politics is an institutionalized practice exercised by individuals, organizations and states, while the political exists as a wider sphere of activity embedded in the directive structures of a society and in the conduct of humans as 'political animals'. Politics effectively takes place in the sphere of the political wherein the agency of things – material and immaterial – is determined and exercised as they are perceived, and become directly or indirectly influenced, by a political ideology. There has been a general societal perceptual failure to distinguish between the political and politics, in large part because, as Claude Lefort has pointed out, the latter acts to conceal the nature of the former.[4]

Although design is not usually associated with politics, other than via, for instance, image-making, branding and the associated production of promotional materials, it is, in fact, profoundly political. In contrast to politics (as enacted by the political actions of activists, parties, governments and policies) design gives material form and directionality to the ideological embodiment of a particular politics. As the history of architecture and design confirms: cities, hospitals, prisons, offices, factories, homes, parks, public transport, utilities, infrastructure, public information and so on, all arrive with forms lodged in particular sets of ideological value that are predicated on how human beings should be viewed and treated. In this way, design and the designed function politically. As such, design expresses power materially and in ways that shape how people interact and ontologically prefigure their material culture and economy. For example, as we learnt not least from Michel Foucault, the form of a prison designates a specific regime of discipline and punishment that places both its staff and prisoners in a structure of designed compliance.[5] Likewise, but in a very different setting, the form of a family home is indivisible from the particular nature of family life.

Although design totally infuses the material fabric of the world around us, it is almost always rendered invisible by the very thing(s) it brings into being. The existence of 'designer' buildings and products themselves confirm this – they affirm, and by implication, conceal, the anonymity of that which they are not – the vast mass of unattributed designed structures and things.

Usually, the enormous and omnipresent power of the political, as the operative of the force of design, is present only via its silent structuring agency, as opposed to overt signs and statements. Yet there are, of course, times when the political, politics and the designed all meet in very visible ways: a river is proposed to be dammed; a new road is proposed that will require demolishing scores of homes; a city council proposes to add another runway to the local airport; a historic building is levelled by an unscrupulous developer.

In a world of rapid urbanization, increasing population pressures, structural unsustainability, plus the likelihood of increased conflicts over natural resources and a massive explosion of environmental refugees due to climate change, the relation between design and the political will become more apparent and more important. In the face of this situation design has to be made overtly and proactively political. Design has to become a politics. For design to become politicized, it has to directly confront politics.

Unpicking the Common Moment

Environmentalists tell us that our planet is in crisis and has to be saved. In truth, over millions of years, the planet has suffered and survived traumas beyond our imagination. The reality is that human beings have been directly and indirectly responsible for inflicting enormous amount of damage on the planetary environmental systems and it is 'we' who are in deep trouble if the environments that have supported us turn into hostile places. There are but two possible futures: humanity defutures itself into oblivion (and a damaged planet evolves according to the determinants of this condition); or, humanity transforms its mode of planetary dwelling (by being itself transformed or by its numbers being very dramatically, un-naturally culled).

Our concern will be with learning how to become other than we are and how to shift the balance of our actions to sustaining all we depend upon. This means our propensity to destroy enacted predominantly by a will and practice to create must be surmounted.

Currently, for all the research and rhetoric associated with endangered environments and species, human beings are profoundly ignorant about what they actually destroy and with what consequence. It is still the case that as we continue to grow in numbers and worldly destructiveness, we simply do not see our monstrous nature. Consider that in the space of less than 20,000 years, as a species, we moved from being around forty or fifty million nomads living by hunting and gathering, to six-and-a-half billion technologically hyper-extended, super-consuming beings.

As suggested, to present such a bleak view is not to assume humanity is doomed; rather it asserts that: to have a future there has to be a critical mass of people willing to fully face what 'we' are and the problems we humans continually create; and, second, that informed redirective action has to be taken to alter 'how and what we are' and 'what we do'. Clearly there is a significant difference between the collective 'we' designated as humanity and the collective 'we' of a critical mass of redirective actors who, as we shall see later, have to be aware of the pitfalls of acting and being tagged as another 'revolutionary vanguard'.

Democracy: First Pass

Democracy (in its difference) has de-legitimized the voice of 'the common good' and abandoned the development of conditions able to create a social ethos. Moreover, notions of subjects coming into being in a culture of collective concern for the collective good have been devalued as socialism was cast into the dustbin of history. What the implosion of 'socialist states' actually evidenced was the failure of a politics to realize a political idea rather than the failure of the idea itself. Yet to say that the future of humanity depends upon recognizing and engaging the collective concerns and the collective good is no invitation to repeat political errors of the past – which is to say these imperatives have to become elemental to a new, rather than being attempted to be bolted back onto an old, politics.

The media markets politics as a commodity and politicians as salespeople. In this setting, democracy in the developed 'democratic world' has degenerated into televisualized 'consumer democracy'. This directly connects to the notion of 'consumer sovereignty' – politics dominated by a reaction to 'consumer demands'. Democracy marketed as a commodity is continually turning in a vicious wheel of political fortune powered by the televisual. As C.B. Macpherson argued several decades ago, consumer sovereignty is one of the distinctive features of capitalist democracy.[6] To be made media-digestible and electorally saleable, issues arrive before an electorate stripped down to 'the simple' and, whenever possible, in forms that appeal to base interests (like economic self-interest, nationalism and discernable, if sensationalized, fears). As a result, what is voted upon is abstracted from what actually requires to be decided, especially in the long term. It does not enable informed choices to be made about major, critical, futuring issues. Instead, hollow gestures abound.

There is, of course, also globalization's underside wherein cultural ignorance or violence, or both, are continually exposed (or even created) to underpin the deployment (or imposition) of democracy as 'the desired' political ideology of a globalizing 'free' world order and its individuated subjects. Although not blatantly asserted as such, pressures are applied to adopt the institutionalized secular politics of democracy, not just to establish the economic order of globalization but also to displace theological and mythological identities that constitute other modes of human being. Democracy employed toward these ends is an instrument of naked and age-old imperialism. So while globalization is a market pragmatic to attain what capitalism always strives for (the highest returns at the lowest costs from the largest possible market) it is also something more.

From the perspectives just outlined, globalization and its politics of democratic universalism are at best divisive and at worst imposed progenitors of violence.[7] The way in which Muslim societies have been viewed and engaged is one example of its character.[8]

Undemocratic Democracy

Fundamentalism is of course not merely an 'external' problem. Neoconservative Christian fundamentalism taps into a longstanding strain in democratic politics, named by Karl Löwith as the 'the politicising of life' (in recent years, as we shall see, this has been named as biopolitics).

Here is a politics in which political difference is neutralized and governments become administrators of public, and increasingly, private, spheres of life. As such, governments act as the defining agent of which life has, or does not have, a value. Subtending this politics is an authoritarianism masked in the garb of a representative political process. It takes place in the name of, for instance, national security, national interests or public health. Increasingly, and post the 'war on terror', 'democratic' regimes assume sovereign power and act without the constraint of public accountability. The most overt example in recent years is the conduct of the US at its Guantanamo Bay detention centre in Cuba. Notoriously, this place was created to function outside the law by the exercise of a 'state of exception' by authoritarian executive power.

It is not just that holding hundreds of suspected terrorists in this detention centre for years on end without trial has been a travesty of justice, including a contravention of *habeas corpus*, but also that this process deliberately and symbolically diminished the humanity of detainees – reduced to what Giorgio Agamben calls a condition of 'bare life'. Although the physical abuse of these people received massive media attention, it was the CIA's model of psychological torture that has perhaps most damaged the image of the US. For instance, letters to loved ones and friends were censored, not simply for sensitive information or political content, but to rid them of any signs of affection – so that emotional isolation would be total.

The population at large is not exempt from the externalization of this abuse of power. Under the authority of 'the state of exception' every citizen is *de facto* a potential security risk; thus not only is a national surveillance system established to focus on 'high risk' racial and political groups, but also laws are created to allow people to be taken into custody, detained and interrogated without charge. The US Patriot Act of 2001 became the model for this practice – adopted, with variations, by a number of other states, including Australia. While this kind of legislation garners passing media attention, it quickly folds into the background of everyday life in democratic societies.

In the age of the 'National Security State', everyone is a suspect. Surveillance becomes a flexible and pervasive practice – terrorism, violent crime, drug dealing and white-collar crimes are now no longer neatly divided domains. State paranoia begets paranoia. What such a development evidences is that the types of actions that characterized infamous hard-edged totalitarian states are now being accommodated within the soft totalitarianism practices within many Western democracies. The distinction between 'liberal' democracy and repressive regimes is not nearly as clear-cut as it is still often thought to be.

Now to Design

Design is both integrated into the narrative and specifically addressed at the end of most chapters. The actual political forms that design can take have been detailed at length in a companion publication – *Design Futuring*.[9] This book extends that book's project by presenting an approach to the redesign of politics and elevating 'the political' by giving recognition to design as a particular political form. Such a focus does not imply exclusivity – clearly there are other fields that could and should be viewed in this way. Moreover, as indicated already, this text aims to open up a field of thought and action needing to be developed and occupied by many thinkers from a total commitment to advancing the intellectual means of extending 'redirective practices' toward Sustainment. It's a risky business. But without a proliferation of path-finders willing to expose their work to critique and for others to take it further, all will be lost.

While design is a marginal figure on the agenda of institutional politics, its actual directive force on ourselves and on the world around us makes it inherently and profoundly political. To recognize this, as well as design's implication in unsustainability (which few in the 'design world' do, let alone the wider community), is to grasp the necessity and scale of the task before us: making design a politics. In essence, this means positioning design in relation to the political and then situationally developing it as a particular political practice in its own right. This requires telling a story that begins with how design is framed politically within the coming age of unsettlement.

Content Outline

The book is organized into four parts. Part One, 'Design, Politics and Defuturing' consists of three chapters that place design as politics squarely in the face of the defuturing problems to be contended with.

Chapter One – 'Facing Finitude' – deals with living in the midst of structural unsustainability and confronting this situation. It argues that the solution to a problem demands facing it, no matter how daunting – it has to be 'looked in the eye' without turning away. Against this backdrop, the chapter will confront democracy mapped across: (1) anthropocentrism, the human, selfhood and structural unsustainability as an ontology; (2) the creation of the defuturing processes of design as they deliver the aesthetically packaged defutured ruins of an unsustainable world (design as concealment and design as future-blind); (3) living in a technosphere, as technological beings, with machines of creation and destruction; (4) design, biopolitics and the induction of the human into the waste cycle.

Chapter Two – 'Inadequate Solutions of Now' – argues that current 'solutions' to structural unsustainability are totally inadequate. Following on from the previous chapter, the nature of a plural 'now' is examined in more detail, but with special reference to the universalization of insufficient action in the face of the deep crisis of unsustainability (of which climate change is but one facet). The chapter also examines the two extreme poles from which technology is viewed: faith in its salvational power; and fear of its destructive potential – both of which centre on the use or misuse of design.

Chapter Three – 'Redirection, Design and Things' – presents a picture of what design can actually do. It illustrates a range of design futuring actions that position it with efficacy and as politically strategic. In so doing, the agency of design is inverted – rather than servicing the status quo it is projected with a capability for affirmative change. It does this not via utopian dreams or idealist schemas but via practical action that advances the materialization of futural thought and signals the possibility of another way of seeking and delivering forms of emancipation based on remaking social relations from other times, other cultures and from the creation of 'political things.'

Part Two, 'Re-framing the Political' is formed by four chapters that circle around the relation of problems and solutions.

Chapter Four – 'The Political, Sovereignty and Design' – introduces the need for the design of another political agenda. The approach is historical, opening with a focus on modernity as it rested upon the proposition that governance is underpinned by the sovereign rule of law. The chapter also argues that the defuturing quality of structural unsustainability and the emergence of unsettlement bring the authority and sufficiency of the law as sovereign into question. While not displacing the necessity of law, it is argued that the imperative of 'Sustainment' has to be given transcendent sovereign power. It asks 'how can this change happen in a form of imposition that will not instantly generate conflict?' This question, in significant part, will be turned into a design question.

Chapter Five – 'In the Shadow of Carl Schmitt's Politics' – asserts the necessity of understanding who are one's 'friends and enemies'. It does this by exploring a key idea of the controversial political philosopher and jurist, Carl Schmitt, but in contemporary circumstances. Thereafter it deals with the 'dictatorship of the imperative' – which is where the issue of what is sovereign is delivered at length. Drawing on how design is mobilized in the previous chapter, connections are made to the absolute needs of the present. Against this backdrop, it is argued that a new politics, a politics of design, is vital to stage. By implication this means a showing, an enactment, rather than a theoretical exposition. Such a politics begs to be invitational, relationally connected, collective, and cultural. It comes out of making things otherwise, of redirecting, of telling, of claiming a space of joy and holding what needs to be valued amid the ravages of the defutured and at a time of unsettlement.

Chapter Six – 'Pluralism Is a Political Problem' – directly confronts the extremity of 'the dictatorship of the imperative' (to be understood as the 'rule of Sustainment' that cannot tolerate actions that claim 'the right' to defuture) and the relation between the plural and pluralism. It points out that all design is impositional and directive (it excludes all other than what has been selected to be produced). In this context, the issue becomes 'what is it appropriate to impose to ensure Sustainment'? The answer does not reduce to just one thing; rather the imperative (Sustainment) as a process of making time in a finite world can be advanced in numerous ways. There can be a commonality in difference but this does not imply a pluralism that includes the right to defuture. Clearly the problematic of the relation between democracy and Sustainment now arrives and has to be creatively engaged (part of this demand is for a new political imaginary beyond democracy).

Chapter Seven – 'Remaking Sovereignty' – considers how the rule of Sustainment can be created by design. Specifically it asks a series of demanding questions. What does it take to remake sovereignty by design? What is there to remake? How does what is sovereign become sovereign (beyond the creation of a constitution)? In the context of such questioning, sovereignty names the authority and rule of Sustainment – which is to say politics, economics, the nature of cities, industries, education, ways of life and much more all serve Sustainment before all else. This change can only occur by design. Conceptually, the chapter deals with these very difficult questions by again turning to that arch critic of liberalism and democracy, Carl Schmitt. The challenge here will be to think through and beyond Schmitt rather than with him, and then towards a form, and mode of representation, that can appear credible.

Part 3, 'Design Futuring as Making Time' brings thinking to futural action and, in so doing, reveals the potential of design when taken beyond its existing forms, framings and applications.

Chapter Eight – '*Neu Bildung* for a New World' – looks at design in the context of making 'new worlds, subjects, and ways of learning'. In doing this, it recognizes that worlds and selves are two creations that make each other, not least through formal and informal processes of education. Yet the instrumental mission of education, in the production of the modern subject as modern world-maker, increasingly looks like an induction into error. Unsustainability, and the forms of defuturing that have propelled it, have been created, in large part, by enacting what has been learned. The chapter argues that the remaking of education is no mere issue of 'content' but rather the creation of a culture of re-learning (a *Neu Bildung*). Central to this task is the placement of redirective design and Sustainment as culturally foundational. *'Neu Bildung'* thereby becomes the agency of a futural memory that directs the made and the maker. Redirective design is the anchor of this exercise – bonding 'now' to 'then' as a progression of relationally linked actions.

Chapter Nine – 'On Freedom by Design' – deals with the hardest question of all: the question of freedom. It moves from modernity's assertion of freedom under the law to the future that demands freedom secured by Sustainment. The imposition by design of unfreedom, of limitation required by Sustainment, is the only possibility of freedom available to us. To grasp this apparent contradiction, a series of established positions will be critically engaged: liberalism; democracy and the free subject; the relation between nature, rights and violence; and questions of the universal and the individual. Thereafter the design question to be posed and resolved is 'how, by design, can losses be overwhelmed by materialized gains?'

Chapter Ten – 'Design Beyond the Limits' – takes design practices beyond their existing limits. It acknowledges that Sustainment demands the impossible, yet unless this demand is met there is no future (for us). Under the direction of a politics, the only means available are thinking, design and action. Reiterating – democracy cannot be taken as the end point of political development; myopic anthropocentrism cannot be the high point of human being; the disengagement of capital from the fundamental processes of exchange upon which life depends, together with the idea of continual growth, cannot be taken as the basis of an enduring economy. There is everything to design, but not merely by the design of more things.

In all, the book sets out to show: how design can become a more powerful, political and affirmative agent of change; what it is that is fundamental and so vital to sustain by design; the need to create a new political imaginary and to think beyond democracy. But above all, it makes a powerful case for design as politics. It does so at what is perhaps the most critical moment in the entire history of humanity: a moment where we, as finite beings in a finite world, find ourselves confronting our finitude.

Finitude is no easy idea to grapple with. As limit, it is indivisible from mind as well as from the unknowable limit of matter in time and space. Yet it is more: it embraces our individual being as finite substance of creative limitation not just in terms of space and time but in the realm of being (crudely, 'all that is') itself. In so far as for 'there to be being' there has to be 'non-being' – otherwise being could not be brought out of concealment.[10] Thus while we can use a definition of finitude grounded in space and time, we have to go beyond this limit and acknowledge finitude as that which divides that 'which is not made present' from 'a discernibly making present' – in other words the concealing of being from its unconcealment. In this framing, unsustainability is the concealed negation of being. To reduce unsustainability to the likes of environmental damage is not only to fail to understand its agency but to massively underestimate the danger it poses as it rides the cusp of our being-in-being.

Part I

Design, Politics and Defuturing

Unsustainability is a condition that is reducible to a damaged global environment and its ecologies. It is equally: a notion of economy based on perpetual growth; war as a machine able to deliver the total destruction of human and animal populations; a mode of social being disarticulated from any enduring means to sustain it; a breakdown of that interdependence upon others we call community; and a way of seeing 'need' based entirely upon self-interest. In all respects, sustainability has arrived as a structural condition – and by design – via: technologies and systems that knowingly or unwittingly generate negative environmental impacts; an unrestrained use of natural resources; the deliberate destruction of tradition, ritual, systems of belief and the sacred in order to impose 'the modern'; forms of development that break up the social fabric; and the transformation of culture into a commodity vista of objects and images that project the realization of unrestrained desires as the basis of a meaningful life.

So defined, and in all instances, unsustainability arrives by design, and as such it negates futures, it takes our time as finite beings away. In so far as unsustainability is the most extensive form of destruction of all that human, and many other forms of life, depend upon, it is the most political of all things political. Yet because institutionalized politics is governed by expediency, unsustainability is simply placed in 'the mix': under theorized, under engaged and under prioritized.

The next three chapters knit together to form a counter view. They contain two case studies, but what needs to be understood is that there are no case studies currently available that fully or adequately illustrate the analytical perspective and theory that the book puts forward. Quite simply, the theoretical perspectives are currently ahead of the nascent practices represented by these case studies (which is not the same as saying that there is a clear theory/practice divide).

I

Facing Finitude

To begin with, a series of key concepts will be introduced in order to understand the character of 'now.' When faced with the difficultly of trying to evoke the new, one can invent new terms and languages or bend what already exists. The concepts about to be presented draw on both options because it is contended that the new situation in which humanity finds itself cannot be adequately understood by currently available conceptual language.

Structural unsustainability names a condition of mind and action that materially erodes (un-measurably) planetary finite time, thus it gathers and designates the negation of 'the being of time', which is equally the taking away of our future. It embodies a process that has become elemental to modern economy, culture and politics. This process has been named 'defuturing', and what it produces as 'the defutured'. In our age, structural unsustainability is of such a scale that it marks the opening of a new epoch in human worldly habitation – an epoch of unsettlement, wherein being and being-in-place become perpetually insecure.

Defuturing and the Defutured

Defuturing has a history with a burgeoning narrative of things, structures, industries, processes and ontologies.[1] It brings into question the 'rights of man', ancient and modern, to appropriate planetary resources and to destroy terrestrial, aquatic and atmospheric environments of biological dependence without any futural account. More than this, defuturing has also nurtured desires and conduct that have sanctioned the erasure of cultures of material modesty, fostered global inequity and condoned the use of unchecked mass destructive violence as an expedient politics. In myriad ways, defuturing has legitimized the sacrifice of the future for the wants of those people of the present who are, or aspire to be, affluent.[2]

Over the past two centuries, bonded to the protection and extension of privilege, defuturing has been amplified by industrial culture with its technological instruments of resource appropriation, unchecked production and politico-economic global colonization. These activities have, of course, been dominantly facilitated by the burning of fossil fuel, which has dramatically increased greenhouse gas emissions and accelerated global warming. The climatic consequences are becoming more apparent and more unpredictable.[3] That our designing actions (we being the unknowing populations of excess) are the cause remains largely invisible. Moreover, in relation to global warming, for all the time and money spent on climatic modelling, there is not a single scientist on the face of the planet who knows exactly what will result from the currently unfolding situation, or when. What they do know is that there is a serious situation getting even more serious, and that their warnings are to a great extent being overlooked.

No matter who or where we are, we live in a world in which political regimes uphold economic systems and interests that negate the future. This has neither been planned nor happened by chance. It is the result of incremental designed action and thinking without vision or critical reflection over a long period of time. The most basic failure is a global system of economic exchange that is actually disarticulated from the 'nature' of fundamental exchange.[4] Defuturing is effectively situated within an economy that is disconnected from the very exchange processes that give all that recurs its transformational dynamic – it is disconnected from change that serves the being-of-beings (the order of continuity). While one can claim that historically, this situation arrived unwittingly, the ways in which global economic and political practices are disposed toward defuturing mark it as a visible process of negation. By implication, and by degree, almost every one of the world's political, economic and cultural leaders refuse to confront this situation – such is the power of pragmatism as it occupies the professional political mind.

At best, all that even the most progressive nations do is to trade on the basis of reducing environmental impacts while upholding the existing economic paradigm. Yet market and political mechanisms (like carbon trading or tax, pricing structures and environmental regulations) are just not enough. The degree to which such actions fail to grasp the nature and force of defuturing, and embrace the imperative of Sustainment, begs detailing. There are three fundamentals that Sustainment rests upon:

1. The creation of, and movement to, a new economic paradigm that abandons the notion of continual quantitative growth.
2. The retrofitting of the material world as made so far (the actual scope of this task is huge and currently obscured by the ongoing creation of ever more things, including 'green things' such as buildings and products).
3. Recognition that structural unsustainability is an ontology, which means that causally and essentially the unsustainable has become elemental to existing and extending modernized human being.

From the perspective of the first two fundamentals of Sustainment, many of the problems to be faced cannot be completely solved. From those problems that can be, many will take a long time (climate change is the most obvious example – because the elimination/transformation of the fossil fuel economy will take many decades, plus greenhouse gases have an atmospheric life of over 200 years).[5] Many of the solvable problems can only be solved by insightful and committed action, which again is currently lacking in large measure.

The dynamic of defuturing is just not being registered in political and public consciousness, and its continued globalization as an ontology is still far from being recognized. Without question, positive progress depends upon acknowledging and addressing this situation. Problems cannot be solved unless they are confronted and currently they are not.

The De-bounded Space of Defuturing

It is easy to give the impression that defuturing is undifferentiated – this is reinforced by its proximity to the broad and sweeping notion of unsustainability. But it is always contextually situated and needs to be thought trans-spatially. Its form of appearance in north-eastern Africa is one thing, its appearance in New York, Dubai or Tokyo is another. Likewise, we also have to realize that globalization and technology (especially communication technology) have dramatically shifted the way geopolitical, cultural and economic *and social* space is bounded.

Recent United Nations Development Program reports have indicated that while there have been significant reductions in the numbers of poor in some poorer countries, especially India and China, the actual gap between the rich and the poor is widening in the world at large.[6] The absolute poor are actually becoming more entrenched in their position. And as the 'global financial crisis' that unfolded at the end of the first decade of the century showed, holding onto the new-found wealth by the many who had acquired it was a tenuous exercise.

While the differences between the affluent and underclass of 'the rich world' (graphically illustrated by the social tragedy that unfolded after Hurricane Katrina hit New Orleans in August 2005) begs acknowledgement, the division is starkest in the informal economies of Africa, Asia and Latin

America, in which hundreds of millions of people live on a dollar a day or less. In contrast, there is the commodity-hungry new middle class of 'the newly industrialized nations'. This latter class has been assumed to be the route to becoming, healthier, long-lived, well-housed, better educated and with a falling birth rate. Superficially it is easy to criticize the desires of these aspirant classes, but they are not so much a problem as an expression of its symptoms.

First, the disposition toward defuturing has become inherent in the way of life of middle and aspirant classes. It arrived not as a result of a collective moral flaw but as an inscribed condition of being-in-the-world – it is a reflection and projection of a globalizing world of manufactured desires, with accompanying objects and images, to which people *en masse* have been exposed, albeit with different consequences. Second, and indivisibly, currently there is no other desired future on offer, certainly not one able to deliver social and economic equity as framed by Sustainment.

No matter where in the globalized world the people of this proto-cosmopolitan class live, they can increasingly be found living in the same kind of houses or apartments, shopping in the same kind of supermarkets, eating the same kinds of food, dining in the same kind of restaurants, going to the same movies, listening to the same music, wearing the same kind of clothes, doing the same kind of jobs (often for the same companies), driving the same cars, flying in the same kinds of airlines – and so it goes on.

The appearances of defuturing not only arrive in spaces of excess but equally those of poverty, evident in the everyday life of the world's undernourished, unhealthy, illiterate, slum dwellers. Slum life can be socially vibrant but it also implies lack of physical infrastructure, reticulated potable water, sanitation, drainage and waste collection. In such an environment, life can be a vicious circle wherein people lack the ability to replenish the environments they exploit and deplete.[7]

Against this backdrop, globalization cannot just be claimed as a force of human emancipation able to solve planetary environmental problems while creating conditions for universalized democracy.[8] Globalization is part of the structurally unsustainable and acts to defuture. Neither biophysical environmental impacts nor poverty can be ignored. Both of these negatives converge, and will increasingly do so as climate change bites deeper and multiplies the number of 'environmental refugees'. The current projection is of the order of 200 million by 2050, with the figure of 500–750 million being talked of by the end of the century.[9] Currently the international community struggles to deal with a global refugee population of a mere 26 million.[10]

Just in relation to one problem – sea level changes – research presented at the Copenhagen Climate Congress of March 2009 doubled the projected level of rises. It was claimed that this would eventually displace 600 million of the coastal dwellers of the world.[11] Since this meeting the situation has been reported to have significantly worsened.

These figures have been presented, debated and revised now for over a decade by organizations as diverse as the International Red Cross, the World Bank and the Intergovernmental Panel on Climate Change (IPCC). While there is undoubtedly a great deal of uncertainty about the actual numbers, it is evident that a process is already in train, with serious implications. Planning the evacuation of a number of Pacific Islands is already underway (because their fresh water lens is in imminent danger of saline incursion from rising sea levels), with some people already having left. Likewise, tens of millions of people in Bangladesh are perhaps only a few decades away from being inundated. What has commenced will escalate to the movement of hundreds of millions of people, adding up to an unprecedented redistribution of the human population and a logistics exercise like none ever before. It proffers the prospect of widespread chaos and conflict due to mass crossing of borders by huge numbers of people in search of food. Strategic military planners around the world are already directing attention to such situations, and are influencing the policies of governments – although the rhetoric is still 'muted', with the implications of decisions not being made explicit.[12] For example, one can view the expansion of the naval forces of several nations beyond the conventional notion of threats from prospective hostile nations and as a contingency in the face of massive fleets of refugee ships heading towards a nation's territorial waters. Bluntly, the initial action to be expected will be under the banner of 'border security' and will be aimed at keeping people from arriving on land.

The kind of events outlined form part of a picture of climate-induced demographic change that will not only result in enormous numbers of people being physically unsettled, prompting enormous logistical and design challenges, but they will also have other consequences ranging from global conflict to the very psychology of human beings changing (as uncertainty, insecurity and unsettlement become dominant features of their psyche).

Climate change events will probably dramatically alter how human beings view and occupy their world. Sustainment implies a new economic paradigm that enfolds redistributive justice to meet this situation but its initiation requires major directional political and economic change. This change is neither just an option nor utopian but an absolute necessity. Within it, equity, justice and conflict reduction are no less a priority than establishing the care of natural resources and halting the destabilization of the planet's atmosphere. Such change is clearly not going to come via enlightened self-interest, neither can it come from within the limits of democracy as it is.

This imperative for global socio-economic and environmental change cannot be understood in purely geospatial terms like centre/periphery. The hegemonic condition named as 'the West' is as much a condition of a particular kind of subject as it is a politico-geographic designation. The West is no longer a bounded space. Moreover, the demographic make-up of populations within almost any particular geography is not just plural, but post-national and made up of fragmented allegiances and identities. Mostly, feeling this situation travels ahead of knowing it.

Beauty and the Wasteland: Living in the Ruins of an Unsustainable World

For the privileged, defuturing often happens under an aura of elegance. And while we live amid the ruins as well as the edifices of the modern world, our eyes are deceived. So many of the celebrated material signs of success are actually marks of failure and evidence of devastation, but in the form of the beautiful – the elegant house with four 'state-of-the-art' bathrooms; the stylish kitchen packed with 'smart' appliances; the wardrobe full of designer clothes; the vaulted marbled foyers of trans-global accountancy corporations; the global fleet of sleek private jets of the ultra rich; jewel-studded watches; extreme performance sports cars that cost three or four times the wage of a well-off worker in the West – and so the list cycles down to the goods on sale in all the 'high-end' department stores, boutiques, car showrooms, and so forth, of the world.

For the West, the once-dark underside of modernization is all but gone (be it that all that was once modern is now old and often becoming dysfunctional). The grime of smog-filled cities, slums, mountainous slag heaps, horrendous industrial diseases and injuries are no more, but this is not so for many of the 'newly industrializing nations' who now do so much of the West's manufacturing. The ability (or at least the attempt) of the West to become 'clean and green' depends, in significant part, upon exporting its 'dirty' industries to newly industrializing nations and to unseen places in even poorer nations.

For modern people, from the Industrial Revolution onward, the world seemed to unfold as an endlessness procession of attainments — industrial processes, ever more sophisticated technologies, wondrous materials, elegant products, well-appointed homes, freeways, medical science, vast buildings, fresh and processed foods available irrespective of season, instant global communication and so on. This world was, and is, clean and liveable. Horrors remain, but Western industrial production has rendered many of its industrial processes environmentally invisible. The true performative nature of things is concealed – 'beauty' conceals the 'beast' (such as the combustion engine, the over-serviced engineered building, coal- and oil-fired power stations, nuclear plants, and the toxic heavy metal/earth metals of the components of many electronic products). At the same time, existing design practices feed an increasing hunger for 'stylish' manufactured goods, even if 'green', all travelling at speed towards landfill.[13]

So much that defutures goes unseen not only because an aesthetic of concealment has 'evolved', but equally that seeing designed 'things' critically is antithetical to commodity culture and even to most designers – perhaps not surprising given that most architects and designers still remain uncritical service providers. To re-emphasize: living in a structurally unsustainable world needs to be understood as living amidst elegant as well as overtly recognizable forms of disaster.

Biopolitics

French social philosopher Bruno Latour asserts that there has never been '... any other politics than the politics of nature, and there has never been any other nature but the nature of politics.'[14] He wants to end nature as the foundation of politics. Quite clearly 'nature' is not going to go away – it is not a consensual object nor is it reductively fixed as humanity continually naturalizes the artificial. Certainly, what is called 'nature', how it is defined and understood, varies between cultures, including the cultures of the West.[15]

One can highlight the significance of what will be named here as biopolitics, critically analyse the various constructions of nature and propose alternative figures or discourses, but no amount of deconstructive blood, sweat and tears will erase the ontological hold the idea of nature still retains – in so many ways, bio-centric nationalism rules.

Essentially, biopolitics means 'the politicization of life'. It marks a move away from the centrality of the body politic (institutionalized politics) to the politicization of the body – whereby 'natural life' is brought into a calculative regime of power. Ultimately, biopolitics is predicated upon the erasure of the essence of what has been understood as humanity ('social being' as opposed to 'bare life').

All human beings arrive in the world as an animal (*zoe* – bare life) and are made human (*bios* – social being) by their socio-cultural world of becoming. The dominant Western narrative of humanity is that it constituted itself by placing itself outside nature (*phusis*), eventually establishing a condition of exteriority and (illusory) independence ('human nature') from 'the natural world'. Other accounts and understandings have existed, still exist and often remain exposed to overt and covert attempts to erase them. Even so, a difference between bare life and a life brought into being by socio-cultural authorship is a commonality linking all peoples.[16]

The work of Michel Foucault from the early 1950s until his death in 1984, explored historically how power came to be exercised in dispersed, multiple and often subtle ways, especially in the areas of law, medicine and sexuality.[17] He argued that from the seventeenth century onward, capitalism required the management and control of bodies. Specifically, this economy needed healthy, passive and compliant bodies within the system of production and planned, controlled urban space. Effectively, techniques of power over the body and its biology permeated all social institutions: the military, family, medicine, education, workplace and prisons. Direct control, supervision, surveillance, regulation, measurement, and above all, the internalization of normative behaviour, infused the techniques of power. At the same time as being acknowledged as a pathfinder, Foucault has also been criticized for failing to develop the concept of biopolitics that he placed so much store by.[18] Moreover, he did not address the most extreme example of biopolitics in the modern era (the concentration camp) – as pointed out by Giorgio Agamben, currently Italy's most celebrated philosopher.[19]

Extending Hannah Arendt's analysis of totalitarianism, Agamben makes clear that the camps exemplified the convergence of the reduction of human life to 'bare life' with a system of absolute domination outside the rule of law.[20] What this did (and does) is to normalize a 'state of exception' and thereby suspend any form of political accountability. The imposition of the 'state of exception' was not an aberrant historical moment; it has been used consistently by desperate regimes in the 'developed' and 'developing' worlds (most recently in the US's detention of prisoners in Guantanamo Bay, as noted earlier).

In displacing human-administered forms of power with technological mechanisms, biopolitics is being dramatically expanded. Unquestionably, science, politics and nature are now being been brought into a relationship whereby 'life in general' is no longer just governed by the natural order but is increasingly open to technological direction (including of bodies). In this respect, human destiny is being further removed from political determinants, the management of space and the 'laws of nature'. The very conditions of being are becoming exposed to major and often defuturing forces of transformation.

Central to the contemporary moment are a range of actions that, as Giorgio Agamben says, '... constantly redefine the threshold of life and so distinguish and separate what is inside and what is outside, what life has value and what does not.'[21] He argues that as we cannot return to what we were, to our naturalness, we have to change and go forward but under our own direction.[22] But, as is being said, our agency is being checked and then negated by the union of biopolitics and technology. These ontological designing environments clearly bring the power and very possibility of self-direction into question.

The most terrifying aspect of this situation is not simply the prospect of what threatens but the refusal of the situation by a deeply embedded condition of unknowing that has become intrinsic to us. This unknowing is indiscernibly evident in institutional politics, which, while having some sense of crisis, displays neither the ability to grasp nor the means to imagine what is so crucial to comprehend and engage. If one seriously reviews existing political ideologies, institutions and practices in relation to global circumstances, it becomes clear that they are simply not adequate to resolving, let alone engaging, the scale and complexity of existing and imminent problems. Flawed reactive methods of organization, economics and politics are applied to environmental and geo-political situations well beyond their reach.

The insufficiency of reason continues to be mobilized to isolate and engage specific, but inadequately analysed, problems. While rationalization – the application of a faith in reason – can and does designate the non-rational, it mostly lacks the means to address it. Moreover, the attempted application of political solutions frequently fails to acknowledge the disjuncture between the conditions that problems are embedded in *and* the extant agency of available political structures – nations and parliaments. These institutions are not organizationally appropriate nor are they practically capable of dealing with problems of the planet's population, terrestrial environments, atmosphere, oceans or economic system. But they pose themselves with this capability. Additionally, the order of time in which policy and action is framed is so often massively at odds with the kind of mid and long-term planning essential to redress deep and critically embedded structural problems.

The actual organizational means to engage problems of defuturing with some chance of success will have to come from a broader and more informed understanding of causality and a sense of relational complexity. Such means need to have the ability to undermine bio-political and technologically in-scribed networks of power. Most starkly, it is vital that a politics arrives that can undercut the propensity to recourse to war.[23]

Current political approaches, such as international agreements and sup-port for sustainable technologies, are feeble instruments in the face of such scenarios. The pragmatism of such actions overlooks the crucial need for a new political imaginary in the emergent epoch of unsettlement. In the con-text of Agamben's key remark that 'in modern biopolitics, sovereign is he who decides on the value or non-value of life as such' such a political imaginary has to focus on thinking and gaining the power to sustain life (as *bios*) by finding a way to make Sustainment sovereign.[24]

The Biophysical Shadow: Feeding the Body

According to Malthusian theory, the growth of the world's population would outstrip the planet's ability to produce sufficient food and disaster would fol-low. While the manner of presentation of such thinking now looks naïve, it has retained a critical insight and opened an issue that can now be explored with more salience.

Certainly, there are dire problems in feeding the world's total population but this cannot just be reduced to the ratio of population to the volume of food production. The problem is as much to do with: chronic material im-balances between the rich and the poor; inequity in food distribution; the nature of world trade; poverty; and the politics of agricultural production. The numerous food riots of 2008 were not due to a global lack of food but to its cost, localized supply problems and the use of food crops to produce combustible fuels (ethanol and bio-diesel). The material-economic basis of humanity's deepening structural unsustainability is not merely a biophysical question; it is embedded in conditions of ignorance, severe inequity, extreme social injustice and conflict over political theologies and the ownership of natural resources.

All this is to say that paradigmatic political shifts and ontological transformations equally require fundamental economic realignments – currently, the dominant mode of (capitalist) exchange is disarticulated from the systems of exchange upon which organic life depends. All the arguments about maintaining a healthy economy, upholding standards of living, keeping the market buoyant, increasing productivity, building the nation's wealth and so on, are, in the last analysis, signifiers of a process of destruction without renewal. There is limited recognition that the renewable path is an appropriate one for energy, but almost no realization that what is actually needed is a renewable economy. Such an economy would address destruction (intrinsic to creation and economy, wherein renewal is possible) as it has become devastation (the condition of the wasteland as assigned by Nietzsche, in which there is eventually nothing to renew) and its cost (in every respect), as much as the issue of production (including food).

Facing Democracy

Proponents of globalization put democracy forward as the most highly developed form of political life. Democracy has become *the* normative figure against which all other socio-political ideologies are judged and positioned on an evolutionary scale. But this picture of the 'stages' of political organization is flawed. To start with, there is a need to restate the notion of democracy as fractured. It is not a unified political ideology.

Democracy's difference travels back into its history and across its contemporary appearances. Before outlining these differences, there is a basic distinction to make between a 'substantial' democratic process and the 'formal institutions' of democracy. In most instances, 'democratic' practice is not the same as that which speaks, legislates and governs in its name.

There is a profound difference between the Greek founding moment of democracy (the direct exercise of decision by the power of all members of the elite) and contemporary democratic models, wherein the power of an enfranchised populace is circumscribed within the limits of liberal democratic representational pluralism. The Greek system was specific to the empowered class – those who were the acknowledged citizens of the *demos* (the people). The process functioned as a direct democracy – every issue requiring to be decided went before everyone with the power to vote. Thus, the ability of the *polis* (the city) itself to function was predicated upon the willing of the *demos*. While there is a profound difference between the modest scale of the Greek system and the expansive representational model of modern democratic politics, the founding moment remains important to re-examine.[25]

Modern concepts of democratic process were prefigured in medieval Europe by the use of the law as a restraint on the power of the sovereign, and later, by the creation of consultative processes. The most celebrated document, in this regard, was the *Magna Carta* granted by King John of England in 1215 (it guaranteed human rights against the excessive use of royal power). After this, democracy did not gain much political momentum until the late Middle Ages when proto-communist European serfs revolted in pursuit of land rights. Their revolt lacked any theory, structure or democratic process as we now know them, but it did register a demand for (what were to become democratic) 'rights'. Equally, this moment marked a schism that has remained within political theory and culture ever since. This can be characterized as the divide between 'the rule of the people' (socialistic democracy) and 'the rule of a representative legislative body' (social and liberal democratic government). Here then is a lasting tension between 'democracy' as a means to acquire power, versus 'democratic process' as a means to retain it. But there is also another tension to acknowledge: one that lies within the illusory 'rule of the people'.

The English Revolution (1642–51) was an attempt, in common with a number of other civil wars, to replace the sovereign monarch with the 'sovereignty of the people'. However, in this case, and others across the range of revolutionary struggle, the power of the people mostly remained inchoate and illusory. Though rhetorically mobilized, 'the people' are rarely present and active at the centre of power – they are an absent signifier. Yet the elite that creates and fills this void continually acts to hold the representation of the people as sovereign before 'the masses' named as 'the people'.[26] What is held in tension by the ruling power then is an 'image of the rule of the people' and 'the people's recognition of this image as an illusion'. An open question here, with contextually different answers, is the degree to which 'the people' become complicit in maintaining the illusion.

In the first instance, these differences were conceptually played out in works like Thomas More's *Utopia* (1516), which advanced the democratic ideal of a classless operative society. His democratic model was based upon commonwealth and was also communistic. A century later (in England) ideas of social justice were fused with democracy and promoted in the influential writings of John Milton and John Bunyan. Their ideas were enacted by radical groups like the Ranters, Diggers and Levellers who struggled against the propertied class – their aim being to gain 'an equality of goods and lands'.[27] The key event of this moment was the fated English Revolution led by Oliver Cromwell and his 'New Model Army' with its ambition to create a Commonwealth. Prior to this were the conflicts in Europe triggered by Martin Luther, the unfolding of the Reformation and the fusion of the ascendant Protestant religion with a new and radical politics.

Illusion, Representation and Aesthetics

Modern representative liberal democracy, as has been suggested and will continue to be shown, is vulnerable to the fundamental criticism that it is not, in essence, democratic. Historically, this criticism has been made from many political positions and over many centuries, not least by Jean-Jacques Rousseau in *The Social Contract or Principles of Political Rights* (1762).

Parallel to the political activism of the seventeenth century was the theoretical development of democracy, most notably by Thomas Hobbes, John Locke, Rousseau and, thereafter, Thomas Jefferson. In all cases, as political historian C.B. Macpherson made clear, the democratic ideal was bonded either to the creation of a classless society or to the operation of a single and absolutely dominant class society.[28] In this context, the political ideology was initially formed and mobilized to create not only a new mode of governance but also to form new kinds of subjects of the state.

In contrast, what arrived in the nineteenth century was the notion of democracy gathering all classes and representing their interests. James Mill, Jeremy Bentham, John Stuart Mill and the spirit of utilitarianism were all players in this move. At the core of this thinking was the desire to bring liberalism and democracy together within a single ideology to enable the rise of an inclusionist pluralistic society. At exactly the same time as liberal democracy was being conceived and assembled, the communistic model of democratic process was being recovered and refurbished by Karl Marx. One of the common criticisms of the dominant proponents of democracy, including criticism by socialists, was that they continually failed to acknowledge that 'first and foremost' democracy should be participatory rather than representative.[29]

The assertion of rights was a central feature of political developments in the formative period of modern democracy – most evident in the American Declaration of Independence (1776) and the French Declaration of the Rights of Man and of the Citizen (1789). These were the structures that led to the formation of elected representative legislative bodies based on universal suffrage. But equally, they installed the conditions of the representational paradox.

This paradox goes to the core, and it can be defined as a disjunctural representation of 'the people' being represented. Essentially, and in most democratic nations, the people's rights are constitutionally inscribed. The elected representatives claim to represent the interests or concerns of their constituents via their rights having been constitutionally given and represented. Effectively, 'being represented' meant 'being a represented entity within the directive regime of a representational object'. In turn, this meant that 'the subject being represented' was abstracted while the elected representative took the upholding of the representation (the constitution) as primary and representing the needs of the subject as secondary – thus the symbolic took precedence over the concrete (which is not to say the concrete was totally ignored). If we bring the 'abstraction of the subject' together with the 'illusion of the people' we can see that there is a void at the centre of representative democracy. Claude Lefort's characterization of democratic power maps onto this observation. He concluded that power is absent at the centre of democratic government because the people, state and nation are constituted as image, and while politically mobilized as a locus of power, they are in fact in themselves 'empty places' – and thus mere representation.[30]

Power is continually exercised, but not democratically. In conformity with Foucault's thesis, it is dispersed – for instance, into the military, departments of taxation, treasury, transport, health, education, and so on. While none of these entities operate democratically, the claim is that they function under the direction of policies and an *appointed* minister of government who has been democratically elected. But accountability in this structure turns out to be primarily to 'the national interest' – which dominantly means capital and national security – rather than being to democracy, which gets covertly and overtly (in the case of 'the state of exception') negated. Effectively, the representational character of 'democracy' is deployed to deflect the gaze from government as operational pragmatism.

The Concept of the Political, possibly the most influential of Carl Schmitt's works (on both 'the left' and 'the right'), argued that parliamentary democracy reduced politics to an aesthetic – a representational interplay (and as such, the negation of the political). The pragmatic response to this reduction was that there are political ends that can justify such action.[31] Such a position is none too distant from pragmatic justifications for suspending democratic process to manage the complexity of everyday life, or for the imperative of national security. Obviously such thinking leads, for example, to attempts by 'democratic' regimes to legitimize acts of torture.

This briefly sketched account of the plural forms of democracy exposes a number of things: the error of assuming a linear development from the Greek democratic ideal to present day political forms; the existence of utopianism as one of democracy's undercurrents; the structural relation between democracy and communalist communism; and the reduction of the political to an aesthetic. As Schmitt made abundantly clear, there has never been a rule by democracy '... that did not recognize the concept of the "foreign" and that could have realized the equality of all men'.[32]

The dominant strains of democracy are numerous, spanning political positions from 'right' to 'left' and include democratic rationalism, capitalistic, liberal, interest based, deliberative, communicative, subsidiarity and radical. They are surveyed at length in many textbooks and by many more specifically focused engagements.[33]

Being Political and a Crisis of Democracy

What design brings into being not only influences the nature of the world we human beings inhabit but equally affects what we become as actors within that world as its makers and un-makers.

The usually hazy sense that billions of people have of themselves as political subjects has been constituted through induction into a culture in which political ideology has material substance. Here, then, is a structured context in which to view the designing power of democracy as political institution, political theory, symbolic power, an idea lodged in the everyday, idealized practice and rhetoric. There is a huge schism between the popular idea of the exercise of democratic rights by individuals and the actual exercise of power by democratically elected governments (evidenced at its most extreme via the exercise of absolute executive power overriding the sovereign power of the rule of law when a government declares 'a state of exception').

Against the backdrop of 'the war on terror,' the 'state of exception' and those laws that curtail basic freedoms in the name of the interests of 'national security', what is thrown into stark relief, as indicated earlier, is a willingness of the governments of many 'democratic' nations to suspend already diminished processes of democracy. While these actions have generated a considerable amount of concern, it is what they signal in relation to unsettlement and deepening structural unsustainability that allows a coupling of democracy and crisis. In short, there is an impending situation in which measures likely to be taken will be totally authoritarian. This crisis of human freedoms is being precipitated by an inability of democratic politics to act with sufficient foresight and vigour to curb the dominant defuturing elements of the capitalist economy and stave off the crises they trigger.

As we move forward, it will be demonstrated that democracy, at least as it currently exists as a handmaiden to globalizing capital, cannot 'make time', and thus cannot politically transport humanity to viable futures. On the basis of what it promises, democracy removes itself from the ability to impose those limitations upon which all future freedoms will depend.

Critiques of the multiple forms of democracy have been longstanding, complex and from the full range of ideological positions.[34] Yet to bring the issue of structural unsustainability to democracy is to confront its very foundations. No matter whether the focus is on democracy's direct or representative forms, the issues remain the same. Will 'the people' elect a government with a mandate to impose the limitations upon which Sustainment would depend? Or alternatively, can a politics beyond democracy, based on the delivery of Sustainment, be created (and if so, what role in this politics can design play)? These two questions will travel throughout this book. But to begin with, the relation between capitalism and democracy needs examination. To do this we will draw on a 'radical conservative', Joseph Schumpeter, who was a contemporary and almost a kindred spirit of Schmitt. Schumpeter did not resolve these questions but his contradictory arguments, which, while centring on an elitist form of pluralism, significantly contributed to making the issues evident. In common with other conservative critics of his day, he saw democracy as a global inevitability but not as long as it was bonded to liberal capitalism.[35]

Superficially, Schumpeter appears to be an enigma. He upheld the power of conservative elites while embracing socialism, yet as his biographer John Medearis makes clear, he had a mission and strategy that bridged these seemingly opposite poles.[36] This mission, in essence, was to facilitate capital's transformation from its liberal affiliation to (his notion) of democratic socialism. The intent was to transpose elites from one context where they were losing ground to another where they could gain it. Thus democracy was seen as without social meaning and as a pragmatic means rather than a value in itself.[37] Schumpeter viewed liberal capitalism as unstable and composed of multiple tendencies that drew it in directions that undermined its own interests; in particular, it embraced mechanistic rationalization at the same time as extending attachments to irrational beliefs that were against its own interests.[38] Likewise, liberal capitalism also diminished the power of those social and entrepreneurial forces that empowered it. To counter these trends, he sought to elevate marginalized entrepreneurs as change agents able to break the hold of those forms of rationalization that had displaced the historical function of democratic politics and of thought. In sum, his project was to overthrow an ideology that he believed claimed human beings as inherently rational.[39] He went so far as to assert that the attack on tradition, by capitalist modes of rationalization as it affects 'our minds' would actually destroy capitalism itself.[40]

To understand Schumpeter's position one has to grasp the distinction he made between the *capitalist system*, which for him was simply its operational mechanisms and the *capitalist order*, which he regarded as the form of civilization and its institutions (all that capitalism upheld).[41] In this context, the instrumentalist capitalist modes of rationalization invaded the capitalist order and started to undo it. This order was, of course, the object of his primary attachment and to be safeguarded by the elites with which he was aligned. So what he was striving to do was to displace liberal democracy as the betrayer of these elites. His version of democratic socialism was a regime controlled by an elite. In the face of the inevitable onward march of democracy, Schumpeter believed it possible to emplace elites to tame democracy's power and preserve traditional (conservative) values. He believed these elites would be able to compete for and win the popular vote. To understand his faith in elites one has to recognize Schumpeter's contempt for, and indivisible bad faith in, 'human nature'. He viewed the 'masses' as an unthinking herd that lacked 'the potential to reflect, discuss, persuade, and act in common'.[42] He dismissed the kind of argument put forward by John Dewey, that there is an imperative for democracy to educate 'the masses', on the basis that it is not in their nature to be educated.

It's easy to write off people like Schumpeter and Schmitt as fascist reactionaries (which in some respects they were). However, we dismiss their insights at our peril. Drawing on past and present critics, a powerful case can be made against the ability of liberal parliamentary democracy to curb the excesses of capitalism, its failure to exercise social responsibility and its implication in environmental *devastation*. Likewise, the violent imposition of 'democracy' in the name of liberation has considerably diminished its credibility and moral authority. Above all, the degeneration of democracy into authoritarianism has been frequent. As already signalled, the concern is that with the expected levels of social instability (and violence) in the wake of impending climate change effects, the state of exception will become a state of permanence.

With the prospect of instability and authoritarianism increasing, an affirmative political order is absolutely crucial. What this order turns on is the extent to which there is a general willingness to 'sacrifice freedoms' to secure that fundamental freedom which is Sustainment, and thereafter to realign political forces. Although there is a great chasm between the democratic idea and democracy in practice, such is the prefigurative (designing) power of the idea, that people sacrifice their lives for it. Yet if one would wish to claim an object of belief for which to sacrifice, after due consideration, one would surely choose Sustainment (*de facto* the future) over democracy. To give these remarks more of a critical edge, they need to be put in a broader frame that allows us to move through the kind of socio-political and economic contexts outlined. The aim here is to be able to imagine other possibilities.

Context one is 'now' and could be called 'the expected'. It reflects the predictable disposition of the world's dominant political regimes and the power of capital to strive to maintain the status quo (be it with a few concessions to reducing environmental impacts). The likely trajectory of this disposition is for a reactive response and crisis-like imposition of severe restrictions on industry and everyday life following the arrival of extremely critical environmental circumstances, not least as a result of a changing climate, creating, for instance, a crisis of global food production combined with tens of millions of environmental refugees on the move.

Context two is a 'might be' and is futural and nameable as 'the desired'. It is based on a realistic view of where transformative action could begin from, while recognizing that for viable futures to be secured change has to become radical. It would start by maintaining (but not growing) the status quo, and at the same time, establishing a 'change community and change platform (by design)'. This strategy would seek to grow the new economic paradigm out of conditions sustained by the one it sought to displace (which is the essence of platforming).[43] The creation of this platform would initiate not just material transformations but onto-political shifts as part of a much larger design agenda of change. This is the agenda of 'design futuring' underpinned by the key notion of 'redirective practice'.

While new 'green' technologies and products continue to gain media attention, what really deserves a huge amount of time and effort is retrofitting the vast world of human creation around us, so as to direct it away from the structurally unsustainable towards Sustainment.[44] Quite simply, the existing world within the world has to be dealt with. What redirective practice responds to is the absolute need to deal with both the structurally unsustainable 'nature' of human being and the material world that such a mode of being has already created.

Configurations: The Human and the World

As indicated, a confrontation with structural unsustainability demands a seismic shift in political, economic and cultural agendas. Yet there is an equally large, or perhaps even larger, confrontation to be had with what 'we' are and have become. This confrontation is vital, not least because of the overwhelming need to fully understand that the essence of structural unsustainability is 'us'. This is to say *it is a product of how we are* and the way we act in (and on) the world.

Anthropocentrism, the Human, Selfhood and the Political

For Hegel, it is both fundamental and altogether worthy of astonishment that human understanding (that is language, discourse) should have had the force (an incomparable force) to separate its constitutive elements from the Totality. These elements (this tree, this bird, this stone) are in fact inseparable from the whole. They are 'bound together by spatial and temporal, indeed material, bonds which are indissoluble.' Their separation implies the human Negativity toward Nature of which I spoke, without pointing out its decisive consequences. For the man who negates nature could not in any way live outside it. He is not merely a man who negates Nature, he is first of all an animal, that is to say the very thing he negates: he therefore cannot negate Nature without negating himself … Thus human Negativity, Man's effective desire to negate Nature is destroying it – in reducing it to his own ends, as when, for example, he makes a tool of it (and the tool will be the model of an object isolated from Nature) – cannot stop at Man himself; insofar as he is Nature, Man is exposed to his own Negativity … It is the very separation of Man's being, it is his isolation from Nature, and, consequently, his isolation in the midst of his own kind, which condemns him to disappear definitively.[45]

What Georges Bataille says here not only illuminates an idea running though the entire history of human thought, but also exposes the unknowing that travels with anthropocentrism – an unknowing that casts a shadow over virtually all human knowledge, not least science. Bataille, the leading figure of an assemblage of mostly French heterodoxical writers and thinkers of the mid-twentieth century, had a clear sense of the political implication of confronting what 'we' really are as 'a shattering' with profound consequences. Such confrontations underpinned almost all of his writing – which is one of the reasons why he is still read and remains influential among 'progressive' circles.

Staying with the dichotomy between 'man (nature)' and 'man (social)', Jenny Elkins returns us to our already registered concern with bio-politics. Drawing on Giorgio Agamben, she points out that politics has to become a 'politics of being' (which is non-exclusionary and not a politics of human-designed rights).[46] A biopolitics that simply centres on the human *as* being, in a defuturing age of unsettlement, is just another form of negation. All this is to say, often contrary to rhetorical appearances, that the body politic is being reduced to a biological mass to manage politically. The more unsettlement bites, the more this will be so.

While national and global conflict and economic and environmental problems have been given an enormous amount of attention in the literature of politics, the questioning of the 'nature of human being' has received scant consideration. That the nature of human being is not universally the same (but ever is getting treated as such), this observation is graphically illustrated when we consider the ontological differences between Western secular and the religious (Islamic) subjects.

At its simplest, the secular modern perspective and belief is that one lives in a social milieu with the power to exercise free will, whereas the orthodox Muslim believes that one has to live according to the will of God. Such understandings imply two very different modes of being: for the former the human is a socio-political being; for the latter the human is God's servant on Earth. When democracy is imposed on an orthodox Muslim's culture it does not just arrive as a political imposition but as the destruction of the very sense of self.[47]

Added to this view is the globally dominant perspective of all people being fundamentally the same (evidenced by the discourse of human rights). Difference is only acknowledged at a super-structural level, epitomized by multiculturalist understandings whereby difference becomes reduced to customs and tradition, food, dress, music and visual arts. Fundamental differences in world view, value systems, mythologies, cosmologies, psychologies, morality, emotional mindscapes, and so forth all go by the board. Yet, if the world is perceived in radically different ways, being-in-the-world cannot be regarded as, and equate to, being-in-common.

The empirical facticity of the world may be beyond dispute, but it can never be experienced and viewed independently from the perceptual frame of cultural difference. For those cultures defending their right to maintain their difference, globalization is just the latest face of colonial violence.

'We' actually live a dilemma – notwithstanding debate on the issue of community, we cannot (continue) to be without being together (for we are of the totality) yet we exist in difference (affirmatively and as a condition of the negation of others).[48] So framed, a 'politics of being' (beyond) us demands learning and living a 'commonality in difference'.

It is just not possible for modern human beings to be non-anthropocentric and remain human – anthropocentrism is elemental to the essence of our human being. The only futural option 'we' have is to take responsibility for what we are, acknowledging our interdependence as elemental to what the great phenomenologist Maurice Merleau-Ponty called 'the flesh of the world' and expressing this by enacting the practices of Sustainment. By failing to recognize what we anthropocentrically are, existing politics clearly negates such responsibility. Dominantly, 'environmental politics' is complicit in this negation, not least via its biocentrism, which treats the environmental symptoms of human actions as if they were causes; whereas, absolutely unambiguously, 'we' are the cause.

Unquestionably, there are many problems that require fundamental transformations of our mode of being-in-the-world as a species, such as: how we treat our immediate environment; where we live; how we live and travel; what we eat; what we buy; what waste we generate and how we deal with it. This all adds up to an urgent need to start creating cultures of Sustainment able to establish values and conduct that act to secure, rather than negate, futures. Taking responsibility for our anthropocentrism demands two strategies: making the imperative present as an idea able to be thought and designing into being a politics of accountable conduct (here the relation between one's actions in the world, their impacts, limits and sacrifice could be made explicit and indexed).

Effectively, by design, irrespective of individual disposition, and in a condition of Sustainment as sovereign, all registered voters become accountable for the manner by which they utilize resources and with what impacts. Freedom here becomes a freedom to do what one likes within the conditions of limitation that secure that potentiality that is futuring.[49] The shift implied in this prescribed conduct moves from unrestricted 'consumption' to a delimited expenditure of non-renewable resources, but with an unlimited expenditure of those that are renewable. In essence, responsibility for one's actions is here transformed into making every enfranchised subject the environmental manager of their self. Moreover, the greater the ability to design one's life within this condition of limitation, the greater the degree of one's freedom. The claim is not that such action solves the problem at large but that it engages one's self as a problem.

Unfortunately, current political theories, institutions and practices totally fail to recognize this imperative. In short, democratic theory and practice are currently not only incapable of establishing an economy, society and culture able to secure sustainable futures but also unable to hold political subjects accountable for their actions. Put baldly, there is no correlation between for whom or what one votes and one's political conduct. Politics is thus reduced to simply exercising one's vote. In contrast, what is being outlined here is the displacement of a political gesture without accountability (voting as exercising self-interest that validates an anthropocentric impulse in a culture where individualism has become an ontology of unaccountability) to living with political accountability as a materialized foundation of responsibility for one's self. While such action will probably only be adopted by a small minority, this can actually be reframed as the potential arrival of a large number of change agents able to deliver modes of ontological design (to masses of people, if not 'the masses').

The oft-posed question 'what can the individual do?' is addressed not by prescribing a particular course of action but by suggesting the enactment of a perceptual politico-realignment and an ontological shift. Rather than an individual being political by acting politically it is a matter of one's being 'being political' – which effectively means the subordination of one's self to the collective of a politics, but from the perspective of 'a change community' bonded to that 'community of difference' that seeks to advance Sustainment. Thus one can act alone as a plural figure of the collective. In contrast to the individual as a lone actor seeking an action that will make a difference, or as a member of a political party or interest group who complies with the rules of the collective, the individual being who has become a political being within a change community only has the commonality of belief directing collective action in difference. In sum, it is possible for the individuated subject to cease to be that invented political-philosophical entity we call an individual and become a truly political being.

2

Inadequate Solutions of Now

'Now' is a time unlike any other in human history. For the first time in our existence 'we' discover that we are responsible both for putting the future of our planetary existence (and much else) at risk, and for dealing with this situation (if we can). Two questions thus loom: 'is it too late to stop doing what we destructively do?' and then 'do we have enough time to adapt to the circumstances of the devastation we have created?' Empirically, we lack affirmative and clear answers to either question. Yet politically, we still have to act, be it without certainty. We must strive to take our fate firmly in our own hands. So acting implies a new kind of politics and the political deployment of design by both designers and by those who knowingly or unknowingly make design decisions.

Antonio Gramsci was imprisoned by Mussolini between 1929 and 1935 for his communist and anti-fascist politics. Although sick and in pain he maintained his sanity by constructing an inner life through writing. Of many the insights that his prison notebooks communicated, one is especially pertinent to what will be said here.[1] That insight is the distinction he made between 'common sense' and 'good sense'. Gramsci equated 'common sense' with the mobilization of generalities, unexamined assumptions and unquestioned beliefs in circulation in any given society, while 'good sense' was the product of empirically grounded knowledge and learning from critically reflective experience. The latter is obviously the way in which 'common sense' is often thought in English.

Unfortunately, it seems as if 'common sense' as 'good sense' fails to inform the conduct of many who occupy the highest echelons of political leadership of the world's powerful nations. Crudely, acquiring and employing a lot of money, trying to touch populist nerve endings, using street cunning, appealing to the self-interests of voters and doing political deals all seem to be the dominant ways that political power is gained and mobilized. Thoughtfulness, intellect and sensitivity toward 'the state of the world;' extending one's imagination and acting with integrity appear not to count for much. That there are historical exceptions to the dominant contemporary rule of mediocre political leadership does not invalidate this sweeping criticism. Let's be frank: much of the rhetoric of professional politicians – as they speak of democracy, freedom, the family, nation, sustainability, and so on – especially when an election is in the offing – confirms this judgement. So much of what we hear amounts to little more than a collection of platitudes, sound bites and clichés.

One could imagine the trite answers to the two questions posed a moment ago tripping off the tongues of the army of speakers of 'common sense'. Yet the two seemingly straightforward questions that opened this chapter unfold to reveal a perplexing complexity. 'Is it too late …?' and 'do we have enough time …?' Both questions necessitate a rethinking of how we understand time.

Characteristics of a Plural 'Now'

Scientific, universally coexistent and experiential modalities of time all simultaneously mark a moment, but it is not the same moment. Time is not just relative but also plural. Any claim to time being universally singular is discourse specific, thus no consensual view can be asserted.

The measurement of time by the caesium-beam oscillators of atomic clocks has not only put the accuracy of timekeeping beyond the grasp of what most of us are able to imagine but it has also widened the gap between quantified and experiential time. Whereas the measurement of time is scientifically calibrated and universal, the experience of time is differential, event-based and subjective. Time is change.

The moment of 'now' is a key figure in the relative nature of historico-experiential time. How 'now' is experienced geographically, biologically and politically is, at one level, registered by the notion of uneven development and at another by natural cycles – my nation is not at the same 'stage' of development as yours; my culture is older or newer than your culture; my seasons are not your seasons unless you also live in the ranges of south-east Queensland, Australia; and my body may have more or less time than yours. Thus while we share the same 'now' my 'now' does not match yours.

The past is equally problematic. It can be said that the general socio-economic conditions of one nation's past are often another nation's future. Socio-economic and inter-generational cultural differences within a nation, city or community are also temporally differentiated at any given moment. So if time is that 'in which events occur', as Aristotle suggested, it is clear that we move across and between similar and very different events and thus encounter 'now' as fractured. Yet between a reality-posited hyper-measured moment of time and the experiential difference of the changing moment of 'now' there exists something else that is momentous.

No matter the differences of our circumstances as individuals, cultures or nations, we now share a time that is new. We all share a continual moment of the diminishment of time. The actual finite time of our life on the planet (and the life of much else) is being reduced by our own destructive actions as a species. While our 'being-in-time' cannot be quantified, it is still being quantitatively negated.

Now is a new time: a time of 'unsettlement' in which we are starting to live. It is a moment when the destiny of humanity and its future modes of worldly occupation are not only unclear but still unimagined. What is certain is that we cannot continue to be and be as we are.

The most overt sign of unsettlement, as said, will be the hundreds of millions of environmental refugees created by climate change as the century rolls on. The coming changes are going to be as significant as the establishment of human settlement itself, which, of course, underscored the rise of the modern world. What then are the design demands of this situation? Can we even begin to envisage them? What kind of socio-political visions can we bring to a task of a magnitude for which we currently have no measure? Before responding to these questions, the issues need grounding politically.

Democracy 'Now' and the Universal

Familiarity with the general idea of democracy does not necessarily mean that it is actually understood.

The West's attempt to make democracy globally hegemonic went along with global modernization theory of the late 1940s, which directed early United Nations policy, as it was predominantly shaped by the USA. Democracy and capitalism became the bonded agents of the 'free world' as it was configured in the liberal notion of the free market, animated by the powerful.

The economic and political expansionism of this era bled into the contemporary project of globalization. The idea of *under*development was imposed upon *un*development, which often meant that a subsistence economy was destroyed and 'poverty' arrived. Even the politically critical narrative of these events didn't see that this was establishing a trajectory toward structural unsustainability (as a condition of inequity, and as a consequence of projected and partially realized development). Thus one of the 'attainments' of globalization has been the universalization of the unsustainable.

The leading nations of the international community (as was the 'G8' and so forth) are snared in a debilitating contradiction that the discourse of 'sustainable development' tries, but fails, to conceal. On the one hand they remain totally committed to global economic expansion within a system predicated on the idea of perpetual economic growth. On the other hand, they are aware that environmental impacts (especially those created by global warming as accelerated by greenhouse gas emissions) are a threat to their developmental objectives. 'Sustainable development', in this setting, is a 'have your cake and eat it' strategy. It comes down to a proposition that says 'all that needs to be done is to instrumentally reduce the impacts of the technologies used and then carry on business as normal (be these technologies generative of greenhouse gas emissions, toxic waste, etc)'. Thus, sustainability and growth (the cake) can coexist within the digestive system of the existing economy. But 'sustainable development' will not work. This is because: market expansion (the product of growth + globalization) will tend to outstrip product or technology improvement – the environmental advantages of hybrid cars, for example, are wiped out if the number of cars on the planet doubles (which would be the aim of a car industry recovering from a global recession). The desire for 'consumer culture and products' that a globalizing culture generates means that the actual material impacts of a continuously growing global population ever speeds resource utilization (and negation) – the 'impact population ratio,' (a multiplier of the base number of people on the planet times their resource uptake) continually increases. Thus the impacts of existing and projected economic growth, in its current form, are far outstripping impact reduction measures. Moreover the fundamental issue of human-centredness (anthropocentrism) goes unrecognized and thus unengaged. In other words, the created ontological disposition of people to be unsustainable (because that is how they have been culturally constituted as economic and political subjects) is in no way checked by sustainable development. People will always find a way to be unsustainable unless they are ontologically designed (by being in another kind of experiential 'world') to be otherwise. Basically, the notion of growth as the basis of the global economy is actually indivisible from an unchecked desire for 'more' by almost all subjects of such an economy.

Parliamentary democracy (in all its forms) is not only unable to confront this situation, and thereby put itself in a position to deal with the human-centred causes of structural unsustainability, but it contributes to the worsening of the situation. It is effectively stymied by its bondage to capitalism (as it is) and by its pluralism and popularism. The political survival of the ruling party has become dependent upon economic performance – China, with its two systems, is just as locked into this as any 'free world' nation.

Being critical of democracy as a politics goes beyond its inability to deliver the changes needed to establish a culture and economy of Sustainment. There are long-running criticisms from other quarters, pointing, for instance, to the destruction of tradition and belief systems, the imposition of electoral machinery before the institutional infrastructure of civil society is developed (like properly organized political parties, a system of law, institutions of governance and an adequate basic education system), and its ability to be appropriated by elites seeking to maintain an existing system of power (and its inequities).

Passing over Technology Now

Just as democracy is an everyday fact, which, because of our limited knowledge of it, remains mostly unknown, so also is technology. Dominantly, technology is regarded as if it were external to us and simply available as a tool to use. This illusion needs to be shattered.

For all humanity, technology was born with the use of tools which, unwittingly, came to be employed to reshape the given world. This moment marked the commencement of proto-human beings making a world in the world – which in turn would make them (as it became the world into which they were born and acted). However, for technology to become an object of consciousness, the idea had to be brought into being – it had to come to mind. For the West, the narrative that claimed to do this was 'productivism'.

Productivism was a mode of thought created by the pre-Socratics in order to know and represent *phusis* (the way the Greeks named 'all that is'). It was based on the idea that all matter, elements and causal forces could be understood as structures constituted by processes of structuring. It was a mode of thought that took materiality beyond its apparent objectified form. Prefiguratively, thought was brought to materiality in a way that posited its nature as over-determined structurally, and thus available to be directed elementally as form. In other words, things were seen as more than they appeared to be. It followed that productivism (as a mode of mind directive of action) formed the essence of design as intuitively enacted. This means that things were seen to be able to be directed to become something other than what they seemingly were – they could be produced by an intent to transform (design).

Effectively productivism was the precursor of reason and its practical application. It was amplified and fully realized in the Enlightenment, especially via analytic and calculative thought of that great thinker Gottfried Wilhelm Leibniz (1646–1716) and by experimental science in general. At this moment, a way of knowing transmuted into a far more powerful means of creating, re-creating and re-designing 'things' that were able to be understood structurally. Such thinking was foundational to the rise of technology as we now understand it. It marked a transition to a method of producing information by theory. As such, it took making beyond basic empiricism's dependence upon trial, error and observation. In turn, this led to productivist theory becoming inscribed in a technology itself (a very early example was the Jacquard loom, invented in 1804, which used information carried by punched cards to control the longitudinal pattern of the fabric being woven).[2] Productivism thus first structured making via systematic mean, eventually leading to the creation of technological systems themselves. No matter what they produced, such systems have been absolutely crucial in the constantly accelerating metabolism of the unsustainable. Productivism dramatically increased industrial production's dependence upon, and creation of, destruction.

This brief account of productivism marks the passage, over millennia, from a perception of things as products of their structure to the industrial production of things based on the manufacture and manipulation of material and immaterial structural elements.

Accompanying productivism was the arrival of what Martin Heidegger named as 'standing reserve' – all worldly resources simply being available and at hand to be employed at will. While 'resource' management now goes some way to acknowledge this situation, it fails to ask the most fundamental ethical question – 'does what is being created justify what is being appropriated and what is being destroyed?' In relation to technology, resources and products, one cannot just deal with how they appear and are used instrumentally – they always have consequences beyond immediate use, and thus are always ethically charged (and so raise ethical questions).

One of the more serious consequences of technology becoming hegemonic (its current status) is the way we, in our anthropocentricity and global differences, give way to it. 'We' do this in the belief that the technology exists to serve 'us', that it is neutral, under our control and gives us the ability to save ourselves from what threatens. This uncritical relation to technology blocks recognition of its agency beyond immediate instrumental functions. Most significantly, what goes unseen is how technological things dramatically and ontologically design us and now, increasingly, technologies themselves. While this has always been a tendency (the tool user has always been a product of his/her tool, as well as a productive user of it), as tools/technologies have become more prolific, complex and powerful their biophysical, metaphysical and cultural designing power has also grown (correspondingly, human ability to control technology's designing has diminished).

Technology continually changes what technology is. In turn, technology continually changes the nature of the material world and beings in that world. Technology thus 'bit-by-bit,' unceasingly and incrementally redesigns itself, 'nature,' world and beings. There is now nothing that is not technologically contaminated; there is nothing that in some way has not been touched by the naturalized artificial (including us). 'We' now know so much of the world via technology, including the world itself as imaged, but our knowing itself has become technological.[3]

Effectively, technology's instrumental appropriation has turned back upon its appropriators and instrumentalized them and their environments. What we have now is a description of an intersecting moment between Schmitt's understanding of technology (a neutralizing force), and what Heidegger called *Gestell* (translated as enframing) – an animatory force stamping out (as with a press) the designed forms and structures of an inanimate 'nature'. *Gestell* is now evident in 'technoculture' as an economy becoming a way of 'life.'[4] This is a fundamental change of the very ground of our being wrought by technology's neutralization of our directive agency. It is enacted by a self-negating political mobilization of 'enframing' (wherein human agency becomes diminished and rendered passive). Thus to become instrumentalized is to become a subject of the political rather than a political subject.

Machines of Creation and Destruction and the Technosphere

In common with design, what technology brings into being mostly goes unexamined by society at large. This is especially the case in the way the form and function of both negate futures – not just in terms of overt environmental impacts, but equally in their ontological formative (desiring) consequences (the world we occupy is undermined by the way we want the world to be). Technology can no longer be regarded as a tool completely under human direction. As the philosophy of technology has unambiguously made clear, there is an indivisible relation between our making of our world with tools and our own self-creation.[5] The use of a tool, for instance, cannot be divided from the acquisition of skill to use it – be it a hammer, computer or bulldozer. Not only is the subject-object relation interactive but over a vast expanse of time the accompanying symbiotic relations have also produced world-forming ontologies (craft workers, artists, engineers, farmers, and so forth) wherein specific practices have inscribed particular modes of being.

As technology has become more complex and further integrated into everyday life, its designing of the self and world has dramatically increased. We now live, as technological beings, in a technosphere that has been integrated with the natural – it is no longer possible to locate the dividing line between them. Biological engineering evidences this most overtly, but technology has also touched almost everything natural by intent or accident, not least our own chemically, prosthetically, surgically and cosmetically modified bodies.

We are, of course, more than body, and whatever we actually are is a fusion of three determinate forces: (1) our genetic inheritance; (2) the ontological designing of all we encounter and engage via the form and content our material culture and its environment (both natural and constructed); and (3) the designing of our being as it arrives through the form of our socialization. It follows that we are the consequence of not purely the biological (our bare life), the social (our politico-theological life) or the technological (our metaphysical modality) but rather we arrive out of our animality and into our hybridized being human as a result of a relational assemblage.

Thereafter, technology continues to weave its way into our life and 'we' become deeply embedded in techno-culture – which is now environmentally elemental to, and a key element of, 'our' *habitus* – the structuring of that which structures our thinking and acting as we, in turn and in our difference, ourselves act as a structuring and structured force.

An inversion is occurring. Increasingly, we humans do not simply extend our selves and our will via technology but technology now extends itself through us – we think it serves us but more and more we serve it. Passively, and in myriad ways, modernized life means acting on technological instructions that are conduct directive – how we communicate, travel, cook, wash clothes, take pictures, extract money from our bank, monitor our health are just a few examples. User-enablement, convenience or even pleasure all mask this surrendering of our selves to being ontologically designed via technologically compliant action. To know that a good deal of software as a product of programming also programs its users, and to dismiss this fact, simply registers the extent to which, ontologically, 'we' have unwittingly accepted becoming technological.

Without question, arguments over whether or not technology is neutral are long over. This is not because its non-neutrality has become recognized but because technology has become a 'naturalized' environment – in its omnipresence it has become taken-for-granted, it has neutralized us. Notwithstanding this situation, as Carl Schmitt recognized many years ago, it remains pressing to expand on how technology is seen in relation to structures of power. Schmitt argued that technology rather being neutral acted to 'neutralize' in so far as it took power (other than its own) away.[6] This neutralization resulted in it becoming more and more powerful as a *neutering* instrument of human agency. This is confirmed within the populations of most nations – there is now *no* widespread fear of, or even critical concern about, technology. It is simply trusted.[7] Neutralization has led to naturalization. Any critical distance between 'us and it' has gone, thus any notion of the human/technology relation as polarized between domination or liberation has evaporated. Certainly, there are still a few technologies recognized as harmful, not least technologies of war. Notwithstanding this, almost all critical narratives examining the dangers of technology have disappeared. So long as it complies with legal and technical standards, the market selling technology now operates without constraint. Yet, know it or not, humanity is now actually deeply entrenched in a 'double bind'.[8]

While initially it appeared that technology was adopted to amplify the power of the body and to stave off the dangers of 'nature', it increasingly became employed to attempt to dominate the natural world (which is now retaliating, albeit unknowingly, with a vengeance). This misdirected history is now producing conditions that might well end up threatening the very viability of life itself, including our own life (at least as we know it). Rather than recognizing the most immediate events marking this situation fearfully, and meeting them with grave concern, the dominant disposition of governments and their economies is the reverse. They support the proposition that technology is an available and developable means to 'save' the day – it is treated as an object of faith. This disposition of restricted vision in turn folds into a lack of political imagination. Effectively, and within a culture wherein technology has become hegemonic, the processes of technology's neutralization and concealment by design have combined to further remove it from critical and essential interrogation. The degree to which technology is of political significance is directly related to its invisibility and increased agency as directive of bodies, work, culture, environments and futures.

Fear and Technology

Reflecting on what he had learnt from the political philosophy of Thomas Hobbes (1588–1679), Schmitt, viewed human beings as essentially danger-ous. Moreover, the ability of men to recognize this danger, and then become frightened by it, created a 'need for security'. The development of 'the nation state' was thought to be the means to deliver this security (although, as we know, it could equally remove it!). The price for this security was obedience to the state. But as John McCormick, when recounting Schmitt, pointed out, this established '... fear is the source of political order'. Thereafter 'human beings once confronted with the prospect of their own dangerousness will be terrified into the arms of authority'.[9]

The fast-vanishing fear of neutralization via technology, as already men-tioned, implies a technologically induced loss of memory. This effectively denotes a technologically induced transition from a state of knowing to a condition of unknowing. Counterwise, there is also the fear of the enemy, of war, of the unknown, of the other – fears that ever remain strong by virtue of the relation of the state to media technology as the source of the appearance of what is feared. While there is a clear distinction between fear arriving via (media) technology and a fear of technology itself, the situation gets blurred by the media particularizing certain technologies (like weapons of mass de-struction – which is a socio-political, rather than technological description). Additionally, fear of dangerous technologies (like nuclear) is sought to be as-suaged by technology and its representation (thus improvements in nuclear technology are mobilized to reduce fear – the fact of more nuclear plants, and therefore more nuclear targets, seems to escape 'under the radar').

The speed of techno-political change continually overtakes the events it brings into being. For instance, while technology universalized war, and ended its containment within clear boundaries ('the battlefield'), this, in large part, removed the distinction between weapons and non-weapons (a long range bomber and a passenger aircraft become bomb; the armoured tank and the petrol tanker; the body of the armed soldier in action and body of the terrorist armed with explosives). Events associated with, for instance, asymmetrical warfare, drive already rapidly changing technologies (the relation between 'improvised explosive devices' and the nature of light armoured fighting ve- hicles is an example of this). McCormick makes it clear that technology has moved from being an economic instrument to becoming a means to structure social life as an operational techno-structure.[10] This transformation and el- evation of technology means that the issue of its relation to freedom and unfreedom arrives with ever increasing significance, even if it does not have a high profile. Technology now poses three fundamentally linked problems, into which both Heidegger and Schmitt had particular insights.

The first is Heidegger's recognition of enframing (*gestell*) as a structuring that, in the end, places everything at the disposal of technology, including human beings. One of the implications, as Fred Dallmayr recognized, was a change in the thinking of freedom, from 'freedom from' to 'freedom to'.[11] Of course, there are a host of delimitations between 'freedom from' and 'freedom to' however it is in the locus of freedom where a second problem arrives. As we have already partly recognized, what technology discloses, as major structure/structuring of world(s) and being-in-the world(s), is that anthro- pocentrism has been 'set free' as a disembodied ontological designing force. Thus anthropocentrism has become reified and has fused with technology. In effect, this means that the 'will to power' that Nietzsche showed to be a defining characteristic of the 'nature' of anthropocentrism, has become partly dislocated from human being and relocated in auto-replicating techno- structures (which can be understood through Heidegger's notion of 'will to will' with its transfer of metaphysics, as thinking, from subjects to objects). Such disembodiment implies a soulless re-embodiment functionalized in the operative mindlessness of the technological (the ramifications of what is oc- curring are profound and still largely uncontemplated, especially politically). As indicated, it has become increasingly difficult for contemporary critiques of technology to be developed, given voice and gain an audience.[12] The hege- monic condition of technology reaches deep into contemporary culture and is expressed via forms of techno-culture. This poses major semantic problems for the language of humanism and its ability to speak of the designing agency of the decentred non-human.[13] Added to this are massive disjunctures in modes of 'being-in-the-world' that are starting to open up (not least between emplaced and displaced peoples). Certainly, the call to accept responsibility for our 'being anthropocentric' needs to recognize the delimitation of 'human' agency as well as the displacement of key characteristics of anthropocentrism into the technological. Obviously, such change demands a radical rethinking of how 'we' designate the relation between the 'human,' 'nature' and 'technology' – not least because there is a considerable gap between the actuality of determinate forces and what we generally believe acts to determine.

The second problem is the widespread belief that technology has 'saving power' – this reduces technology to an object of faith; such faith is a fundamentalism. Heidegger's evocation of technology having a 'saving power' was based upon gaining knowledge of the essence of technology (its causality) by watching over it to catch sight of 'what comes to presence'.[14] Here, it is knowledge that saves, but with the acknowledgement that knowledge cannot exist independently from what has to be known (technology).

The third, linked problem centres on the possibility of contestation given the neutralization of human agency (as physical and intellectual labour) by technology (cf. Schmitt). This is not based on hope of liberation from it (for 'it' has become so infused with the worlds in which it has a presence) but rather the recognition that we need to become 'strangers in our own land'. Although standing on the structure and system of technology (as it exists as ecology and environment) contestation requires acts of rediscovery, mapping, navigation and judgement in order to create a state of manufactured estrangement, one that alienates. This alienation allows it to be recognized that, in a condition of hegemonic technology there is no position of detached observation; however, the creation of such a state of manufactured estrangement, does provide the basis of a critical view.

Just as there is a crucial need to learn how to live with 'nature' so also there needs to learn how to live knowingly and non-fatalistically with technology – as 'it' exists as the naturalized artificial (an other nature). And just as we have 'learnt' not to give way to many of our 'natural instincts' so equally our 'naturalized technological instincts' have to be curbed (like unthinkingly driving to the local shop rather than walking; assuming one has to respond to the arrival of a 'technological improvement'; or more generally, reaching for a power tool when a basic hand tool requiring a little more effort would serve just as well). Such learning requires a key place in the culture of Sustainment.

The Enlightenment installed a faith in technology as a liberatory force (what has been named here as a fundamentalism and what Schmitt called 'the religion of technicity').[15] This faith is totally misplaced. Technology is always ambiguous – it both solves and creates problems. One can neither deny the non-life force of technology nor demand anything from it. Contrary to the view of it as a mechanism of utopian delivery, it needs bringing into a critical presence as an entrenched power that threatens.[16] Hobbes' natural condition of 'Warre' has, as the naturalized artificial, arrived in a new form. It is with some irony, that we reflect on what Schmitt had to say in Leo Strauss's *Notes on Carl Schmitt's The Concept of the Political:*

> The self-evidence of today's widespread faith in technology is based only on the fact that people were able to believe that in technology they had found the absolutely and definitively neutral ground ... In comparison to theological, metaphysical, moral, and even economic questions, which one can quarrel about forever, purely technical problems entail something refreshingly objective; they allow of solutions that are clear.[17]

As we have been implying, the very appearance of ideologically inflected neutrality was an underscoring ideology inherent in the utopianism of modernity's vision of bringing 'the world' into one developmental moment. The 'purely' instrumental and 'neutral' application of technology created the machine forms and products that took on signs of what was deemed as modern. At the same time, technology, as has been acknowledged, and as Schmitt knew full well, although framed by the rise of the secular (and counter to its projected neutrality), became a complete object of faith and thereby exercised its power to neutralize. One could say that nothing conceals the emergency of the unsustainable more effectively than the blinding and enduring power of this faith in technology as salvation. Just as technology provided the means to bridge the difference between instrument, structure, spirit and matter so also did it remove any discontinuity between the socio-political and the mechanistic.

In the past few decades there has been a move from the 'party machine', to the 'media machine' and then, as Schmitt put it, to 'the machine that now runs itself'. The media 'window of' (rather than 'on') the world puts its goods on show for the mostly jaded consumers, and these 'sovereign consumers' opt for things that flash before their eyes. As long ago as 1927 in *Public and its Problems*, John Dewey expressed concern about this. In viewing the complexity of a modern, mobile and culturally diverse society, as its members stood before the challenge of making sense of emergent technological and scientific forces, Dewey found the political machine and the people wanting. His idealized answer was education – for democracy to function it needed more social knowledge. Clearly the gap between 'the conditions of his concern' and 'knowledge' has now widened enormously. We now live surrounded by complex questions that have a profound impact on futures (both ours and others). These include questions of 'natural resource use and abuse', climate change and adaptation, biophysical environmental and personal health, 'hyper-consumption' and the content of school and university education. Yet an electorate only really understands (or in many cases even cares about) a few (or any) of these complex issues. Moreover, the amateurism of the 'professional' politician is incapable of grasping and dealing with this complexity. This is because their primary interest is the horizon set by the political institution (the party) and its re-election and, second, because complex problems get passed down the line for public servants to deal with. In turn, public servants are mostly conformists, concerned with keeping up bureaucratic appearances and the day-to-day 'running of the state machine' plus looking after their careers.[18] Mostly, the politicians mouth provided 'answers'. The professionalization of politics, the job, is but one more nail in that coffin we call the status quo.

Design and Vision

We have traversed a landscape of the present in which we have situated ourselves as observers and actors in a unique moment of human worldly occupation, addressed as 'now'. Within this moment we find ourselves confronting the need to deal affirmatively with the consequences of human-induced planetary devastation. In this situation, we find democracy, as an unfamiliar familiarity, deeply implicated in the problems of 'now' and seemingly incapable of extricating and transforming itself. However, for the moment, it is technology to which most of our concern has been directed, not least to expose the error of placing faith in it as a neutral 'saving power'.

There are now two further questions to consider. What can be demanded of design practices, and the designed, in this situation – can we actually envisage what they are? And, what kind of socio-political vision can we bring to engage the massive transformative task (a task of magnitude for which we currently have no measure)?

From what has already been said, two general answers to these questions are apparent: (1) there is the demand to respond to 'making time' in the face of structural unsustainability's defuturing trajectory; and (2) there is the linked demand to respond to the coming epoch of unsettlement. To meet these demands is an enormous challenge embracing both reactive and proactive approaches.

Reactively, there is the task mentioned in the previous chapter: dealing with the world of human creation – by redirecting 'what already exists' toward Sustainment. To think this requires passing over not just the extant material fabric of human creation, but also its accompanying cultural ecology or ecology of mind – for it is here where we find defuturing embedded. The scale of this challenge can be seen by considering the fate of the city, which is in large part a product and a harbinger of technology. The city is created by technology, metabolically functions (and dysfunctions) by technology, serves technology and when necessary, is defended by it. Whatever the fate of the city, technology will be involved. The city is likely to be responded to in three very different ways.

There are those cities that will be able to be 'metrofitted'. Metrofitting is where retrofitting is taken to another level by modifying the city's built fabric, technologies and economy to deal with existing and coming problems (not least the adaptation to a new climate).[19] Then there are those cities that will have to be abandoned because they will not have enough water, or will be inundated; or because extremes of heat or cold render them uninhabitable. Some of these cities may be able to be moved (in whole or part) and then retrofitted in the new circumstances while some may be simply stripped of their reusable materials. Transporting or forming anew the economies and cultures of such cities will be as much a challenge as moving them materially. The third imposition turns on those people who will experience the extreme forms of unsettlement resulting in total loss of home and city. These people (problematically named as environmental refugees) – of whom there will be tens, then hundreds, of millions – will need new cities. These will have to be built rapidly and on a huge scale. At the same time, homes will have to be equipped and new economic and cultural infrastructure will have to be designed and provided. And then there is, of course, the challenge of moving people themselves (see case study below). How, for example, can the projected sixty million environmental refugees from Bangladesh by mid-century, be moved without major conflict? Where do they go – geographically and climatically – and to do what? These are questions without parallel. Effectively people, like all refugees, will come from and arrive into a condition of unsettlement, but on a scale currently beyond imagination.

Proactively, the design of cities and 'invention' of a cultural and material economy able to absorb huge numbers and then deliver social stability, well-being and Sustainment is an absolutely enormous challenge.

This kind of economy will require a radical mind that moves away from the notion of perpetual growth towards a situation in which quantity is displaced by quality (itself redefined, elaborated and culturally infused). Here, political vision has to totally merge with the practical tasks of addressing the performative, material and cultural character of what is needed and produced. This also means that the whole rationale and form of 'production' for 'consumption' is remade. Here, production is re-conceptualized, becoming far more articulated to responsibility for what is produced (contributing not just to sustaining the bio-physical environment but equally to skill and knowledge, and thus to a social ecology). Consumption equally requires intellectual and practical investment to become truly metabolic.

From one perspective, this new economy could propose directional changes, such as, at its simplest, the creation of long-life products exchanged with a much higher economic and cultural value. Such products would require innovative financing (perhaps many would be leased, some come with job packages, and others, like furniture and appliances, could well be included in mortgages). Clearly, these products would transform the way made things are seen, used and valued. From another point of view, the domain of services could be expanded to embrace a far wider range of product maintenance activities. Likewise, there are a variety of 'producer service' activities that beg major development: local food production; local water management; natural environmental improvement and remediation; child care; waste management; technical support and maintenance services for IT, renewable energy systems and buildings.

Connected to this, the very idea of craft invites remaking, but not as some kind of romantic revivalism. What is desirable and perhaps possible is an elevation of skills and knowledge to command current materials and technologies. The aim would be to invest what is produced with far greater care, character and aesthetic durability (beauty divested of fashion and bonded to constructed appearances of Sustainment).

In essence, the general aim has to be reconfiguring the relation between production and consumption. Make production more fulfilling and attractive, make what is 'consumed' actually consumed or enduring. Services need wider, more diverse social and economic functions than they have had to date; and management of resources has to be brought more directly within the remit of the everyday. While the actions outlined start to be introduced, much has to be eliminated, not least useless and negative (harmful) products. Likewise recovering resources from waste, while countering the waste of human resources, the profligate expenditures of energy and phasing out a whole range of parasitic professions propping up the existing economic status quo. In all cases, such action does not start from zero – there are existent traditions to draw on and build on.

Beyond addressing instrumental needs, such an economy would equally centre on a major development of forms of cultural production and exchange that would aim radically to alter the balance between cultural production and consumption. Such activity, rather than being marginal, minority participatory practices, would be positioned as key elements of everyday life. Music, dance, writing, visual arts, industrial and hand crafts here beg to be seen as not just means of pleasure but a basis for creating and exploring new ways of seeing and learning about previously closed worlds. The quality of a culture, both in terms of the forms and content of everyday life (language, cultural exchange, rituals and so forth) and specific cultural practices, thus become elemental to that remaking upon which a quality economy would depend.

Of course, all that is posited here is a suggestive and rapid sketch of what a design-transformed economy could look like and begin to do. In reality, what is signalled is a huge project that requires massive planning and a vast amount of effort, involving the work of hundreds of thousands of people for a decade or more, all directed by thinking towards *a socialized capitalism subordinated to the sovereign power of Sustainment.*

Such a project is even larger than indicated, for it also implies fundamentally addressing global inequity, which like the excess associated with wealth, is elemental to structural unsustainability.

In all, it also implies the creation of a heightened critical sensibility (not least of technology) and the launch of a project of writing a new economics – a project nothing to do with environmental economics or sustainable development, but rather a far more fundamental exercise that would be central to the task of developing an economy of Sustainment – this a project that should start now!

Who leads this task? The answer here is that designers, among other professionals, could and should take on a good deal of the responsibility. Clearly, they do not have the conventional economic expertise that is required to be remade but they could provide the practical visions that newly constituted creative economists should help to design, test and realize. Obviously, once again the ambition proposed is vast but in the end it is a far more appropriate and practical option than trying to keep the defuturing status quo in place.

Whatever sense of an agenda has been evoked, the actual agenda is much larger. At the same time, one cannot imagine it arriving in total or as a revolutionary overthrowing. Rather, it is possible to envisage the building and linking of 'change platforms' by 'change communities' that both expose and demonstrate directional change, while liberating powerful and transformative ideas – ideas that go well beyond the scale and manner of 'alternative movements' of the past. All that is indicated here is but one strategic option in what has to be a strategically plural construction of the political.

Case Study: Moving Cities

This is a case study of a practice that will become of increasing significance. A postscript to the study supports this claim.

City Move was an international design project undertaken between 22 March and 3 April 2009 to conceptualize and plan the move of the Lapland city of Malmberget, in the 'county' of Gellivare (also the name of the adjoining city).[20] Malmberget is 120 kilometres inside the Arctic Circle in northern Sweden. It is a mineral-rich region that has been mined for several hundred years. Ultimately, the move will likely affect up to 20,000 people.

The reason for the move is that below the city is an iron-ore mine. At the time of Malmberget's construction the extent and exact underground locations of the distributed magnetite ore-bodies were not known. Magnetite has high iron content, is magnetic and is in demand as a high-quality ore: it is an economic asset deemed by the Swedish government to be more important than the preservation of Malmberget.

The mine is huge. It is 1,000 metres deep and has an extensive underground road system down to this depth (it is possible to drive to the base of the mine in a bus). The decay and erosion of old workings, combined with nightly blasting (which occurs around midnight every night, followed by a small localized earthquake) have created a very large and expanding 200 metres deep pit (known locally as 'Gropen'). Notwithstanding a backfilling program of five trucks a day working around the clock for a projected ten years, the pit is swallowing the city. The deeper the mine goes, the greater the problem becomes. Even if the pit is eventually filled, it is doubtful if the land would ever be sufficiently stable to allow public access.

Northern Sweden, as said, is mineral rich. Iron, zinc, copper, gold and silver are all mined in the region. Mining iron ore in the area by LKAB (now owned by the Swedish Government) started in 1890. Initially, all mining was open cast but the mining of iron ore in the modern period has been underground. The problem of the expanding pit has been around for over forty years. Yet it has never been squarely faced. Certainly, the mining company LKAB, the municipality and the people have never effectively come together to cooperate in order to solve the problem. Some houses have been moved, whole areas have been demolished, and the pit has been fenced off. The actual process of moving houses proved to be costly, impractical and mostly a failure (some of the brick houses simply disintegrated). The practice has now been abandoned.

De facto contradiction ruled: the community, while having its existence threatened by the mine, is also dependent upon it. In this respect, the city has become a monoculture consisting of the direct labour force, sub-contracted labour and suppliers. The number of people dependent on the mine means, for all intents and purposes, no mine, no economy, no future. More than this, working at or for the mine has over-determined the cultural life of the city. Because of the high wages, young men opted to work for the mine, rather than leave and gain a tertiary education. Young women either took jobs as truck drivers at a nearby open-cast multi-mineral mine (they are favoured because they have been shown to be less hard on the trucks' gearboxes as the men) or they left to seek education or employment in southern cities.[21]

The Frame as Given
The forty participants in the City Move event (including the author) were from seventeen countries, and from a wide range of design and related disciplines. Although all arrived with the expectation of actually moving the city, the situation was far less clear. The project brief posed the problem as being more about moving the community than built urban fabric, and while leaving the location of the 'new city' open, there were many limitations on where it could

go. Dominantly, the brief asserted a need for the community's fears to be countered, change to be faced, issues of insecurity addressed, a desire to move be created and concerns for 'the little people' be recognized. In every other respect, the brief was vague (organizational means, process, cost and timing were all omitted). Above all, the impasse between the mining company and the municipality on the funding of future action was not resolved. This problem has a history, especially in relation to questions of compensation for the loss of homes.

The brief requirement was that solutions were to be presented in a standardized exhibition format – to national government ministers (two), LKAB, the municipality and the community.

The Event
The participants were divided into six teams with the same brief, although approaches taken varied. Some focused on new visions, others were more conventional and centred on eco-tourist development and ideas arising from consultation with local people. This case study will present a summary of the 'Feel Free: Organize' group (the author's).

The group dominantly understood the problem as having three aspects:

- the community's lack of cultural and economic diversity (the place was a monoculture);
- the city's geographical isolation (120 kilometres inside the Arctic Circle and well over 1,000 kilometres north of Stockholm) with a population that seemed to have a very limited awareness of the world beyond the region; the city was shrinking as the mine swallowed it up and as its ageing population was becoming depleted;
- the forces of municipal and corporate power had demonstrated a failure to grasp, name and engage deep structural problems.

This understanding was gained by talking to representatives of LKAB, the municipality and the community (including young people). From this, a response was formulated. It was not based on designing the technical means to move the city, or conceiving a new city to inspire. Rather, it devised and developed a cultural, economic and political process to enable a new city to come into being, supported by an organizational model. This combined a development and design process encompassing new industries based on meeting specific socio-environmental needs and a university campus supporting the strategy. Effectively, the approach was an applied, proto-exercise of design as politics. A slightly more detailed account of the elements of the proposed process should make this clearer.

The first stage, with local and outside input, would focus on the creation of 'cultural capital' (knowledge and power of imagination) and experiential capability to gain a collective, but not uniform, view of affirmative futures – these to be projected via carnivals, festivals, exhibitions, drama, music, dancing, educational workshops, social events, etc. The aim was to create common experiences, perceptions and conversations able to breakdown the monoculture, while establishing new social links and imaginary futures – moving from conditions of limitation to ones of potential.

The second proposed stage was forming a 'futures corporation' (owned by all the social, economic and political elements from which the community was constituted). The intent of this corporation would be to bring everyone together organizationally to support and facilitate:

- linking all formal and informal community development actions, including forming new networks;
- forging common goals based on common interests;
- generating the knowledge and resources needed to drive cultural and economic innovation;
- proposing actions, forms of development and new industries able to trigger the birth and organic growth of a new city.

The project presentation outlined how a 'futures corporation' would be designed, formed and operated (with an appropriate decision-making process).

Stage three illustrated the kinds of industries and institutions that could provide the foundation out of which a city could emerge. These illustrations included the creation of a 'local area renewable energy network', a new kind of university campus, a 'rapid city building construction industry', and an arctic artificial sun industry (based on a large reflector inside a helium-filled balloon).

All these stages were brought together to show the community how to move from uncertainty to certainty, accept change and create possible futures. More than this, it showed how exposing the global implications of the project could break 'introspective localism'.

The Feel Free: Organize group recognized the importance of global issues on two counts. First and most generally, many of the international participants were involved in the project because they recognized that moving cities would become an increasingly common need and practice in the future – they wanted to learn more about the process beyond the local and the immediate. Second, LKAB, while seen from a local perspective, was working in a global market and this market was recognized as being able to be co-opted into delivering solutions.

The Frame Expanded
To understand the global and local connection, some more contextual information is needed.

- The group noted that mining (especially open cast mining) generates vast amounts of waste (mostly rock) – in the Gellivare region this being over 98 per cent of the extracted material.
- To add value to their resource, LKAB turn the magnetite ore into pellets, which are taken by rail trucks to ports to be shipped to customers around the world. The trucks return empty.
- Iron and steel mills exist in the region. One of the main waste materials from their blast furnaces is 'slag' (it is mostly limestone and functions to extract material contaminants). Slag is a cementitious material – it is very similar to cement and it can be (and is) used as such.
- Notwithstanding logistical challenges, it would be possible to turn waste rock from open-cast mines into an aggregate, bring slag to this material via rail to make concrete, and then, with formwork, produce pre-cast building products.

- It was pointed out that such building products could be used in the creation of rapidly constructed cities – the context here is climate change. Recently adjusted figures (cf. the Copenhagen meeting of March 2009) dramatically increased the expected rate of rising sea levels. Current ad hoc ways of dealing with refugees are not viable in the face of such a crisis – many rapidly constructed cities will have to be built.
- The industry proposed for stage three of the 'city move' was thus not just pre-cast concrete 'tilt-up' building component manufacture. Rather, it had three elements: rapid-city and prefigurative design services (adaptable, off-the-shelf city plans, including infrastructure); pre-cast building components for commercial, business and domestic structures; container transportation and logistics. Obviously, much complexity goes along with the planning, initiation and development of such an industry. Recognizing this complexity, it was proposed to create a campus of an existing Swedish university to specialize in moving cities, rapid-city design and construction and related socio-cultural and economic issues.

The key point of the proposal was to bring local and global needs for delivering sustainable futures into convergence. This would encompass the form of a new city, a new economy and a revitalized social fabric. Furthermore, it would break the monoculture of Malmberget; inject 'new blood' and knowledge into the community.

The ability of the 'City Move' project to embrace the kind of approach outlined was circumscribed. The organizers (the Swedish Industrial Design Foundation) should have insisted on a more coherent brief from the municipality; a formal exercise of problem definition was needed; the formation of the design groups and the establishment of a design process, should have been far better facilitated. Limited time and expediency meant falling back into popularism and pragmatism (whereas the complexity of the problems begged a great deal more analysis, theoretical rigour and conceptual exploration). It would also have been better if the form of the final exhibition presentation had been permitted to be appropriate to the kind of solution being offered. Notwithstanding these limitations, a good deal was learnt by every one of the participants, the project did trigger local dialogue and progress toward all parties working together has been made.

Postscript

In October 2009, Gall & Medek Architects, Brisbane, in collaboration with the Design Futures Program, Griffith University, Queensland College of Art, made a submission to a design ideas competition initiated by Gold Coast City Council for a Cultural and Civic Precinct Master Plan. The City of the Gold Coast is one Australia's major tourist resorts. Rather than conform to the given brief, the submission proposed transforming the city, including moving a significant segment of it. This proposition was based on responding to existing coastal erosion on the Eastern seaboard of Australia, the fact that a good deal of the city is based on a flood plain and the expectation of substantial sea level rises and storm surges in coming decades. A contour of 4 metres was drawn (based on a maximum 2-metre sea-level rise and a 2-metre storm surge). Design decisions were based on 'designing in time' and what had to change to deal with this situation – this meant designing back from an assumed future.

The submission, named 'Gold Coast Two' had three key elements.

- The creation of a satellite city with a link corridor to the residual Gold Coast City. This would be both an area of residential relocation and new industry development. Movement would be via a coordinated process of destruction of the old to be abandoned and creation of the stages of the new city. Some of the old would be moved to the new, plus it would partly be built with material 'mined' from the old.
- City reconfiguration: elements of the abandoned the city above the 4 metre line, as well as some tower blocks, could be transformed, linked by bridges (which could be built upon) and/or serviced by boat. This reconfiguration would also be given a strong symbolic dimension wherein the memory and story of the rise and transformation of the Gold Coast

could be marked and told. It would also include a major food production component (fish and urban farming).

■   The creation of a floating suburb associated with the formation of a new industry. This suburb would be formed out of clusters of floating homes in sheltered spaces in a newly formed, inner Gold Coast archipelago. The homes would be plugged into service conduits (power, water and sewage). This form of dwelling would act as the focus of a major research and development project to underpin the establishment of a new industry. Effectively, the creation of such a suburb would provide the marketing environment for a potentially worldwide industry (which might be based at the satellite city).

Woven into these elements would be a number of new 'economic and cultural drivers'. Two kinds of cultural institutions were put forward to illustrate the potential of this kind of development: an inter-cultural resort and a multiversity.

The inter-cultural resort aimed to dynamically illustrate an emergent global post-national culture that would be essential to create to help avoid conflict from climate change – this by showing cultural futures as pleasurable experience, new knowledge, entertainment and adventure. It would export this content and message locally and to the world.

The multiversity would generate and trade on all the knowledge developed to create the whole 'city move, new economy, new culture' experience – this together with generating the knowledge required to live, work and survive in a world with a changed climate. The multiversity would recognize and exceed the limitations of universities and their disciplinary structures.

Based on the quality of the provocation and ideas, the Gold Coast Two submission was named 'supplementary winner' and awarded Aus$18,000. The Australian Broadcasting Corporation produced a radio programme based on it.[22]

3

Redirection, Design and Things

Designing has to be grasped and made present as an activity that extends well beyond the rubric of designers. Designing goes ahead of all that we intentionally bring into being, thus it is integral to all forms of prefigured human productive action. More than this, it is also the consequence of much that is produced – designed things, functionally, operatively, go on designing with positive or negative consequences for users and often society as a whole (the coal-fired power stations is a graphic negative example of this). Despite this, it has proved enormously difficult to gain widespread recognition of the importance of design.

Without being consciously directed, and for many decades, two forces have combined to work against this recognition. First has been design's designation as a particular domain of knowledge and practice that has restricted how its agency is perceived. The design professions have been complicit in creating this delimited view. Second has been the ultra-reductive way the media and much of the academic concern with design has characterized it. Dominantly, the approach has been to reduce the presentation of design to aesthetic concerns, with a focus on taste and style. Added to this has been the delimitation of an already circumscribed presentation of the field to just a few areas of practice – mostly architecture, furniture, fashion, graphics and 'designer' objects. The vast bulk of that which is designed – its character, function and consequence – goes by in silence.

Two observations flow from this: far more people in many more domains of thought and practice need to pay greater attention to designing and the designed. For, writ large, the designed prefigures the nature of those things that are determining the fate of the world that we are bringing into being. As such, it is determining our fate. At the same time, much more attention needs to be given to what designers do.

Currently the design profession, in all its diversity, is unambiguously a service industry bonded to the economic status quo. But for it to become an affirmative force of redirection towards Sustainment (and in so doing, contribute to remaking a politics beyond democracy) it has to become truly futural and political – which implies design becoming more dynamic, more powerful and more able to communicate the significance of designers to society in general. This means that the way designers think the culture they create and the practices they establish have to break radically with existing and dominant patterns. The obvious question is: how can this change happen? Clearly the answer begs practical and situated responses but all such responses need to be based upon a solid and critical conceptual base. What follows aims to be an explicit contribution to bringing this base into being but, of course, within the wider context of the entire book seeking, in other ways, to serve this end.

The Agency of Design Redirected

The development of a viable political theory of Sustainment is one thing; the design and creation of the institutions to materialize such a theory is another. Clearly, between this theory and its institutional realization a means of enablement has to be created. The project of Sustainment carries such a means: redirective practice. This is a meta-practice that can be understood as a gathering of practices under a common understanding and intent within which design is situated as a powerful actor. In its emergence, redirective practice acknowledges the imperative of dealing with 'what already is' and turning it towards the future with sustaining ability.[1] The example of 'metrofitting' given in Chapter 2 is a clear instance of this.[2] Rather than seeing the problem of the unsustainability of almost all the world's cities as something to be addressed just by architectural, transport, energy and industrial based solutions, 'metrofitting' equally embraces the transformation of how risks are identified and mapped, how the city functions as a 'semiosphere', how it can be managed as water catchment, used as a location of food production and treated as an environment that invites modifications in how, where and when we work.

Positioned between things as they are (the structurally unsustainable as normalized) and Sustainment (a project and condition in which the process of making time is normative), redirective practice has vast futuring potential. Realizing this potential requires intellectual impetus and the communication of the situated attainments of actual projects across many disciplines. The demand and opportunity for the practice will be most dramatically seen as the global condition of unsettlement become more apparent. In this situation, there is a pressing need to rethink, redesign and reinvent the very 'nature' of urban and rural life (and the relation between them).

Equally by design, as a practice of redirection, there are a vast number of things to destroy, recover, remake, change and create for Sustainment to be possible. Although, again, the conceptual challenges are daunting and practical difficulties formidable, a capability already exists to bring to such tasks. However, this capability (capacity) begs major development. By far the largest challenge will be bringing redirective practice to the remaking of the institutionalized political domain. The key to doing this, will be the establishment of what will be explored later as the 'dictatorship of the imperative of Sustainment' – for unless Sustainment becomes sovereign, the political, as futural, will always be negated by the politics of the status quo.

Breakability

Unquestionably, there are substantial political fault lines within the status quo into which wedges of affirmative change can be driven. Recognizing this, and having appropriate wedges available, is obviously crucial for design as politics.

If anyone doubts that radical political change is possible, they have failed to learn the overwhelming political lesson of the twentieth century. It was a century littered with the ruins of regimes with political ideologies that were deemed to be 'iron clad' and historically unshakable. Certainly, the lesson of Berlin in 1989 was that there are no politically constructed walls that cannot break and crumble. It is with this knowledge in mind that one should view the defuturing character of the structurally unsustainable: climatic events and the tendency of capital to destabilize are already making cracks appear. But these cracks will only increase and deepen unless appropriate transformative action is taken, which is why our concern is focussed upon the entelechy of Sustainment (action affirming its potential to become actualized). Here, and from lessons learned from deconstruction, there is clearly a need to hypostatize what can be actualized.

Sustainment requires the identification of those critical moments within which it is possible to make vital decisions that open the way to redirective transformations. Strategically well-directed and theoretically informed action can be prefigured in response to this moment once it is recognized. The current moment, our 'now', exists between recognition of crisis and the actual circumstances turning critical. Effectively, this moment is ambiguous and of unknown duration (from some perspectives, the moment of turning has passed). So while affirming the absolute need for action, actually taking it rests in a state of undecideability. Because of this, there is a danger that decisions will be taken too late: when crisis turns to breakdown. All one can do in this moment of *aporia* is to contemplate the situation and make ready. A politics of design cannot make this moment appear more overtly or graphically. What it can do, though, is to confront attempts to cover over dangers, establish proto-communities of 'change agents' and make a *chorismos* (a separation, a space of withdrawal) that can alter the proximity of change agents to the familiar (be it of worlds, pleasure or things). Such action produces a self-created condition of alienation wherein one becomes an outsider while remaining on the inside of the situation from which one is recoiling.

Such political action can also help affirm a commitment to the value of 'that which has to be sustained'. Thus, in essence, a politics of design, so disposed, is the designing of the redirective designer into a position of critical action.

No matter our power, working toward Sustainment is always *dioxis* – a striving towards something that is ineluctable. To be able to be what we need to be, we have to be captured by what we strive for, which means that we have to be open to *orexis* (a striving that is a willing, felt as a desire). In other words, Sustainment is not just a condition that 'we' try to bring into being but rather it is also something we become. To become such a being is not an act of will, nor is it the action of a single individual hurling themselves in the face of the forces of defuturing. Rather, it is the acquisition of a learned exemplary disposition, attuned with Sustainment. At its most basic, what is being said here is that 'we' need not only to work to create Sustainment but equally to embody it. So although Sustainment requires instrumental action, designed direction and practical wisdom (*phrönesis*) to come to be, it equally needs a political ontology wherein politics becomes a lived mode of being that infects its institutional forms. Certainly, Sustainment must never become *soteriological* (a doctrine of salvation) but should remain as a striving.

While evoking a thinking and language of another time (and in so doing, symbolically reiterating the past as a site of relearning for the future), what has been said equally expresses thinking futurally.

Advancing Futural Thought

To go forward we have to go back to examine the particular character of the milieu formed by, and in, Western culture and economy out of which contemporary design emerged – which means critically looking at the substrate upon which design stands (the ideas and values that constitute its cultural and economic foundation). Notwithstanding that this foundation may be elusive, it is present as a post-Enlightenment deposit – an afterlife of Enlightenment philosophy embedded in everyday life. Put simply, we all think and act out of a philosophical heritage – we do not have to know anything about the Greeks, Kant, Hegel, and so on, to be affected by their thinking.

Claims abound that philosophy is in ruins. Three situations support this view: (1) the loss of the impetus and potential of post-structuralism and deconstruction (as they offered a revitalization of thinking philosophically); (2) a continued decline in the status of the humanities (and thus the teaching of philosophy) due to the global drift towards instrumental and vocational education combined with the displacement of philosophy by (and as) science; and (3) the shrinking of the institutional space of 'the serious' within Western culture as it has embraced 'entertainment'. In the light of these claims, the dominance of instrumentalism is evident (instrumentalism has effectively become the intellectual base of materialist culture; as such, it reduces things to pure utility wherein, for example, the symbolic becomes just a means to valorize commodities).[3]

The counter claim is that philosophy has to recreate itself in the face of the cultural lacuna that is elemental to, but an under-recognized aspect of, structural unsustainability. There is a need to create new cultural spaces within and outside the academy that can embrace practical philosophy. This acknowledges that Sustainment cannot come to be without innovative thought itself becoming a redirective practice. Before elaborating further, we need to retrace the steps that brought us to where we (as readers) are.

Backwards to Go Forward

For those of us from the Western tradition, the imperative to think anew returns us to reconsider a turning point for Aristotle (when critically looked back at, and built upon, pre-Socratic ideas and then looked forward to a practical philosophy based on ethically effective action as it informed politics: the sphere of choice).[4] His Janus-like perspective yielded a reflective, critical way of thinking based on educated opinion combined with rigorous interrogation of what he observed in the world around him (this, as a basis for projective 'scientific' knowledge). From a retrospective viewpoint, Aristotle created a mode of thought (obviously, before there was a division between scientific and philosophical thought) in which philosophy and science coexisted. This enabled him to retain an engagement with the fundamental questions of first philosophy (most basically, questions of 'the why' and the 'what is') while turning to what was to become the modern question and preoccupation – 'the how'.

Put at its simplest, the scientific method, of which Aristotle was a precursor, developed and gained ground, while his reflective, ethical and political agenda was, in the main, cast aside. This is one of the reasons why the instrumental question of 'how' came to dominate Western metaphysics and gain hegemonic status. One of the most significant consequences of this turn was the reduction of objects (via science) to material qualities, systemic function and so on. The endless productivist project of learning and disclosure, while delivering a huge store of knowledge, has equally been accompanied by darkness. So much was concealed and forgotten, including the symbolic environment that objects contributed to and from which they gained their cultural agency. Effectively, and notwithstanding the agency of design, the objectification of objects diminished the qualities of their being and 'our' perception of them. Ironically, a great deal of modern industrial design was preoccupied with the symbolic meaning of objects, but dominantly from a discourse of bringing culture into economic service (especially through the object as sign generating increased exchange value).[5] Such secular symbolism has little or nothing in common with the more fundamental spiritual landscape populated by human beings, and their interaction with artefacts. This landscape, in all its difference, was the site of the creation of the material cultures and plural worlds of meaning of all the varied human societies. Contemporary 'cultures of consumption' are oblivious to the objectification that renders spirit in-animate and conceals the symbolic essence of things (their cultural agency). All the branding, and notions of 'emotional design', as they are claimed as symbolic actions, evacuate culture in the very act of its appropriation and injection into the instrumental.

We, as a modern(izing) global constituency, are now at a historical juncture wherein we know so much but fail to grasp that we equally understand so lit-tle. The past, present and future of the destructiveness lodged in our ontology (previously identified as the defuturing character of our anthropocentrism) goes by un-confronted. As a result, so many of our collective mental and physical efforts to deal with the structurally unsustainable continue to be misplaced. This situation will remain dominant unless we embrace a politics of design able to bring the remaking of our selves and things together.

The latter has to be based on establishing a level of global equity that reduces 'the standard of living' (as currently conceived) of affluent nations while improving the economic quality of life of the poor by just, empowering and futural means. One can but re-emphasize, Sustainment cannot be at-tained without equity.[6]

Yet it is doubtful if there is a single elected politician on Earth who is at-tempting to think and present the enormity of the structurally unsustainable and the fundamental political transformations that it demands. The green political parties of the world are no exception here. In common with all other environmentalists, they represent a biocentric mode of understanding that displays little comprehension of the worlding of the designed, the complexi-ties of ecologies of mind, the relational complexity of the 'naturalized artifi-cial' that sustains us, or the impacts of the political economy of the sign. The necessity of a radically different kind of politics and a new economic paradigm simply does not arrive within either mainstream or alternative politics.[7]

In the Company of an Other from Elsewhere

Thinking, learning and design all draw from cultures of others and provide another means of going back to go forward. It is not that they offer something to appropriate via an approved act of borrowing, or by theft, but rather that they simply provide another kind of *chorismos* – another denaturalized proximity, another confrontation with alienation.

Western society has a history of publicly projecting its thinking, innovation and making as a series of attainments (or even 'solutions'). Notwithstanding genuine accomplishments, it equally displays a lack of ability and rigour in comprehending what is vital to sustain of mind and matter and why. Once 'what there is to do and how to do it' have been identified, Western society is enabled to instrumentally act. For all its attainments, the West's limitations fold into age of technological hegemony. The lack of wisdom of the knowledge claimed by the 'information age' is a clear example of this. As the rhetoric of knowledge has been inflated so the culture of learning has faded.

The dominant industrialized sensibility of this age is hostile to – and seemingly incapable of – thinking that which is not instrumental (technological). Equally, 'information', as it functions in tandem with digitized 'knowledge', operates with debilitating reductionism that flattens 'the culture and history of modes of knowing' from knowledge itself. Going well beyond early critics (like Theodor Adorno and Max Horkheimer), cultural instrumentalism directly and indirectly turns 'knowing' into the servicing of economic ends, while making a major investment in appearances. The dominant sensibility of this age lacks insight and vision beyond techno-culture. It is mostly anchored in either the already pictured or in a restricted system of picturing (belied by an enormous technological facility to manipulate images). Increasingly, visualizing is predicated upon an ethnocentric disposition toward a universal/universalizing visual language.

Within the dominant tradition of Western metaphysics, what cannot be said clearly, rationalized with precision and inducted into a consensualizing discourse, is regarded as of a lesser value or mystical. This historically inscribed reduction has contributed to the current situation, which has elevated the status of calculation. 'The measured' is deemed as truth and difference is neutralized by pluralism. This pattern has been exported, but without any account of what is being threatened or destroyed. As, in a particular setting, David Hall and Roger Ames point out:

> What is achieved in the West by dialectical accommodations of distinctive viewpoints is realized in China by institutionalized 'vagueness'. By refusing to stress the univocality of concepts or the hypothetico-deductive or axiomatic systematization of theories, and in the absence of a strict delineation of a variety of cultural interests, the Chinese have not so persistently raised to the level of consciousness the presence of distinctive semantic contexts, nor have they foregrounded the sort of dialectical conflicts among opposing theoretical contexts to nearly the extent this has taken place in the West.[8]

Classical Chinese culture was not predicated upon the agency of the mind of rational subjects but on the designing of aesthetic forms and traditions directed by a sage. The sage can be understood here as an authoritative person who advanced to become an exemplary person and thereafter transcended selfhood as discourse. The thoughts of Confucius, for instance, while associated with an historical figure, became independent from the specificity of his being. This tradition was not sustained by 'a will' but by the dynamic relations of cultural structures, material practices and material forms (and thus, as artifice, pleasure, ritual and lifeworld was a powerful agency of ontological designing).

While the form and content of historical appearances fall away, there is still much to learn from China's past (and from other cultures) as it (they) guided and sustained the culture for millennia. In particular, it is possible to find rich and complex relations between time, directionality, 'the being-of-beings' and the 'being-of-things' that all suggest the value of opening up an anthropology of ontological design predicated upon examining the 'worlding of beings', which neither folds into utility, symbolic relations to things nor mechanistic determinism. At the very core of Classical Chinese thought was the notion that all *things* are dynamic, everything changes and that this is the way (*tao*) that all force, the idea of 'flow' was being recovered by the Greeks revisiting pre-Socratic thought via Heraclitus. (Aristotle strove to bring systematic thought to flow, as *kinesis*, to disclose *phusis*. His thinking was to lead to the reification of *phusis* as 'natural' – later to be subsumed to the laws of physics and the organicism of biology. However, as Heidegger showed, Aristotle's thinking and understanding of causality does not coincide with the now ruling mode in which it has been cast.)[9]

A Question of Things

Things and objects are not divided by organizing principles, inertia, social or material form, the abstract or the concrete. Rather they flow into each other, are in dialogue and are the resultant matter of discourse.

In so far as design as politics posits things with enormous significance, it is again worth giving a little more attention to the significance of the place of things in classical Chinese thought, for here the issue of anthropocentrism powerfully reasserts itself. To do this we turn to François Jullien's deep understanding of how ancient Chinese culture understood things (which cannot simply transposed into a Western tradition and a 'thingness of the thing').[10]

One of Jullien's most significant projects was the exposition of the significance of *efficacy* in Chinese culture. He explains it at length via an examination of the act of origination as carried forward by the continual transformation of things through their propensity to take on a life of their own.[11] In this respect, efficacy directly connects to the questions of action and inaction, which are inextricably bonded together in ancient Chinese thought. The Chinese never shared the West's view that directed action could change reality. This is one of the most profound differences between the cultures.[12] Considering this, 'the efficacy of things' can be understood as a process that is mostly not a visible or strident force but predominantly discrete and virtually unseen. As the origination of something, it simply happens un-noticed as the being of the thing itself unfolds.[13] For instance, the best of leaders act without being seen to do so. Jullien goes on to conclude that this 'propensity thus provides the key to the actualisation of things'.[14] The ancient Chinese story of the three physicians, recounted in Thomas Cleary's introduction to Sun Tzu, *The Art of War*, graphically illustrates the point.[15] Action so characterized is a with-drawal into 'acting-without-action' – which is acting (be it in medicine or war) while giving way to the recognized evolving agency of the unfolding 'thing' (the condition of 'respondence').[16] It thus means acting based on allowing the weakness, flaw or entropic character of 'the thing itself' to run its course. Now from an ecological, ontological and ontologically materialist point of view, this understanding confirms a circularity of designing whereby 'things design the designing of the design of things that design.' Thus ontological designing (a way forward to positing a responsibility with things) can also be slated back to Aristotle (as an idea he both travelled toward and away from).[17]

Jullien opens his chapter in *A Treatise on Efficacy* with a discussion of Aristotle's pronouncements in his *Physics*, where he argued for the primacy of first causes. This idea travelled from being a Greek universal projection to the Western imposition that flowed through to the making of a universally modernized understanding of science and technology overriding cultural difference.[18] Interestingly, Jullien points out that the 'Chinese tradition had scant interest in causal explanations, and showed a distinct lack of enthusi-asm for myths.'[19] He also emphasizes the importance of etiology (the science of causes) in the Western tradition. This preoccupation with causal explana-tion was both prefigured and extended by science, forming a lineage from the earliest mythological narratives of things, functions, worlds and spirit to the proto paradigms of contemporary astrophysics and theoretical biogenetics. All of this thinking is vested in a particular model of reality that is taken to demand functional description. In contrast:

> The Chinese interpretation of reality in any realm, and even where most generally specu-lative, thus appears to proceed through the understanding of things. One starts by identi-fying a particular configuration (disposition, arrangement), which is then seen as a system according to which things function: instead of the explanation of causes, we have the implication of tendencies. In the former, one must always find an external element as an antecedent, and reasoning can be described as regressive and hypothetical. In the latter, the sequence of change taking place stems entirely from the power relations inherent in the initial situation, thereby constituting a closed system: in this case we are dealing not with the hypothetical but with the ineluctable. In the context of natural phenomena and in first philosophy, this *ineluctability* of *tendency* or *propensity*, depending on the word

chosen by the first Western interpreters of Chinese thought as they tried to convey its originality. Thus Leibnitz, attempting to refute Nicoló Longobardi's arguments declares: 'The Chinese, far from being at fault, deserve praise for their view that things come about through their natural propensities.'[20]

Although as indicated, the idea of flow was halted by a preoccupation with causality in the Greek tradition, it was more resilient in ancient Chinese culture, as evident in the significance given to the notion of propensity.

Political Things

It might seem that, in our account, 'things' have displaced a concern with the political and to a lesser extent, design. Not so. The political returns as a 'thing', be it informed by learning from the Chinese. Sadly, this is a learning that almost all of contemporary Chinese culture has mostly forgotten as a result of the 'cultural revolution' that took place between 1966–9 as well as the more distinct but enormously damaging 'clearing of the past' (physical and psycho-social) that commenced in the mid-nineteenth century to make way for a 'modern future'. Conflicts over the modern, which deemed all aspects of tradition as a bar to progress, were bloody. They dramatically shaped the nation's history, this being graphically illustrated by the Taiping Rebellion (1850–64). The Rebellion, led by the mystic Hong Xiuguan, had the intent of using China's past to direct the form of its future. Hong Xiuguan brought a peasant army and a number of secret societies together to oppose the modernizers, especially the Self-Strengthening Movement (1861–94). Between twenty and thirty million people died during the course of this conflict, with about the same number dying in a famine that followed.[21] As Joseph Needham's huge project of documenting the *Science and Civilisation in China* (commenced in 1943 and spanning over half a century) indirectly evidenced, the value of the past was continually neglected or overlooked in favour of modernization. While neo-Confucianism and gestural celebrations of the inventiveness of ancient China in part acknowledge the past, these 'developments' do not add up to a historical consciousness able to critically inform future actions at any level. The cultural violence, damage and neglect wrought across a century and a half was enormous and continues to have serious consequences for the form of the nation's culture and its sustaining ability.

Our concern with the political is, of course, overshadowed by the imperatives associated with the structurally unsustainable. Given this, it might seem that discussion of Taoist notions of efficacy, propensity and causality have been an unwarranted digression. Again not so: they are crucial to thinking a *way* forward. Having said this, if the lesson of structural unsustainability as the product of unknowing action is to be learnt (which makes it a problem lodged with the thinker rather than the thought), the defuturing propensity of the structurally unsustainable world of human creation has to be made tangible. What this means is actually disclosing how particular forms of designing and making our world within the worlds are future destructive. Yet in its omnipotence the quality of this world is not at hand – it is not merely 'out there' as an identifiable object. Yes, there are all those overt symptoms of the structurally unsustainable that preoccupy environmentalists and environmental technology; but equally there is the over-determination of our anthropocentric being as it does not see both the destructive dimension of artifice and the misuse of so much that actually has an ability to sustain. This is why, as has been pointed out, the essence of the structurally unsustainable rests with the mode of our being, rather than just with the form, matter and use of the things of our creation.

The political that is intrinsic to 'the moment of decision' carried by the nature of the propensity of things is clearly far removed from its association with 'the politics of now'. Likewise, as we shall discover via Carl Schmitt, friends and enemies are not defined in relation to an arbitrator who takes sides but in relation to the question of absolute decision. Equally, democracy moves away from ideology linked to choices of individuals and political parties to choices of alignment with particular directions of 'the agency of things' as they are articulated to the multiple and plural forces of Sustainment. In contrast to environmentalism, as a particular politics within the 'democratic process', a decision bonded to action lodged in ontological designing comes from 'political things'. This centres on things arriving with a propensity towards 'sustaining ability' within a political economy of Sustainment. Therefore it is not a matter of directly confronting the seemingly impossible challenge of the structurally unsustainable – a challenge that is predominantly hidden by the objects of engagement of 'sustainability technologies'. Rather what has to be given way to is making the decision (a moment of responsive rather than directive action) that emplaces Sustainment as sovereign. This marks a move from projective action to 'respondence' (as indicated, this term is put forward as in-action, which is how the other of action translates from Chinese Taoist philosophy).

As decision opens the way to respondence, the possibility arrives of being directed or at least being waylaid by things that sustain. But at the moment the possibility of realizing this objective is blocked by three linked obstacles: (1) the inability of the Western rationalist paradigm and its hegemonic technology to recognize the consequences of its action; (2) the problem of Western intellectuals disengaging from their existent ecology of mind so they can move to another philosophical foundation; and (3) the dominance of a mode of democracy that has become a 'vote for self-interest'.

Once more, we find ourselves standing in the shadow of the seemingly impossible: the political and practical challenge of overcoming the unsustainable demands the imposition of the unfreedom of Sustainment made sovereign. Once more we have to consider this imposition at length.

Designed Things

There is a very short, modest and true story from a not especially unusual village in Timor-Leste. It is a story about the men of the village and was told by the son of the village baker. To understand it, one has to recognize that this new and small nation has a bloody distant and recent past. A long time Portuguese colony, it was occupied by Indonesian forces when the Portuguese departed in 1975. They stayed for twenty-five years and during this time killed about 15 per cent of the population. After gaining independence the nation experienced a period of violent and civil unrest. Now back to the village.

The baker and many other men only work during the morning. In the afternoon – every afternoon – they make music. The music they make is with a few old guitars, a violin and song. They sing in their native tongue, of life, hopes, pain and dreams. From the bricolage of things of the past they are making the new, they are singing their way into the future. Their sons, in a different idiom (the visual), are doing something similar. Likewise, once colonized, people all over the world are doing the same thing. Pleasure, coping, suffering and ontological design are all embedded in such activity. Cultural production (be it music, dance, growing food, tending animals, building longhouses, and so forth) is productive of community and thus of Sustainment. In these simple observations, in the example of the baker's village, are to be found some vital design lessons.

Making a path to the future is a common enterprise directed at the common good – what overwhelms this as a political/ideological statement is that the cultural reality of the structural unsustainability of advanced industrialized nations gets posed as the future. It covers over dreams and manifests a forgetting. It forgets that community is about an exchange of knowledge and skills; that the likes of purchased childcare and aged care are indicators of an inoperative community; that work and pleasure can exist as a continuum; that the working day is something that has been taken out of the control of working people; that making was as much a social as an economic activity; that the past and the future are stories to be told; that design is as much carried in tradition and memory as in economic practices of the market.

Designed things as designing beg to be seen in a richer context. It is not a matter of exchanging the complex for the simple. Rather, it is a question of realizing that the loss, the sacrifice that Sustainment demands can be met with a new richness, a recovery (getting better and retrieving) of that which was seemingly lost. The designing to be sought is for a quality of being in which the nature of one's life improves from a base of poverty, whether that poverty is embodied as lack or excess.

Case Study: Sustainable Design Education in a Post-Colonial Context

Timor-Leste is a small, newly independent nation still suffering in the shadow of its colonial past and recent violence. It is about 650 kilometres north-west of the Australian city of Darwin. The nation occupies a divided island – the western side was part of the former Dutch East Indies and is now Indonesian territory (with the exception of a small Timor-Leste enclave of Oscusse). The nation had been colony of Portugal for several hundred years. When Portugal withdrew suddenly in 1975, instability developed. Indonesia took advantage of the situation and invaded.

Indonesia's occupation was brutal – the official estimate is that between 1975 and 2000 over 187,000 people were killed – this, in a nation of just over one million people. When the population turned out *en masse* and voted to become independent in August 1999, there was an enormous backlash from pro-Indonesian militia, resulting in several thousands deaths and a vast amount of destruction. Responding to this situation, albeit somewhat belatedly, Australian troops were dispatched to establish peace – they were later incorporated into a UN force. Although the military presence has now been reduced and partly replaced by a UN policing operation, there is still a major UN involvement in the nation (from several UN agencies).

Since 2002 (the year the nation became officially independent) there have been several moments of instability – in particular, riots in 2006 associated with the actions of disaffected Timorese troops and, in February 2008, an assassination attempt on the life of President Ramos Horta, which left him seriously wounded. He recovered after protracted medical treatment. Australia still has around 600 troops in Timor-Leste – they are expected to remain there for some time. Having left once, and then having to return in 2006, withdrawal is unlikely until it is clear that conditions are really stable. The position of Australia towards the nation is explicitly stated in its 2009 White Paper on Defence: 'East Timor is likely, for some time, to be challenged by significant

hurdles to progress in political, security and social reform, as well as difficulties in ensuring food security, adequate infrastructure and employment.
Enduring cultural and political divisions will create the conditions for potential
periodic outbreaks of violence.'[22]

Timor-Leste is also viewed by Australia in terms of wider strategic regional
security, especially regarding its proximity to other somewhat volatile nations
and natural resources. Moreover, the Defence White Paper noted that the
combination of climate change, food shortages, booming population growth
and mobility, public health crises, water shortage, poverty and competition
over energy resources are all growing regional and global strategic issues
(which are projected as becoming significant by 2030).[23] Timor-Leste has the
potential to be seriously destabilized by these impacts (and in some respects
it already is).

While Timor-Leste has a substantial resource – revenue from oil reserves
in the Timor Sea – the nation still has serious economic and social problems.
It has one of the highest birth rates in the world, 80 per cent of the population is under 25, around 70 per cent of the people are unemployed (this figure
conceals the complexity of subsistence agriculture), literacy levels are low (especially among women), the education system requires major improvement,
there is a good deal of domestic violence, the nation's infrastructure is poor,
and the environment is degraded in many areas. Above all, poverty is rife.

A Culture of Change

It is against this backdrop that the idea was conceived of seeding a Timor-
Leste focused 'creative industry' by establishing an education institution with
a curriculum based on local art, crafts and skills. The people of Timor-Leste
have a rich tradition in craft, especially *tais* (weaving), jewellery and wood carv-
ing. The nation also has a very interesting history of indigenous architecture
and house decoration. Overarching all these practices is a strong graphic sensibility, often with the same kind of symbolic forms being used across widely
different media.

Notwithstanding the material culture of the nation having been exposed to
plunder, destruction and theft for overseas collections, there is still enough

historical material, knowledge and skill in the community to provide a basis for the creation of a major educational resource.

To advance the idea, the author devised a research proposal and submitted it to AusAID (the Australian national aid agency) via Griffith University in Brisbane.[24] Funding was gained for three years to research curriculum content – with a need for later funding for institutional development.

Creative Industry, Sustainment and Equity

It would be unrealistic to claim that an indigenously based, export-orientated, creative industry in Timor-Leste can solve the nation's problems, but it could undoubtedly make a contribution to cultural and economic development. This industry would need to be developed with a focus on the quality of what is designed and made so that design and craft products can be put into the international marketplace in sufficient volume to create a good income stream. Done well, this approach could be expected to: have an extremely low impact on the natural environment; establish an educated and well-treated, dispersed workforce; and deliver affirmative visual messages on new ways of seeing and making craft, while raising the positive international profile of Timor-Leste. Overall, it could provide a normative example of what could be achieved by modest investment in the creation of a viable, sustain-able and culturally constructive industry (it could also advance gender equity, assist in 'nation building' and add to national pride).

Designing of the Designed

The project, and a good deal of its research, turns on the realization of two immediate objectives: conservation of knowledge and skills and creative product innovation that flows into the larger ambition of seeding the development of an industry that provides young Timorese men and women with not just employment but with futuring prospects.

Because so many cultural artefacts were stolen, destroyed or lost during the colonial period, during Indonesian occupation and in more recent upheavals, conservation of craft skills and knowledge, together with documentation of traditional aesthetic forms, is very important. This involves both archival research and seeking out craftspeople around the nation with specialist skills (these people to be invited to give demonstration workshops). Culture, of course, is a living entity: within it things change. Change has to occur for the culture to survive. The nature of tradition is that things change slowly and undramatically; the nature of chaos is that things change quickly and unpredictably. When a new nation is created, patterns of development with processes of measured change need to be developed.

The approach of the project includes exploring methods of designing new imagery that incorporates old and established artefactual forms as a foundation upon which to conceptualize new objects; the fusion of old and new visual languages; and the creation of new ones – all directed toward the post-research aim of empowering local creative producers in accord with appropriate aesthetic, ethical and economic standards.

A 'Design as Politics' Perspective
From a 'design as politics' perspective the project sets out to establish two designing forces. The first comes from the establishment of an indigenous base upon which to construct the content of the education model. This is in contrast to the way art and craft industries have developed in many post-colonial nations, as a cash economy that transforms, and often devalues, the meanings of artefacts, rituals, and so forth, for indigenous producers, while leaving them culturally stranded.[25] The second is to significantly increase the role design and craft can play in nation building beyond the construction of iconic forms of 'national identity'. This can include the provision of a model of 'low impact' industry development; the elevation of craft practice within an economy beyond its traditional and limited forms and functions; and the formation of 'producer communities' that are able to bridge existing subsistence ways of life, urban poverty, and high investment industrial development. In so doing, what it is actually being said, is that design action is political action that can establish realizable social, cultural and economic circumstances that in turn, can lead to structural political change.

Beside delivering a model of environmentally low impact, ultra-light industrial activity, in essence, what designing an indigenous creative industry designs is: an economy of micro-economies (that could be micro-financed) within a system of distributed production feeding a culture of entrepreneurship able to lead young producers toward small business formation; a milieu of images and objects that can be used to carry an appearance of the nation to global audiences; and, of course, a proliferation of useful and beautiful objects that invite pride and care. On this last observation what needs to be understood absolutely is that craft, created and presented within the context outlined, is not merely the stuff of specialist galleries, niche market shops in the affluent cities of the world, or village stalls (which is not to say that it would not be available in all such settings). Rather it is something intended to proliferate in the everyday life of people anywhere as one of the markers of an affordable 'quality' economy. As such, it is ceramic kitchenware, a children's wooden toy, a woven wrap, bathroom tiles, a necklace, a hand made flute, a turned wooden fruit bowl, and so on – but with every object saying 'admire how well I am made, recognize the culture out of which my form and appearance comes, and acknowledge that I am a marker of the coming culture of Sustainment.'

Part II

Re-framing the Political

The human is an epistemological construct – 'man' is an invention produced out of the knowledge s/he has created as it assigns attributes of humanity. Whatever we are, we are what we name ourselves to be. Indivisibly, we are born one thing (an animal, an inhuman being) and become another by being inducted into a culture. Constructivism has the day. The search for what is essentially human has been longstanding but as Jean-François Lyotard asked, 'what if what is "proper" to humankind were to be inhabited by the inhuman?'[1] Historically, the mantle of the human has constantly fallen away to reveal another, ugly being.

Humanism is a particular discourse within this history of naming. In its earliest Western form it asserted knowledge of 'man' complemented gaining knowledge of God and celebrated the humanity of Christ; in its modern form, emanating from the late eighteenth century, it sought to privilege a concern with human interests. However, as the work of Michel Foucault made clear, in actuality this development rested on a shift in disciplinary control towards bio-power linked to new disciplinary technologies. These technologies were elemental to the rise of industrializing capitalism and its need for 'docile' bodies. This moment also overlapped with the ascent of democratic modes of representational politics wherein pluralism increasingly enabled the same to pose itself as difference.

The four chapters of this part of the book turn on the nature of the political and what was (and now needs to be) politically sovereign. In so doing, the question of liberalism, not least as challenged by Carl Schmitt, will be engaged, as will the problem of pluralism. However the overarching concern is with considering sovereignty for its remaking in the frame of Sustainment.

At its most basic, Sustainment names a futural process. It is that time in which potentiality is possible and as such, it is ontically fundamental. In a situation where defuturing has reached a quantitative point whereby 'our' finitudinal horizon is rapidly accelerating toward us, making Sustainment sovereign is not a matter of choice. It is a precondition of our being. Its arrival depends upon it being delivered by design.

4

The Political, Sovereignty and Design

Design as politics is not just another issue to add onto the existing political agenda; rather it is a politics in its own right with the potential to transform the nature of political action.

Restating

The unfolding situation of unsettlement arriving before humanity in the early decades of the twenty-first century is serious, with climate change set to become an uncontained problem (which means it will increasingly cluster, connect and amplify other problems). In particular, besides direct environmental impacts, it will increase levels of social instability as the number of environmental refugees and competition for natural resources dramatically increase. Evidence supporting this assertion comes from many sources, not least from strategic and defence planners.[1] This prospect is of particular concern in existing areas of instability, like the Middle East and south-east Asia. The greatest danger accompanying this trend is a heightening of conflict combining with a proliferation of nuclear weapons.[2] The continual growth in global population (mostly in the poorest nations), the level of inequity around the world and the extension of globalization all combine to add more risk to this already dangerous situation. Moreover, both economic stagnation (which means low investment in environmental technologies) and economic expansion (which means increased greenhouse gas emissions) have negative climatic consequences.

Against this backdrop, the question to be asked is: 'can existing democratic politics and practice cope with these challenges?' As the results of the 2009 Copenhagen Climate Change Summit unequivocally illustrated, the answer to this question is no. As intimated earlier, the kind of action needed to address the situation seriously would be deemed a recipe for electoral disaster and undermine democracy's subordinate relation to capital. One could expect a continuation of weak action until the arrival of a full-blown crisis, when a state of emergency would be then imposed. At the very best, it is likely that only a partial recovery from the situation would be possible. The complexity and demands of the situation are totally at odds with how politicians think and act, as well as the division of knowledge of ministerial portfolios and government departments. Thus the interests of representative democracy, and its degeneration into 'consumer sovereignty', are antithetical to striving to gain the means to secure 'the future'. Currently, there is simply no ground upon which to make the vital and hard decisions to direct appropriate action. Responsibility, unavoidable sacrifice and ethical action are all deferred. But at present there is clearly not another political ideology superior to democracy. One can have little faith in political scientists solving the problem. So what do 'we' do?

Certainly, it might be possible to shift action away from politics towards the political – which means shifting efforts from engagement with institutionalized politics to engaging the political nature of the world around us (hence design as politics). At the same, time 'creative communities' could and should put themselves before the challenge of developing new, realizable (rather than utopian) political imaginaries – the corrective to utopianism always has to be: 'unless a means to realize the vision exists, or can be created, it is merely an empty gesture.'

Notwithstanding the magnitude of the problems, and the fact there is no position of exteriority from which to engage them, it must be remembered that at base 'we' are the central problem. Even if a revolution was possible there is no agency to conduct it or ideology to guide it. Likewise, reforming the status quo is not an option – its defuturing impetus is too deeply embedded in the structurally unsustainable. The only real option is 'radical redirection' by redirective practices, including design. This implies redirecting ourselves, and the world 'we' have brought into being. To do this requires disclosing existing foundations of thought, practices and institutions (social, cultural, political and economic) and then remaking, supplementing and re-orientating them around three directive figures:

- relational connectedness (the basis of economy);
- new limitations (the basis of future freedoms); and
- the common good (the basis of a transformed ontology and socio-cultural life).

Remaking at this scale means taking democracy, justice, and ethics back to their initial and fundamental characteristics and then building new forms of social, economic, political and cultural action in the everyday to deliver new modes of conduct and professional practice. Essentially, living politically (which makes everyday life a continual series of political acts) takes power away from existing institutional politics as it upholds the status quo. The spell of centralized power is broken and the reality of dispersed power is animated in action, and so made visible. Obviously, the act of remaking is not going to be embraced by all but it is not unrealistic to envisage the formation of a critical mass of sufficient agency to make a major difference.

Guided and over-determined by the imperative of Sustainment, the process of redirecting the political means dividing action between foundationally remaking: (1) political subjects, (2) situated political thought and (3) those political things (practices and material relations) that constitute the everyday.

More specifically, and universally, beyond existing 'political activists', five kinds of subjects need to be registered. The critical mass, mentioned above, would arrive unevenly by migrations from a clustering of:

- people who invest their fate in what they believe to be the salvational power of a transcendental agent – these are people of faith having a religious ontology (no matter if they have a God or not) – they constitute communities of believers;
- those members of secular masses who never had, or have lost, faith in the telos of the potential perfectability of human beings and society, for whom politics is merely a matter of alignment with what best serves their self-interests and personal preferences;
- those naïve believers in techno-futures, social evolutionism and 'new age' forces who think a solution will simply arrive out of necessity, spiritual enlightenment or via charismatic leaders;
- refusalists who make the political choice of being a-political – the most overt form of this kind of subject could be called the postmodern cynic;
- democratic pragmatists and idealists who believe their political ideology to be the best of all available options (amongst oligarchy, post-socialist socialism, fascism, theocracy, and so forth).

What all these subjects have in common is a sense of difference and the necessity *to be* (sustained). Thus the starting point politically is to expose this fundamental commonality and make it available as an object of remaking within a politics of care. Here care is not being posed as a humanist attribute but as: (1) an ontological quality of our being (we exist in and by virtue of 'care' as it intuitively keeps us out of dangers inherent in everyday actions – like crossing roads, cutting bread, using power tools, etc); and (2) as the performative quality of ethical things (which is to say things that future).

Essentially, making and remaking things that care (sustaining something essential to Sustainment) is a fundamental political act via the creation and use of political things (practices and material relations) that constitute the political field of the everyday.

It is in that space between the emergence of political subjects and the arrival of political things that situated political theory emerges and acts. It is this 'thinking politically' that the subject brings to things, enabling the political to be reanimated – most obviously one can name design politicized in action as a significant example of this.

More broadly, remaking should be understood not as a superstructural remodelling but a wholesale rebuilding from foundations upward. Notwithstanding the numerous and varied attempts to discredit philosophy's deconstructive project over the past few decades, it is precisely this practice that enable the kind of disclosure needed. Getting to the foundation of things (the underpinning of why they exist and what they do) means working on 'things', so they can be rendered politically naked and then differently re-clothed.

Sovereignty Turned

Thomas Hobbes argued that the sovereign, having the power of subjecting social beings to the law, was merely enacting a process of incorporation whereby laws created to govern people fused with the laws of nature – laws to which all beings are deemed to be subject. This proposition, echoing the relation of *phusis* to *nomos* in the ancient world, was not predicated on nature as a naturalized state of things but rather as immutable external directive force, recognized and made present by and as knowledge. Thus 'nature' was claimed as providing the conceptual foundation for law itself.

The earliest written laws, those of Sumerian civilization, were based on the principle of 'an eye for an eye'. This graphically illustrates that the ground of law was 'natural law' based on interpretation of animal conduct. Effectively, as Carl Schmitt's early project on sovereignty aimed to make clear, the (be) coming of law (however defined) was a response to the unruly and unruled nature of human life.[3] This implied that the law recognized animality (bare life) and henceforth set out to ontologically design and install 'socialized being' as a way of life. Law as limit, or as Giorgio Agamben would have it 'ban', is not the restriction of freedom but the means to exclude chaos.[4] Life, however, as Agamben tells us, is not external to law but within it as 'the ban' – bare life is thus held in check by law.[5] Here, it is power that constitutes the rule of law – often imposed as an act of violence and maintained by violence. Thereafter law, as it has become sovereign, establishes the regulatory authority of the political system.[6]

Alain de Benoist demonstrates, in his historical review of the topic, that the concept of sovereignty is notoriously complex and contradictory.[7] Yet one thing is unambiguous – sovereignty is positioned both 'as the law' and 'above the law.' Agamben echoes this view in his rigorous analysis of 'the state of exception,' when he points out sovereignty is paradoxical because the sovereign power 'simultaneously acts outside and inside the juridical order.'[8]

Acting as the highest power, the sovereign steps outside the law, while remaining lawful, and so retains the power of its direction (hence creating the zone of indistinction between inside and outside the law).[9] A constitution thus gets suspended, or reinstated, by the unlawful lawful sovereign power. The 'state of exception' for Schmitt was any major disturbance of the economic, political or social status quo. Of course, in present times, this could be supplemented by large-scale terrorist conflict, limited or extensive nuclear war, or major environmental disasters. Here we should note the underpinning of Schmitt's insight was the proposition that 'all law is situational'.

We can also note that the sovereignty of every governing authority, be it God, Monarch, Dictator, 'the people', or Parliament, has had its absolute historical ruling moment but the passage to another sovereign authority can never be completely closed. No matter who or what is sovereign, one thing is true in every context: 'sovereign is he who decides the exception.'[10] In so doing, the sovereign is that beyond the law 'to which we are abandoned.'[11]

The exercise of 'the state of exception' has gained considerable profile in recent years, as already acknowledged, because of the executive of the US government authorizing the detention of hundreds of suspected terrorists in Guantanamo Bay, Cuba, many of whom were held for a number of years without due process. Such action has increasingly been employed from the end of the Second World War onward, marking a slow erosion of 'democracy in practice'. One of the earliest and worst examples were the 'concentration camps' created by the British in Kenya in the 1950s.[12] In common with Mau Mau detainees, Guantanamo Bay inmates were excluded from every condition of right and appeal. Their humanity was denied and even erased. As Agamben put it in relation to Guantanamo, they became 'unnameable and unclassified beings'.[13] Moreover, the arbitrary power exercised under a 'state of exception' meant that minor gestures, actions and careless words could have dire consequences.[14]

These remarks, made here under the rubric of sovereignty, lead to a series of troubling but vital questions. In the defuturing situation in which humanity exists (but is yet to fully recognize), what now should be the conceptual foundation of law, given the insufficiency of 'natural law'? All law implies imposed limits to exclude chaos, but given the coming chaos, what limits should be imposed now? Given that 'the world order' neither names nor acts to redress 'the emergency' confronting humanity and the impact of it on 'life' in general, what is the authority that now needs to come into being? How can Sustainment become an institution and sovereign? How can contextually appropriate (rather than universal) limits be differentially applied to serve the advancement of global equity (remembering that for large numbers of the world's population the condition of defuturing has no named presence because their horizon does not extend beyond their pressing daily circumstances)?

These questions sit before us to contemplate. The task they set is daunting. In considering them a number of things are already apparent. What is certain is that there can be no Sustainment, no retained freedoms, without stringent limits enforceable by law (the failure, internationally, of effective voluntary controls on greenhouse gas emissions proves the point). Clearly such law has to be universal and based on equity, justice and commonality across difference. The tokenism and gradualism of current processes toward international agreements to limit the forces of devastation are totally insufficient and completely out of step with humanity's fundamental needs and circumstances.

Reasserting the point, Sustainment cannot become the basis of human conduct unless it becomes sovereign. But again we have to wonder how can the sovereignty of Sustainment be made possible and become very core of a transformative project.

Certainly Sustainment has to appear as fundamental and overarching the law of all cultures. Yet if it is merely seen as another Western imposition of disproportionate sacrifices, it will fail to arrive. Effectively, the normative level of development (from nation to household) has to be significantly changed. Of course, many cultures already have values based on the Sustainment of natural resources. A good example comes from Islamic culture (the *Quran* teaches that all living things have an equal right to water).

Contrary to Sustainment being cast as base survival, it needs to be celebrated as a force (of adaptive advancement) able to direct human being beyond itself. It is an idea that centres on potentiality and is beyond 'progress.' However, to make Sustainment sovereign means overcoming the logic, limitations and perceptions of how it has been misunderstood (as sustainability) so far. Sustainment as a project requires a new kind of institutional form: a planetary institution. Here is not the place for its invention. Rather, what is appropriate to point out is that such invention is in realm of possibility (in the under-developed forms of organizations like the UN). To function in the world order would mean ceding to the rule (absolute law) of Sustainment – the rule would be mandatory. Whereas the humanism of the UN is weak, the rule of Sustainment would have to be strong.

This undertaking radically differs from those conceptual projects of the past, like Schmitt's, which sought to transcend sovereignty within the existing geometry of power. In contrast, and as suggested, Sustainment as sovereign sets humanity on another path whereby becoming developed and fully human becomes indivisible from being futural and sustainable. Clearly this implies a labour of economic and socio-cultural re-construction that has to transcend the ways 'we' destroy our worlds and each other, treat everything as a 'standing reserve' at our disposal – and allow the powerful to unjustly treat the powerless.

In practical terms, the politics of Sustainment would mean displacing pyramidal power structures by, for instance, a lateral subsidiarity model wherein both the idea of Sustainment and multiplicities of localized small-scale units of decision making (served from above) become united.[15] But again, the qualification is that 'solutions have to be situationally created'.

It is crucial to emphasize that unlike those political theorists who devote all their energies to conceptualizing what they believe to be a better structural model of sovereignty in relation to the state, law, political organization and 'the people', the approach here, is to explore issues that can deliver content bound to unfolding the idea, project and *law* of Sustainment as enacted.[16]

Imposition and Conflict

The dominant politico-instrumental tendency within the 'developed' world is to objectify the causes of unsustainability and then link them to particular policies, institutions, industries and practices. Responsibility for dealing with problems thereafter is posited with a number of powerful vested interests, not least governments and corporations. However, while the reality of specific concrete problems of the unsustainable cannot be overlooked, they are of course merely symptomatic of structurally embedded causes that are lodged in the very nature of our being modern*ized*. Obviously, this means that they are far more inaccessible and problematic to engage.

Modern human beings constituted a mode of being-in-the-world that increasingly became psychologically, socially, culturally and materially disarticulated from the biophysical and social ecologies of their fundamental dependence. However, our artificial environments – homes, cities, and all the other constructed spaces of our lives – are not ecologically autonomous. In error, we view ourselves as other than all else we deem to be in need of sustaining, yet we are of the same flesh, air, water and genetic matter of so many other life-forms.

Effectively, striving for Sustainment puts us 'at war' with ourselves. The structurally unsustainable invades every dimension of our actual and desired being and infuses our knowledge, actions, cultures, desires, dreams and language. But we mostly fail to see this situation, not least because we focus upon

those means that sustain us in the short term. In so doing, we neglect to sufficiently recognize and value all that is vital for our long-term survival. Blame
does not so much rest with us as flawed individuals as with the world that
brings us into being. In this situation, Sustainment requires the imposition
of directional change. It is not going to arrive out of mass individual self-en-
lightenment or out of liberal democratic populism – electorates are unlikely
to vote for substantial sacrifice, for limits, for sumptuary laws. Hence one
cannot be sanguine about persuading 'democratically elected governments'
to give way to the sovereignty of Sustainment and impose it as law. There is
no other viable option, but how this happens is critical. It is absolutely essential to understand that the imposition of Sustainment does not imply a grey
regime of authoritarian uniformity. Rather it requires becoming a singular
mode of being in, and acting upon, the world, that can be realized in different
ways. Differences in climate, tradition, diet, architecture, occupation – and
all those other things that give a culture its specificity – can remain directive
of difference. What then is imposed is 'commonality in difference' (with commonality going to a dramatic reduction in human destructiveness of all that
being depends upon). So contextualized, two actions can be contemplated.

The first action is the work of communicating the necessity of making
Sustainment sovereign. The current crisis of structural unsustainability does
not appear as a crisis. This 'crisis of crisis' means that a key political question is 'how can the crisis be made to appear?' Existing images don't do it,
statistics don't do it, arguments don't do it – they all simply go to symptomatic
appearances of 'the unsustainable' and lack any notion of Sustainment. What
is actually needed is an expansive relational picture that situates us, and our
political institutions, centrally as, and in, the problem(s). This picture has
nothing to do with blame and everything to do with directional change. It also
has to expose the insufficiency of how 'sustainability' is generally understood,
dominantly projected and defined by science (in its functionalism, science
only shows fragments of seeing and acting upon problems).

The second action goes to the issues of how Sustainment as sovereign is
imposed. The answer is, essentially, by the design of things (material and
socio-political) rather than by force. Our 'becoming otherwise' is a matter of

ontological change. It is a question of changing the ways things are. While design cannot do this as it is, it does have the potential, if it becomes a redirective practice (design as a prefigurative agency employed across a vast sweep of disciplines). Leadership here becomes embodied in particular practices, projects, products, structures, environments, ideas, modes of communication and forms of education as they co-join to constitute a political field. Put all more basically, imposition arrives as a gradual but accelerating occupation of the everyday. A clear example is the design response to the climate impacts upon cities discussed in the previous chapter. Metrofitting cities (retrofitting taken to the level of material and socio-cultural transformation of the city), moving cities, rapid-construction cities and the creation of new urban economies are all examples of the exercise of large-scale redesign and new design projects of the everyday. From a redirective design perspective, this massive and long-time design task is at its very beginning. Its potential power is huge, fusing imposed limits and created solutions.

Design, so framed and directed, clearly has to develop the means of both dealing with the symptoms of crisis (structurally unsustainable conditions) and the cause (our unsustainable selves) while making Sustainment sovereign.

The agenda is vast and daunting but has a starting point. It has to distance itself from the propensity to sustain the structurally unsustainable (which is what a great deal that travels under the heading of sustainability does). Ambitiously, it must learn how to design ontologically to great effect, which implies redesigning the structures that over-determine how human beings come into being (our ecologies of mind and the performative characteristics of the environments we have brought into being that ontologically design us). In truth, if viable futures are to be secured, such an agenda is not a matter of choice.

Democracy, Design, Sustainment, Order

Human beings are not born unsustainable: they are made so by the structures, values, traditions and knowledge into which they are thrown as they learn to be in and of the world.

Consider the following example: when Henry Ford introduced the five-dollar day in 1913 workers traded their freedom to control their labour for 'the freedom' of a higher disposable income. Thereafter, they ceased being tradesmen and became assembly-line workers. The trend of trading control of one's labour for economic 'benefits' became globally normative. The trickle of expenditure of Ford's workers to acquire ever more consumer goods has become a torrent – his action was one of the key triggers of modern 'consumerism'. By the 1930s in the US, and against the backdrop of the Depression, 'streamlining', as a design regime (supported by infrastructure development – especially rural electrification and the arrival of 'hire purchase') took consumerism, as an aesthetically generated desire for modern products, to a new level. The industrialized world (and much of the industrializing) was thereby put on a path to unchecked excess, and what was economically depended upon and what threatened a viable future effectively became the same thing.

Sustainment as sovereign has to confront the materiality of this situation and the powerful desiring machine that drives it: it has to be made a more vital desire. As such, it has to speak to the desire for a future, the needs of the present and to the recovery of those lessons from the past able to provide the basis of contemporary solutions.[17] It has to embrace all images, objects, desires and things that are futural.[18] But in addition to all of this, the imposition of Sustainment, as a reactive process, has to converge with a political order that 'holds what has been created in place within a relational regime'. All things have to be grasped as inter-connected. This is a key design task.

Design: An Order of Governance

In this unfolding moment of human earthly habitation, reordering will almost certainly be a vital response to unsettlement. It will mostly emerge out of need rather than desire, it will be prefigured by a moment of sacrifice and will facilitate imposed Sustainment within a system of governance.

Unsettlement means that things are out of place, are without a place and are uncertain (no matter if things are of the world or of mind). The desire and need for order carries with it a willingness to sacrifice (for security). As the structurally unsustainable bites deeper into everyday life it will certainly bring defuturing into a closer proximity with immediate imperatives.

Already this situation is becoming globally apparent in terms of food – climate changes reducing crop yields, higher prices and the redirection of produce (like corn) away from human consumption towards the production of bio-fuels. This situation is felt as unsettling and a threat to future wellbeing. Increasingly it could be expected that certain freedoms of choice would be willingly sacrificed to gain food supply security.

With a form of governance based upon imposing Sustainment (to which capital and all freedoms are made subordinate) what would (a designed) political administration look like? Without question Sustainment would be relationally connected to every department of administration. Equally, authority would be dispersed into structures able to reorder to create the conditions demanded for advancing Sustainment.

What follows is a notional exercise, not claiming rigour or sophistication. It is not a plan of what should or would be created. Rather it is a sketch of the kinds of things that a regime moving towards Sustainment would probably have to address.

As indicated, the content of the regime would be relationally connected. It would have structures and functions aimed at bringing together *the redirection of: what is to be produced and how* by a new industrial order centred on quality; *all public and market provided services*; *mechanisms of fiscal regulation and control* (possibly indexed to Sustainment goals and under some kind of centralized direction); *the management of all resources and utilities* with frameworks of limitations of scale and impacts; *the form and function of all institutions* of law, education, health and welfare being directed at new ways of knowing, care and responsibility.

All of these elements would fold into the new economic paradigm, wherein quality, rather than quantity becomes normative, and grounded in an 'across-the-board quality development program'.

It is vital that this kind of thinking is not taken to be, and viewed, as a version of the old Soviet model of a command economy, which, while directing a great deal of the economy towards military ends, also subjected industrial production and social life to rigid and mechanistic time-based plans. The regime being outlined would not try to micro-match and manage regulated supply and demand (which the USSR constantly tried and failed to do); while there are impositions, these would be based on empirically confirmed common interests; it would be about advancing the quality of goods and services (an activity almost totally ignored by the command economy) and it would be all about being responsive to conditions of biophysical and socio-cultural dependence.

Likewise, within the structure of relational forms, one could expect the establishment of some kind of (geographic and synergetic) regionalism embracing rural and urban planning, infrastructure, agriculture and 'natural resource management' all coordinated by an 'adaptive design' directorate. Citizenship would be reconceived, redirected and require a form of individual reaffirmation – in so doing, social and Sustainment responsibilities would be defined. National defence would be redefined purely as defence (including the defence of what must be sustained) together with 'support to the civil power' being reviewed and extended. International peace-keeping would also be significant but reviewed and redefined through dialogue with other nations. International trade and relations would centre on 'the export of adaptive solutions'. Export of all primary products would be under the direction of a system of resource management. Population management would also figure large (this would include population redistribution, environmental refugee intake and social justice programmes).

What should be evident is that the imposition of Sustainment would be radical, and although proscriptive, it would sit in the tradition of proscription naturalized. Moreover, while moving away from a model of continual economic growth, even in this most crude characterization of change, what is intimated is dynamic. In fact because the change would be so radical, so experimental, and so much would be at stake, it would be absolutely critical that it be continually reflected upon and adjusted.

The absolutely fundamental issue in relation to such change is not 'will it, and its economy, work?' but 'how, in a situation of diminishing choice, can such change be made to work?'

5

In the Shadow of Carl Schmitt's Politics

The analysis offered here does not embrace the claim of the 'end of politics' (either the end of its developmental potential or its completion within the hegemony of capitalist democracy). Nor does it support the continuity of politics in its current forms. Rather, what it argued is that confronting structural unsustainability is unavoidable. Design as politics can be seen as an element of remaking politics, as a revitalization of 'the political' towards this end.

By engaging the ideas voiced in the first half of the twentieth century by Carl Schmitt, this chapter will expose a radical way of viewing politics as conflict and critique, exposing the contradiction between the claims and actuality of representational politics. Also considered *en route* is a characterization of Schmitt's attack on the serious by entertainment and of his examination of politics as a mode of technology. This engagement will not merely expose the challenges that Schmitt's thinking still presents but will also create a context for considering Sustainment as an essential imposition. Critical focus will then be directed towards a revitalization of the idea of relationality.[1] The chapter ends by placing design as politics in the conceptual space it has created.

Views on exactly how politics is remade vary. Jacques Derrida, so long characterized as a coy and evasive commentator on politics (including the politics of deconstruction) confirmed the imperative to remake it, but how he did this created a problem. In 1994 he wrote on *'time being out of joint'* and the world 'going badly.'[2] Although the context is somewhat dated, his words gain poignancy with the passing of time:

> For it must be cried out, at a time when some have the audacity to neo-evangelise in the name of the ideal of a liberal democracy that has finally realised itself as the ideal of human history: never have violence, inequality, exclusion, famine, and thus economic oppression affected so many human beings in the history of the earth and of humanity. Instead of singing the advent of the ideal of liberal democracy and of the capitalist market in the euphoria of the end of history, instead of celebrating the 'end of ideologies' and the end of the great emancipatory discourses, let us never neglect this obvious macroscopic fact, made up of innumerable singular sites of suffering: no degree of progress allows one to ignore that never before, in absolute figures, never have so many men, women and children been subjugated, starved, or exterminated on the earth. (And provisionally, but with regret, we must leave aside here the nevertheless indissociable question of what is becoming of so-called 'animal' life, the life and existence of 'animals' in this history. This question has always been a serious one, but it will become massively unavoidable.)[3]

Derrida, in the voice of humanism, cries out for an 'other' political. Though he sought emancipation, he failed to embrace the implication of his 'massively unavoidable question' – the question of anthropocentrism, a question that confronts humanity with the responsibility of its being. Seeking ways of engaging this question opens a path to a politics that is both deconstructive and affirmative, wherein the only possibility of 'our being free' is by realizing the obligations to all the others we depend upon.

In the inter-relationality of things in being, 'man' should not be positioned as between the animal and the divine (Derrida's positioning): 'we' humans are positioned in the world of things as designers and makers.[4] The designed, making and the made register an imposition intrinsic to our very being (our *dasein*). Thus the locus of responsibility lies with the ontological designing of 'objectified things'. Our anthropocentrism is materialized by design as 'things' yet we do not see it because it constitutes so much of the form of the world we occupy in the processes of daily life.

Addressing Derrida's 'massively unavoidable' question requires realignment: it is not simply a question of life, animal or otherwise; rather it is now also one of sustain-ability. His question stands before us as the question of our anthropocentric being as it is thrown into a confrontation with the need for Sustainment.

Friend and Enemies

Carl Schmitt begs reintroducing. He was born into a strict Catholic family in north-west Germany in 1888. As an ambitious law professor and radical critic of liberalism, he joined the National Socialist Party in 1933. Thereafter, he became a powerful advocate of the legality of Hitler's regime, and as such was dubbed the 'Crown Jurist' of the Third Reich. In 1936 he was attacked in print by the SS for his Catholic background and his association with Jewish intellectuals; as a result he resigned from his official positions and reverted to his position as a professor at Berlin University. Because of his background, he was arrested in 1945 by the Red Army, held for a short time then released. He was re-arrested later that year by the Americans as a possible security threat and then released in the autumn of 1946. Finally he was arrested once more in March 1947 then again released, two months later. His intellectual fame as a political thinker (which underwent a reinvigoration in the 1990s) has bridged both left and right. It centred on three linked themes: parliamentary democracy and its undergirding of capitalism; technology and instrumentalism; and liberalism (of which he is widely regarded as the twentieth century's most powerful critic). While Schmitt may have been disliked by many and thought to have a 'dangerous mind', the consensual view was that his intellect could not be ignored.

One of Schmitt's best known and most misunderstood ideas was his friend/
enemy distinction (outlined in his *The Concept of the Political* of 1932). He
took this distinction to be concrete and existential, rather than symbolic or
a characterization of an individual disposition. In essence, he understood the
enemy to be the political adversary, collective and a public entity. The enemy
was not a figure of hatred, but rather that to be politically surmounted by the
state or the people so they may freely determine their mode of existence.
Nonetheless, that this 'other' is cast as an adversary (and that a relation of en-
mity is made a prerequisite in giving identity to, for example, a state) meant
political struggle could easily transmute into conflict. In so arguing, a condition beyond the kind of consequences associated with conventionalist space
of politics (the political in its wider sense) could be created. Unwittingly,
Schmitt confirmed 'our' anthropocentric character and the fact that it is at
odds with Sustainment (which requires dramatically reducing, if not totally
overcoming, conflict and its defuturing causes and conduct).

While one can say conflict is anathema to Sustainment, it ever remains
dialectically interlocked with it. Moreover, as Schmitt concluded, the 'an-
nihilation of the other would necessarily amount to self-annihilation'.[5] By
implication, conflicts fold into the 'dialectic of Sustainment' as it rides the
relation between creation and destruction. The unbreakable tension between
the absolute necessity to sustain and the unceasing momentum toward the
destruction driven by the structurally unsustainable is not external to us, but
rather part of our essence (we are our own friend and enemy – the political
conflict is waged within, as well as by, us).

As frequently reiterated, structural unsustainability throws the future of
human being into question. Knowingly or unknowingly, how 'we' act and position ourselves in relation to it determines ontologically if 'we' are the friends
or enemies of all that strives to support Sustainment.

While reason may be brought to comprehend events and the actions of
subjects, the designations 'friend' and 'enemy', and positions adopted toward
conflict, are always emotionally charged. As soon as we are put 'on the line'
and confronted with an unavoidable moment of decision, reason and emotion
(con)fuse. And once the 'battle for Sustainment' begins (by the intellectual

and cultural projects that confront a collective and individual 'taking responsibility for anthropocentrism') the ground shifts.

Positions of opposition are of course not always clear-cut. We, and our friends, are both creators and destroyers who so often 'do not know what they or we do', including to each other. So when Paul Hirst remarks: 'Schmitt is probably right. Enemies have nothing to discuss and we can never attain a situation in which the friend-enemy distinction is abolished.'[6] If you are for Sustainment, all that is not, is an enemy.

Being our own Enemy

Before continuing with Schmitt we need to return to our opening remarks on Derrida's failure to embrace his 'massively unavoidable question' – the question of anthropocentrism. This question not only exposes humanity's need to confront responsibility for its own being but brings to the fore the human condition as auto-conflictual. In creating the denaturalized world of our own construction, that in large part creates us, 'we' unknowingly turned on ourselves: we made our animality enemy.

The *animal rationale* is not so rational after all – 'it' cannot think itself out of its unthinking and unsustaining anthropocentrism. The ontological transformation of becoming another kind of being (which is what human beings who recognize and takes responsibility for their anthropocentrism actually become) is not within the grasp of thinking and an induced alteration of consciousness, *en masse*. It requires major changes in structured modes of being-in-the-world (including how the self is brought into being). In this setting, taking responsibility is not an act of will but a facilitated and habitually inscribed conduct (design). Moreover, responsibility here needs to be understood not as an ability to overcome all that defutures but rather as a prerequisite for resistance – humanity exists in such numbers and with such appetites that it can but be destructive – however, destruction can be a measured ethical decision. It is essentially a question of what is destroyed (because there are things that should be destroyed and things that just must not be, but are). At worst 'we' must create and impose materialized ways to hold our destructiveness in check.

That we destroy is unavoidable. But what has to be made possible is our being placed before a politico-ethical question: 'does what we create justify what "we" destroy?' Is there a more basic and vital question to bring before an economy predicated upon futural accountability? Should not any maker of any thing be placed before such a question?

Unsustainability, when named, usually arrives as a reification of biophysical system dysfunction (normally expressed as environmental or ecological 'crisis'). But, as needs to be endlessly repeated, what goes unrecognized is that unsustainability is essentially a flaw in 'our' being. Bringing this observation to institutional politics means acknowledging that democracy overlooks this situation at its most fundamental – rather than grasping its subjective locus, it objectifies 'the problem' and so conceals the primary site of struggle (the self versus 'the wasteland' within). The inner being of the unsustainable and its external worldly expression are linked. The concept of *habitus* delivers a clear way to understand this. *Habitus* is an exposure of what structures the structuring. It underpins what it is we do (our practices) and the economic and socio-political 'rational' world within which our ontologies are themselves structured.[7] It is the foundation of what is taken to be foundational: it is the designing of the designed.

By implication, in a world made structurally unsustainable, the human instinct of self-preservation (our inherent 'care structure') is being overwhelmed by the negation of our being anthropocentric. To reiterate: 'we' in our sheer numbers (and their technological amplification), simply do not see what we destroy. As a result we have displaced the equilibrium of the 'dialectic of Sustainment' (the balance between (re-)creation and destruction) and allowed defuturing to lead. It follows that unless a reflective ability to confront 'the structurally unsustainable in being' is created – unless it is made an object of confrontation – then defuturing will continue as our normative condition.

Obviously these remarks rest with the issue of forming a new kind of political designing subject authored by a new socio-material literacy able to read *itself* (and its world as an unhomely space of negation and creation, populated by friends and enemies in an unavoidable and eternal struggle). Here is the becoming of the 'the super man and woman' able to design toward another being and conduct a dangerous politics. This politics can but generate enemies. It cannot be conducted in the current political arena. Schmitt, following Hegel and in harmony with Marx, adopted a position against the bourgeois subject that seems simultaneously dated, apt and imminent. He wrote:

> The bourgeois is an individual who does not want to leave the apolitical riskless private sphere. He rests in the possession of his private property, and under the justification of his possessive individualism he acts as an individual against the totality. He is a man who finds his compensation for his political nullity in the fruits of freedom and enrichment and above all in the total security of its use. Consequently he wants to be spared bravery and exempted from the danger of a violent death.[8]

As we shall see when we consider freedom in a later chapter, we can read this via Hegel's position that freedom depends upon a willingness to risk one's life. It's worth underlining that the structurally unsustainable, as an inner-life, leads many individuals to try to secure *their* freedom in ways that undercut securing the foundational condition of freedom (Sustainment) upon which their essential freedom stands. Futurally, freedom will require risking life in the political confrontation that facing the structurally unsustainable structures.

Schmitt's elaboration of the friend/enemy distinction (and his discussion of Hegel's notion of the enemy as a 'negated otherness') can be brought to contemporary circumstances.[9] His distinction equally applies to rethinking 'the political now' as it is *elemental to what we are* and our destiny (rather than an 'externality'). Additionally, thinking the political anew requires overcoming political concepts inscribed in Eurocentrically conceived politics, subjects and institutions.[10]

Another pertinent lesson to be learnt from Schmitt is that being political is not much to do with labouring to acquire power or a utopian quest for an ideal society or even striving for idealized justice but, rather, it is about actively engaging in conditions of opposition over 'that which is critical' (which for

him was largely technology and the form of the state) and for which positions demand to be taken (including positions that designate friends and
enemies).

Being political for Schmitt was a commitment to the serious, which he saw
as being under threat from entertainment. In the present age when every-
thing now has to entertain, such a view is unfashionable, but vital to voice.
Certainly, purely at an instrumental level, there is a strong case that the commodified entertainment produced by the creative industries has two deadly
consequences: it feeds a 'consumer' desire to be continually entertained and
pleased; and it colonizes imaginations blocking the formation of a creative
spirit. More fundamentally, entertainment folds into what Heidegger termed
'the temporality of falling' wherein the present becomes increasingly inau-
thentic as it turns back on itself and, in so doing, 'sucks time dry'.[11] 'Falling'
thus acts to cover over, to conceal, what needs to be disclosed. Put more
directly: the vast bulk of what gets named as the product of entertainment
detracts from our seeing what needs to be futurally engaged – it leads to one
falling into *being in a time of engaged disengagement* whereby the seduction
of the momentary pleasure of mass entertainment negates that potentiality
that is the future, disclosure and truth. The serious(ly) active production of
pleasure is another matter, another project: one to be created to counter what
is delivered *en masse* as it forms the masses who exercise what has been
named here as consumer sovereignty.

Postmodern politics and Cultural Studies (providing intellectual support
for the creative industries) so often celebrate such numbing pleasure. This
effectively condones the recoil from the serious and validates forms of passive
resistance as authentic struggle. This stance, romantically deemed as subver-
sive and progressive in the 1970s and 1980s, now looks at best misguided, at
worst reactionary. Being serious has become the crime of the 'uncool' and,
sadly, Cultural Studies became complicit in this 'coding'.[12] The importance
of a politics of pleasure has been lost in defending its commodified and thus
reified forms. That entertainment destroys or deflects the application of the
mind to the critical and conceals emergency is serious! Unquestionably, there
is a pressing need for serious entertainment.

Dictatorship of the Imperative

As discussed earlier, Schmitt understood that sovereignty's power lies with the ability 'to decide the state of exception'.[13] Currently 'we', no matter who or where we are, lack the authority to act decisively against the rule of those 'democratic' administrations that view unsustainability as if it were just another problem to manage among others. There is no agency with sufficient power to *act* otherwise. All are impotent in the face of this situation, including the international institutions of humanism (especially the United Nations and its agencies). Moreover, these institutions also fail to recognize the significance of 'anthropocentric being' as a crisis underscoring humanity's future. That which is fundamentally critical and essentially at stake, is continually concealed by immediate pragmatic preoccupations (this not least in the financial domain where the response to dysfunction is to attempt to reform and then reinstate the status quo).

Destruction clearly extends well beyond the visible, the felt and moral arguments. Certainly, the environmental movement's critiques, including of consumerism, come nowhere near recognizing the depth of the problem. In actuality, the situation is far more critical than current representations of crises (including climate change) indicate. This is more than the failure of the media to represent the depth, complexity and defuturing consequences of all that is critical. Essentially, the 'crisis of crisis' is lodged in the invisibility of defuturing ontologies wherein *human centredness* and constructed *commodity-based desires* combine to create self-realization as a negation of 'beings together'. Rather than impassioned critique, moral outrage or condemnation of greed and individualism, the problem has to be confronted ontologically (including the ontological designing of 'being otherwise'). So said, there can be no real progress towards Sustainment unless the horror of the sovereign self wherein self interest and anthropocentrism combine to negate both social and biophysical ecologies is confronted ontologically in designing and materially transformative, rather than moral, terms.

A fundamental defuturing disposition embodied in 'the modern self' (mischaracterized as 'human nature') is what 'democratic' regimes currently celebrate as individual freedom. Yet to construct a notion of freedom predicated upon disassociation from collective conditions of interdependence (social and biological) is to create a world-in-the-world of the unfree acting against all that freedoms rest upon.

Not only have modern nations not progressed beyond the attainments of the Roman's capability of circumscribing the unfreedom of emergency powers (existing for the duration of the emergency) but in current intellectual circumstances the fundamental question of decision on the declaration of the crisis as 'emergency' now cannot even be identified. In other words, the trajectory of structural unsustainability (the crisis as defuturing) still remains embedded in an embodied inability of human beings to recognize what they actually are and do. Effectively 'we' have unknowingly made ourselves beings towards our own negation. Contemporary institutional politics does not come to such a conclusion because within the operational discourse in which political practices function, the issue is literally unthinkable – which is to say that the question of being rests outside what it is possible for this politics to think.

Clearly, political history unambiguously indicates that dictatorships are not an attractive proposition; nonetheless, what is 'reasonable, expedient and ethical' is a dictatorship of the imperative of Sustainment – which is a dictatorship of the precondition of all freedoms, including the freedom to act responsibly within the limits of futuring. It is a dictatorship in which all difference other than the right to defuture is possible. Without doubt this proposition is loaded with problems, yet, and unlike the history of those forms of evil dictatorships that we automatically recoil from, the proposition is able to be contemplated and addressed at the most fundamental of all levels: being. It is not a matter of immediate imposition, but of the urgent creation of that unfreedom that is the rule of futuring.

For us humans, our very being is at stake and, in significant part, is in our own hands. But let us be quite clear, the decisionism of enforced Sustainment (futuring) is nothing to do with maintaining an idealized 'state of nature'. Rather what it demands is revealing the crisis of structural unsustainability, breaking the silence of unknowing, and confronting all that defutures while, at the same time, advancing means of Sustainment. There is no assumption here that 'we' can judge with certainty and make infallible decisions, but it is possible to review actions and take responsibility once the need for decision is seen to reside in the spaces between the continuity of ourselves, others and in relation to connections which we, and all beings, depend upon.

Re-presentation

The democratic process of liberal democratic nations is based on a mechanistic-positivistic model of representation in which 'representatives of the people' selected by 'the party machine' present their options to voters. This system virtually eliminates the ability of people to choose beyond an either/ or. So often the choice is no choice (including the option of creating choice). To a very large extent 'representatives' represent the interests of the state, and then the status quo, their own parliamentary institution and its ideology – all in the name of the people. This is obviously not a system of participatory democracy, although *de facto* it is projected as such. The political machine of parliamentary democracy and those who serve it manufactures a picture of 'the real' constructed by economic and demographic data, samples of constructed 'public opinion', projected trends and the like. All this comes with the claim that such appearances of 'the state of the world' are 'objective', albeit that all data are mediated by ethnocentrically framed expertise. This technology of representation ensures 'a return of the same' and maintains the centrality of 'the party' and the state bureaucracy to define: what is to be represented; who are appropriate representatives; and what are to be the processes of representation to which 'the people' are required to comply (if they choose, or are compelled, to vote). It follows that whoever commands the machinery of representative politics, and whoever can muster the greatest amount of money to lubricate it, is in an extremely powerful position to command the choices 'the people' make. All of this was made very clear a long time ago by Schmitt's teacher, Max Weber in his 'Politics is a Vocation' lecture (included in his seminal *Economy and Society*, first published in Germany in 1921/22) as well as in Schmitt's own critique of technology as a negation of the political.[14] Weber pointed out that modern parliamentary democracy is an inherently undemocratic system of government. But as Schmitt observed in his book on Hobbes, the die was cast long ago. As Heinrich Meier points out, Hobbes' view of the state as machine was fully captured by Schmitt when he observed:

> ... the idea of the state as a technological perfected *magnum articium* created by man, as a machine that has its 'right' and its 'truth' only in itself, that is, in performance and function, was first grasped and systematically developed as a clear concept by Hobbes.[15]

Schmitt recognized that the emergent corporate nature of the state made it 'just another large business and that an economic administrative system, a factory and a state are today no longer essentially different.'[16] The balance has continued to swing in this direction with many Western democracies weakening the power of the political state and facilitating its rise as the instrument of a corporate nation. Partly masking this trend has been a representational strategy, including the arrival of a 'new' kind of nationalism and imperialism (cast as the export of democracy and (market) 'freedom').[17]

Latter-day imperialism, manifest as globalized and technocratic liberalism, has a good deal in common with the old style 'free-trade' liberal ideology, supplemented with the power of late modern technological systems and underscored by unprecedented levels of military muscle. Unlike the old imperialism, 'the new' is not predicated on an obvious geography – networks displace a visible centre and culture becomes a significant instrument of power. Of course, resistance to the 'new empire', is also less spatially contained with conflict becoming asymmetrical. In fact, it is increasingly hard to centralize focus on deterritorialized terrorism (national borders do not contain it, its form is plural, while generalized notions, like the 'War on Terror' or conflict between the 'West and the rest' are too vague). It is an emergent, and will be a growing, feature of unsettlement – this especially as whole armies are displaced. Moreover, the terrorist who turns him or herself into a weapon is an absolute figure of the unhomely. He or she is a completely anomic person who lacks even the most marginal place to be, except their last vestige: the place of self-annihilation. In such conflict there is no victory, only repression and a continual drift towards a 'state of emergency' that may or may not fully materialize.

Danger

To be political, as Schmitt defined and affirmed it, is to be dangerous. This ontological condition is but one more thing concealed and eroded by the reduction of politics to administration.[18] Western democratic nations struggle to maintain a politics of political difference. Centrism is now a feature of almost every mainstream political party (evident when one examines policy, rhetoric, gestures and the preoccupation with personality and ego). Popularism demands a politics without danger and actions that call for no sacrifice. In the emergent epoch of unsettlement, all that is politically decided and designed is 'on the line'. Against this backdrop, Sustainment means giving over to action against (our) inherent structural unsustainability.

As was remarked earlier, one element of our nemesis is that 'our' drive to dominate is becoming transferred to our own technological creations. Increasingly, we will find ourselves threatened by things and circumstances of our own creation. It may well be the case that the more the faith in technological salvation, the greater the risk (from both the failure and success of technology). What has made this prospect possible? The direct answer is instrumental reason as the mediation and fusion between human and technological.

Instrumental reason is pragmatic reasoning without critically reflective or relational thought. It is the culmination of the reduction of action to ends without adequately contemplating non-linear consequences. It is an evacuation of truth and its replacement with calculative correctness. It is the failure of reason, as rationalization, to account for what its agency realizes and it is conformity to the preordained. Instrumental reason, once hegemonic, is 'being' become technological. McCormick directs us towards Schmitt's views in his first major work of 1916. Here, Schmitt is disturbed by modernity's constitution of:

... a blind domination of nature and what has come to be called 'instrumental rationality': 'functional means' towards a 'senseless purpose'. Products, whether the outcome of
a capitalist assembly line or the result of a bureaucratic decision-making apparatus, are
spurting quickly and efficiently without any serious consideration of their ethical worth.
Substantive reflection finds no place in this equation.[19]

There is clearly a difference between those dangers which are immediate, physical and passing and those which emplace something which is
fundamentally and structurally dangerous (and often beyond our ability to
recognize). Danger does not always arrive in a garb that evokes fear, or with
forms that threatens. To illustrate we will return to the question of political
representation.

All the World's a Stage

By the early 1930s, Schmitt was warning against the world becoming a world
of entertainment.[20] He placed politics and the state between this world of
pleasure and us. His enemy was the hegemony of amusement (now encapsu-
lated by popular culture). He argued that the loss of seriousness meant there
would be nothing worth dying for – and thus nothing to devote one's life to. His
view resonates with the dilemma of 'human life' in the present age wherein
everything is at stake but certainly, at least in the West, the significance of the
values and meaning of so much has been seriously diminished. The implication of the critique is that life (the way we live) has fundamentally forgotten
what essentially matters, while becoming centred on what is represented as
important (which, for many, is wealth, 'consumption' and commodities). In
this respect, for all their differences, Schmitt, Heidegger, Benjamin, Adorno,
Horkheimer and even Baudrillard were all fellow travellers looking for a way
to think and act in the shadow of metaphysics become technology (instrumentalism) and, as such, dominating pleasure (culture). Moreover, the world
that Schmitt named is one wherein 'the world of the bourgeois is raised to
universality, and expanded to the point of excluding everything else – the
world of the bourgeois who finds his satisfaction in the perfect security of the

enjoyment of the fruits of peace and acquisition'. [21] In the face of this, Schmitt cited the political as '… ultimately nothing other than the affirmation of the moral'.[22] These kinds of views culminated with Heidegger's essay 'The Age of the World Picture', their relevance now considerably amplified by the environment of the televisual, wherein technology, image and thought all fuse.[23] The televisual renders *everything* entertainment: which in turn provides the 'lifeblood' that sustains it. Entertainment is a major feature of its ontology, and the foundation of its economy. Entertainment is its commodifying 'desiring machine', its driving force. The televisual has the ability to convert anything into valorizing attractors – war, sex, pain, humiliation, biological function, hardship, eccentricity, the performance of political figures – all fold into the frame that entertains.

Culture, Commodity, Politics

The globalized entertainment industry dissolves cultural difference – not to the extent that all differences are erased but rather that all cultures become cultures of bricolage. This is different from the processes of change that cultures embrace in order to stay vital. Bricolage is not situated in adaptive change. It is purely a pool of commodified culture into which any buyer can dip. Frequently, it's the consequence of style-driven acts of appropriation. Dominantly, such bricolage neither recognizes nor values established cultural practices, knowledge, identities or environmental cultural determinates (to which, for instance, diet, dress and architecture are responses). This is effectively a pluralism that de-relationalizes culture and potentially sustaining traditions.

It is also the case that the entertainment industry continually appropriates culture and tradition as spectacle, reducing it to a commodity. Political culture has not been immune from this propensity. In relation to politics, television is still an enormously powerful instrument and has effectively turned politics into just another cultural commodity. Elections can stand or fall simply on the basis of how policies or politicians are presented at the level of image. For television, politics is just another packaged product amid the projected mix, competing with other cultural commodities for audiences and market share.[24] The success of the Obama campaign of 2008 can be seen in these terms. It was the result of a massive circular marketing exercise – a huge amount of money was raised to market a visibly different product (against another with questionable 'consumer' appeal) using every possible media option (not least new Internet-based media). This, in turn, enabled an even larger amount of money to be amassed to direct a marketing-created image at a market. The issue here is one of method rather than the quality of a candidate. As a world of defuturing goods and services evidence, the success of marketing does not equate to the quality of the product.

This degeneration of politics leads to what C.B. Macpherson has called 'consumerist sovereignty' – 'democratic politics' reduced to providing consumer satisfaction as just one more commodity among commodities.[25] In this respect the televisualized political creates a sense of politics being directed simply at consumer desires: 'what's in it for me, is this to my taste, do I like the look of this or that politician?' The common good thereby becomes over-ridden by atomized wants, with a singular self rhetorically collectivized in numerous fragmented forms: the tax-payer, motorist, drinker, parent, wage-earner, greenie, tourist, investor, hospital patient, shopper, consumer, and so on. What this means is that our 'selves' are de-relationized to facilitate the appeal to plural individuated interests. In such a setting, the political party that creates the right mix of product, image and audience gets the electoral prize.

Questions proliferate. Is to be serious now to reign against the commodification of culture, while inescapably being interpolated as a cultural consumer? Is embracing the serious a way of taking responsibility for the creation of one's own alienation? Does not the history of political radicalism show that resistance can always be transformed into a cultural commodity? In an age of hegemonic capitalism, and outside anomic or token gesturalism, are acts of political radicalism actually possible? In considering these 'serious questions' we need to remember that the ideological foundations and semiological mast-heads of the left have fallen: environmentalism has either become gestural or incorporated; 'identity politics' is ever trapped in the singularity of its claim; and the space of resistance has been compressed (by a combination of repressive measures under the aegis of 'national security' and by formalized processes of protest that simply demonstrate the state's ability to accommodate gestural action that offers no real threat). All of this predisposes the deeply disaffected to adopt the action of last resort (terrorism).

Notwithstanding the existence of important political causes, there is clearly a serious absence of effective forms of contestational politics. The state has played a key role in creating this situation by two diametrically opposed strategies: the incorporation of resistance as 'evidence' of the spirit of democracy (cf. gestural protest); and the employment of 'extra-political powers' (in the name of 'national security') to 'deal' with what it deems to actually threaten. *De facto*, democracy has learnt how to neutralize a great deal of political resistance.[26] As Schmitt would have so obviously pointed out – to be radical you require enemies; but within the space of the plural, the hyper-conformity of difference (political and cultural) simply replicates the same.

Radical action would, of course, be supported and voted for once a tangible, material crisis arrived. But by then, the action would be too late to counter the long-term consequences of events already in train. While our argument is radical, actually turning it into effective political action is quite another matter.

Again we say: democracy cannot deliver Sustainment, an agenda of 'the future of the future' or a response to the imperative of the dictatorship of Sustainment (which begs to be named and recognized as such). Sustainment as an overarching political imperative – to which all other issues are subordinate (for without Sustainment we have nothing) – means that politics as we know and encounter it (including the politics and practices of sustainability) has to be superseded or totally transformed.

The question of radical action has to be bonded to design but in the eschatological conditions of there being currently no option available to secure our futuring – this because design (as transformed) has major prefigurative potentiality. It is now appropriate to recall Derrida's remark from the *Spectre of Marx*: 'Deconstruction has never had any sense or interest, in my view at least, except as a radicalization, which is to say also *in the tradition* of a certain Marxism, in a certain spirit of Marxism.'[27]

What Derrida points to, even while looking away, is deconstruction's debt to the proto-deconstructive methodology of Marx and the spirit of radicality carried by the Marxian project – which he contrasts with its degeneration into orthodoxy. Here, in deconstruction taken to the limit, is a proto-politics, not only outside the acknowledged frame of Marxist politics but concealed by it – a politics in which radicalism is not a declaration but a consequence. Such a view recasts a reading of the history of Marxism, but also exposes part of its appeal. Equally it also breathes life back into the corpse of Marx at the very moment when it is deemed dead and buried. The ghost of Marx will not walk as a political force; it does, however, conserve the essence of what is radical. Again, connecting with this spirit, radicalizing the radical in the conjuncture before us, is yet another matter that travels with us, but can only come from a conjunctural relation of thought, events and potentiality.

Relationality

Relationality underpins almost everything that is thought and said here. It is a mode of thinking able to engage and deliver complexity. Yet while relationality is an idea with a long philosophical heritage, it has not arrived in Western culture as either a guide to thinking or, more specifically, as a way to think in relation to taking efficacious action. This is one of the many oversights of philosophers against philosophy. Hegel, for instance, is judged as an absolute rationalist, yet writing on the organic and the inorganic, he points out that neither shows itself as 'essential' but rather they maintain themselves in their 'relations' He then proceeds to observe the following (in perhaps the most 'rationalist' of his works) on the relation of organic and inorganic nature:

> The latter is, for the organic Nature, no more than the freedom – a freedom opposed to the simple Notion of organic Nature – of *loosely connected* determinatenesses in which the individual forms of Nature are *dissolved* and which, at the same time, breaking away from their continuity, exist on their own accord. Air, water, earth, zones, and climate

are universal elements of this sort, which constitute the indeterminate simple essence of [natural] individualities, and in which these are at the same time reflected into themselves. Neither the individuality, nor universal element, is absolutely in and for itself: on the contrary, though they appear to observation as free and independent, they behave at the same time as *essentially connected,* but in such a way that their independence and mutual indifference are the predominant feature, and only in part become abstractions. Here, then, we have law as the connection of a [universal] element with the formative process of the organism which, on the one hand, has the elementary being over against it, and on the other hand, exhibits it within its organic reflection. But laws of this kind: animals belonging to the air have the nature of birds, those belonging to water have the nature of fish, animals in northern latitudes have thick, hairy pelts, and so on – such laws are seen at a glance to display a poverty which does not do justice to the manifold variety of organic nature. Besides the fact that organic Nature in its freedom can divest its forms of these characteristics, and of necessity everywhere presents exceptions to such laws cannot be other than superficial, and amounts to no more than the great *influence* of environment; and this does not tell us what does and does not belong to this influence. Such relations of organisms to the elements [they live in] cannot therefore be called *laws.* For firstly, the *content* of such a relation, as we saw, does not exhaust the range of organisms concerned, and secondly, the sides of the relation itself are mutually indifferent, and express no necessity.[28]

These words were first published in 1807, some sixty-six years before the attributed 'birth' of the discipline of ecology through the work of Ernst Heinrich Haekle (1834–1919) on the relation between organisms and environment, undertaken at the University of Jena in 1873. There is a significant connection here. Hegel started his university teaching career at the University of Jena in 1801, which was the context out of which came the words above, and his entire *Phenomenology.* However, this enterprise had been prefigured by his course on 'Nature and Spirit' in 1806, which unfolded into a philosophy of nature that fully developed as Part II of the *Encyclopaedia* 1817. Many of Hegel's lectures on nature were not published until 1841.[29] Clearly, the gap between Haekle and Hegel is narrower than first appeared, especially recognizing that, at the time, to be German and well educated meant, among other things, to have read Hegel. More importantly, what the words above point to is a demand for thinking as a Sustainment, rather than thinking instrumentally or 'correctly' (as philosophy, political theory, etc.).

In the context of what has been said, and linking to questions of biological determinism, it should be pointed out that ecology has a dark history.

Although we are not going to explore this, for it is yet another topic that opens an entire avenue of exploration, we acknowledge it among the many problems that a reconsideration of decisionism has to confront.[30]

Designing into the Frame

Design as politics is a 'practical politics' that is radical in effect rather than gesture. It does not strive only to confront what one thinks but aims at a political confrontation (in Schmitt's sense of facing the enemy) in order to liberate action toward affirmative change ahead of the absolutely critical. Unequivocally, structural unsustainability (in its subjective and objective manifestations) needs naming as enemy. Design, as embedded in, and constituted as, redirective practice confronts this enemy. In this respect, its transformative intent rests with the power of its relational, rather than singular, agency. Strategically, and more specifically, design-based redirective practice and its intellectual underpinning opens another path to (and as) the political by its deconstructive abilities undercutting the ground of currently existing democratic politics and its potential to remake much of what materially stands on this ground.

Design De-signed

All that is designed goes on designing. Thus when what is designed is structurally unsustainable, danger is placed in store. The repositories of dangers in storage are now manifold. They are within our very being, the fabric of the world of our creation (the world within the world) and with the forces of global destabilization.

Design as politics demands new narratives. The meta-narrative is of course Sustainment, but some others have started to be exposited (ontological design, elimination design, platforming, recoding, retrofitting)[31] although this is not enough. We need more stories that are more immediate, engaged, evocative and capable of firing the imagination that designs. Effectively, these stories make possible the narrativiation of design as a political act. Schmitt's thinking can feed such story-telling: his friend/enemy distinction invites reconsidering how political conflict can be understood; how the dangerous is positioned in relation to the dictatorship of the imperative; how the serious can be reanimated in the face of entertainment; and how political representation is a charade.

To illustrate, here are a range of candidates of modes of design generated out of telling a (short) story that resonates with a politics of the serious. Here, a story needs to be understood as a way to put thinking on a particular path; as such, it discloses a way of thinking and a direction open to appropriation. We cannot design in silence. It demands conversation and stories into which design-led redirection can be accommodated and from which it can speak.

The story is the start of that thinking that makes futural and redirective designing possible. Each story ends with questions that open it to elaboration and conversation (and thereafter the creation of a brief).

I. De-warring

What can prevent what Carl von Clausewitz famously called, in his treatise *On War* in 1832, 'the continuation of politics by other means' (war), and how can designers play a part in this?

Military planners see the world becoming increasingly dangerous, with climate-related events potentially triggering large-scale conflicts. Rising sea levels, ocean acidification, loss of biodiversity, drought, bush-fires, destruction from extreme weather events (floods, storm surges, cyclonic wind, hail), food shortages and possibly tens of millions of environmental refugees – besides all the direct environmental and social impacts from such events, there is a fear that they will generate widespread social instability. This might include huge breakdowns in the social order across regions and cross-border invasions by masses of landless and hungry people. Military planners are viewing such prospects with great alarm.[32]

War needs naming as the epitome of defuturing. It destroys bodies, minds, family, environments, cultures, resources and futures. The fighting stops, the bombs stop dropping, the missiles cease to fly, but the destruction continues. War is the most visible mark in the escalation in humanity's defuturing capability. Such is this capability that it now has the potential to destroy the totality of life as we know it. The necessity for proactive measures against war, mobilized against the power of war makers, is immense.

So what can design/designers do in this situation? Obviously they cannot directly intervene and change material circumstances. But they can make the issue visible, generate constructive public debate, build awareness and the political will to put in place policy and planning measures that could help reduce risk and pre-empt critical conditions. This is not projected as minor or token activity but rather, as massive visualization projects wherein key messages are communicated on the scale and dangers of the problems before they actually arrive. Likewise, what actually has to be solved can be directly confronted in dramatic ways. This leads to a pragmatic presentation of possible non-utopian solutions (ranging from: the practical problems of moving vast numbers of people, and to where; the creation of refuge cities (rather than refugee camps); pre-planned economies (part self-sustaining) based on audited capabilities and needs; health and education of displaced peoples; the provision of food; and methods to manage strained inter-cultural relations.

Futuring Questions

How can an image of an imminent war, and its probable consequences, be placed ahead of it as a design-led political intervention? What could an organization formed to do this (like, 'Designers Against War') actually design to create this image?

2. Metrofitting[33]

The polis, polity, politics – the city, civil society, the people – 'metrofitting' is pitched to redirect all that is urban. This concept takes retrofitting into the domain of relational complexity, acknowledging that the major imperative in confronting the structurally unsustainable is to deal with what already exists. As the city is the largest systemic object gathering the diversity of what already exists, it is appropriate to engage, what within it can be deemed as structurally unsustainable. This means retrofitting not just infrastructure (water, energy, roads, transport, waste, telecommunications), institutions, built structures and industries, but also its cultural and social fabric. It also means dealing with the city as a catchment, as a location for the production of food, as a semiotic ecology, as cityscape and sound-scape (the metrofitted city not only has to operate to deliver a high level of Sustainment – it also has to be perceptibly changed: it has to sound different, feel different and be different). Effectively, all the elements of metrofitting cluster in four domains: material environment, economy, culture and community. Metrofitting is the means by which the complexity of the exercise can be named, managed, placed within a time frame and coordinated.

Metrofitting is about putting the city in a position to adapt to climate change; it is about recognizing that means have to be created to enable the existing social ecology of the city to change (how decisions are made, who makes them, and how community is formed or revitalized). It is about the transformation of the city economy (with a bias toward localization and improving the Sustainment performance of industries, products and services). It is also about social justice, equity, cultural Sustainment and prefigurative problem management (like the arrival of environmental refugees).

Above all, metrofitting names the type of action appropriate to the scale of the response needed to the structural unsustainability of almost every city on the planet.

Futuring Questions

The starting point of metrofitting is not an engagement with the city as is, but the act of imagining what a metrofitted city might be like (without falling back into exhausted utopian visions). In other words, transformative action begins with the creation of a story, and thereafter the power of that story. Bearing in mind an unlikely turning of interests vested in the status quo, how could the story be told, and to whom?

3. Chronal

Designing that makes time has to take precedence over bringing things into being (unless these things are about making time). At its most basic, Sustainment it is about making time in the face of the diminishing finitude of human being.

Chronal design starts with an existing design proposition: 'design life'. Products and structures are designed to a specific lifespan (mostly based on warranty periods for components or materials). Their actual life may, of course, go beyond their designated design life. Chronal design takes the idea of design life far more seriously. This means trying to more effectively design the life of something so that it 'lives' in use longer (not just to conserve resources but to inculcate a value for 'the care of things'). Such designing requires more than just designing the thing itself. It might mean, for instance, designing the semiotic ecology in which it will be situated and read; writing a narrative that animates the user's relation to the thing; or totally recoding the thing itself (changing what it means).

At the same time, chronal design can be reversed and be about the clearing of things rather than their qualities. In other words, it's about elimination design – designing out of existence things that take time away. This might be by making or exposing their redundancy, destroying their cultural status, or their perception as desirable (the noisy, nasty, dangerous jet-ski is one easy object to identify for such treatment).

Futuring Questions

Rather than telling yet another story about the designing of a thing, what begs to be told is the design of a thing as change and what changes – this so the designing of some thing moves beyond the realization of an object to the designing of the time of its life. The other story (under the mantle of the dictatorship of the imperative to sustain) is about designing what has to be designed to end the life of a life negating thing. What then can be said about a thing as time? And, what is the appropriate language of forms of creative destruction that make an imminent potentiality of futural things possible?

4. Joyance

Within a new economic paradigm, the existing product stream has to be displaced (as a projected locus of endless pleasure to the extent that there are now people who list shopping as their hobby). The challenge here is the creation and discovery of new things of lasting joy that displace the desire that evaporates once the represented product (the object of desire) becomes the object of ownership. One needs to ask, what gives joy? Obviously the answer will be context and subject specific. But there are some general pointers. It has to be beyond utility (a pleasure to use), provide enhancement (add something to the user's environment or life), provide fulfilment (a move from ownership to attachment to what the object 'gives'), have a particular feel and look (aesthetic appeal) or become an object of cultural investment (its actual value exceeding its exchange or replacement value).

Futuring Questions

What does joy look like as serious pleasure? Who's looking?

5. Re-crafting

Craft has an image that has to change. Craft needs to be seen as a quality of things of the future, rather than a thing of the past! It needs to arrive as elemental to a futural economy and culture.

Craft is a return to making and doing things well, the pleasure of making, the quality of the made, a recognizable aesthetic. It is not posed simply as a product of the hand-made; it can arrive via any technology in which skill can be expressed. Craft is artifice with care that brings something that cares into being – something sacred and secular. It is an object of belief. What is believed is that the value that produced the thing, and is expressed by it, is central to the continuity of life as we know it. To survive, human beings need others, including non-human things as well as people (hence the notion of 'things that care').

Re-crafting brings the making of (and making by) craft into an antagonistic engagement with the existing economic paradigm. Quite simply, it states that the volume of what is made and owned has to be dramatically reduced while the quality of what is manufactured and acquired has to increase. Here joyance and chronal design merge with re-crafting to open into a very different order of things. Certainly such things would cost much more, yet, overall domestic expenditure would not have to increase (because fewer goods are purchased). Moving to a quality-based economy does not imply an economic collapse; although it would mean a reduced standard of living by current measures, but a higher quality of life.

Futuring Questions

Sustainment breaks quality free of relativism and made things free of hegemonic technology, grounding them in a normative condition that once defined, defines quality. The question is how can the theory be converted into something concrete – in other words how can a new idea and form of quality be visualized and delivered?

6. Tonus

Striking the right cord, sounding right – here is the counter to the vacuous project of 'design and emotion' in which designers, under the influence of marketers and mobilizing quasi-theory, seek to imbue products with emotive associations so as to fix a user's attachment and brand loyalty.

Design needs to have a sound – an appealing political rhetoric that can confront the scale of the structurally unsustainable and not be deflected. Design practice needs to redirectively speak and write another way that expresses a will to act affirmatively and politically. It needs to find the fundamental sounds of commonality in difference (all cultures make music, music stripped to basics has to be the music of commonality, the music of redirective and radical change).

Design and emotion has to be ruptured from products and bonded to redirective actions towards Sustainment.

Futuring Questions

'What is it that makes people attached to things?' is the underpinning question of emotionally weighted design and marketing. There are counter questions. How can the nascent attachment to the future inherent in all cultures be brought to the creation of things? How can the representational claims of things, created by an ideologically imbued sign economy, be broken?

This brief review aims to communicate an essential message to grasp. In the unfolding age of unsettlement, new ways of thinking and deploying design will be vital. In this setting, making 'design a politics' is not an option but a necessity. Moreover, this requires the resources of iconoclastic thinkers – Carl Schmitt provides but one example.

6

Pluralism Is a Political Problem

An adequate grasp of democracy requires understanding two of its concomitant elements: liberalism, which we have considered, and pluralism – the concept we are now about to consider. From the outset, the distinction between pluralism and plurality needs registering. Explaining this difference means presenting a reasonably detailed case and making it clear that the plural perspective has nothing in common with a pluralism that asserts the desirability of multiple perspectives.

The chapter will initially discuss the notion of the plural and its relation to thinking – which will include revisiting the ancient origins of the idea. The difference between the plural and pluralism will then be rehearsed, which will lead to examining the connections between pluralism and politics. In this setting, some specific problems that obstruct the ability of Sustainment to arrive under the rule of current forms of democracy will be explored. Finally, design will be placed in the debate and the issue of creating a new kind of political imaginary will be raised.

Our journeying with pluralism may appear take us a long way from design. Not so. Pluralism is deeply embedded in 'consumerist market notions of freedom' that designers now take as given ground. More than this, pluralism has become imbedded in the modern Western psyche as an almost invisible ideological force that appears as a natural way of thinking for both individuals and institutions. As such, in domains like education and the media it is equated with 'balance and fair mindedness'. What follows repudiates this view. Moreover, if one is to understand and change the nature of contemporary design practice then it follows that one has to comprehend what constitutes its foundation. An engagement with pluralism is therefore essential.

The Force of Plurality

Heraclitus was perhaps the most original of the first thinkers of the West. All that remains of his writings are a collection of fragments. Yet the ideas he explored over two-and-a-half thousand years ago made a significant mark upon pre-Socratic Greek thought and thus upon the formation of Western thought itself. Among many things, he indicated that 'movement, change, flow and world' all demanded thinking together.[1] What is plural, and thus relational, conforms to such a demand; it also implies a directional dynamic (wherein destination does not become a set point or end but continuity – a process of Sustainment). Pluralistic thought is that flux which enables a flowing together of fragments of that complex plurality – which, in itself, is beyond our limited ability to see, as well as being counter to the concealment of systematization. All that is addressed as complexity is, in actuality, an unavoidable reduction of 'what is'. The issue here thus becomes one of representational adequacy (a claim of systems thinking and the limit of abstraction). The idea of the plural invites consideration in this light.

Plurality is not a condition of choice; it is the structural necessity from which everything is constituted. The monist singular is indivisible from the many. It is one thing to accept this statement as an abstract proposition; it is another to learn how to comprehend it operatively in the disposition of designed entities and their relations. Such learning is crucial to grasping and mobilizing the dynamics of inter-connection and difference we name as Sustainment.

Hannah Arendt provides us with a point of entry into this puzzle. Arendt contemplated the experiential relation between the 'self and itself' (self-reflection) with the help of the thirteenth-century French philosopher of the will, Petrus Johannis Olivi, proclaiming plurality as 'one of the existential conditions of human life on earth'.[2] She also evoked the Roman notion (which could just as easily have been Chinese) that in order to be alive one had to be with others. Our being human is not singular – we cannot be as individuated, we are interdependent on the other. Moreover, one can say, after Emmanuel Levinas, that one cannot gain a sense of (one's) self without facing an 'other who measures me' and that the creation of one's own identity is indivisible from facing that external to one's self.[3] Those dualisms taken so much as givens – I/thou, self/other – unravel at the behest of the thinking that Levinas commands and fold into what Maurice Merleau-Ponty famously characterized as 'the flesh of the world – flesh of the body – Being'.[4]

Likewise, Arendt's research not only confirmed the view that a mind cannot have a life without the plurality that results from engaging with other minds, but equally 'the many' exists within singularities and as a collective. As Arendt's argument was developed it became the very basis of her ethics. From a contemporary perspective, her position, captured by the notion that 'plurality is the law of the earth' resonates with the essential quality of Sustainment. Unfortunately, she goes on to undercut her position: 'not Man but men inhabit this planet'.[5] A greater sensitivity towards anthropocentrism and non-human others would have directed her thought towards a more complex view. 'The other' upon which you and I all depend is an assembly of 'the many' who form that inter-relational complexity that constitutes life itself. Existence is a universe of interdependent others: human, non-human; animate and inert.

Likewise, and in common with many thinkers, Arendt totalized the human as a 'species being' and thereby fell into that ethnocentric framing which the category 'the human' announces. She negates the violent imposition upon differences that was imposed as the human arrived as a universally projected idea. A more developed position would have been to extend a plural view of life rendering the privileging of man as a problematic abstraction. Reiterating, and more fundamentally, 'we' need to acknowledge our groundedness in the being-of-beings. Our constructed individualism has effectively erased our knowledge and sense of being connected to that of which we are a part.

The nature of individualism is amplified by that drive to direct the self's future. Nietzsche called this drive the 'will to power', which in actuality is the visionless character of anthropocentrism at the very core of those myopic and destructive values we 'moderns' hold so dear. But now 'we' (yet to become the many) find ourselves in a position wherein taking responsibility for, and redirecting, our inherent destructiveness is not a matter of choice but of necessity – if we are to have a viable future we cannot continue to be as were are. We have to become other than we are. Even so, neither learning to care for what must be cared for, nor withdrawing from forms of living and acting that defuture, can occur 'naturally'. Both require designed and managed interventions to enable the creation of a sustaining 'naturalized artificiality' and the imposition of unfreedoms to curb the destruction of what 'sustains'.

Such change heralds a huge politico-ethical meta-project that centres on establishing a 'common good' able to embrace the commonality of needs of humans and non-humans as a 'commonality in difference'. Design as politics is an opening into this project, this especially as a means to exercise futural responsibility against the *telos* of defuturing. Such action requires to be given narrative force. For instance, numerous stories can be told about the disjuncture between the rapid and constant speed of development of the defuturing power of autonomic technology (in the company of the slowness of 'man's' developmental – if not adaptive – capabilities). Remembering, as already registered, that technology is not under 'man's' control or understanding – it is no longer merely a thing, it is an environment of mind and matter in which we dwell. It has become 'naturalized'.

Core Violence

Arendt's view of violence has been extensively criticized. It centred on viewing violence as it is exercised instrumentally and as separated from structures of power.[6] Her presentation of violence – as a sign of the weakness of those forces that exercise it – is criticized as being based upon a claim of the ethico-political weakness of a regime being weakness *per se*. However, what fails to arrive in the debate is a more fundamental recognition of 'the weakness of violence' as it is lodged in the very centre of (plural) human beings themselves. This weakness goes to a more general collective failure to acknowledge the inability of anthropocentric beings to 'see' and take responsibility for their negation of the worlds of their inter-dependence. Effectively, the destructiveness of human being (especially industrialized human beings) can be taken as an indication of an intrinsic violence in 'our' being itself.

To be human is to be anthropocentric and to be anthropocentric is to be violent – here is the core of human violence. It is the price we pay for our denaturalization. But in 'our' destructiveness we are auto-destructive: in destroying that which we depend upon we destroy our selves. To confront what we are and to take responsibility for it means we are effectively at war with ourselves (in so far as these sentiments resonate through Schmitt's life and work it makes him all the more significant). There is no going back, no politics of nature. In order to go forward both we and the political must change and this change can only occur by design.

Evidently, our mode of being evidences acting *in* the world (the locus of our inter-dependencies) as indivisible from violently acting *against* the world (the locus of our own being-in-beings). One would think that the combination of our sheer numbers together with technological amplification of an almost infinite capacity for violence heads us towards an unavoidable moment of nemesis. Yet in this deepening condition of auto-destructiveness, what 'man' violently does still remains concealed from him/herself. 'Our human crisis' (as the crisis of anthropocentrism) denotes an un-named and un-registered condition wherein violence and defuturing conflate. At this point, it should be remembered that irrational and unthinkable levels of destruction (not least war) are directed by reason – and this danger grows.

In contrast to the positives of plurality (as outlined), pluralism, as either a metaphysical or ideological position, accommodates that which it is willing to tolerate, but excludes that which it does not. Contradictions appear as acceptable but outright opposition is not. Appearances are deployed to conceal singular interests often deploying difference to mask the exercise of their authority. In so many ways, pluralism acts to hide the violence of negation, fragmentation and fundamental difference.

Where plurality is an ontic condition, pluralism is a politically and relativistically inflected ideology that, in the company of eclecticism and pragmatism, imposes a disposition toward instrumental solutions. Even more significant to our argument is the fact that pluralism, being inherently institutionally inscribed within democracy, permanently undercuts the possibility of a comprehension of, and engagement with, relational complexity. Pluralism holds what it gathers as atomized, as individuated rather than as collectivities, unities or bonded communities.

Rather than these critical comments implying a call for completely new knowledge, they invite a rethinking of ideas already lodged in the first thinking of the West and non-West.

Recovering a Thinking

The move from plural thought to pluralism seems linguistically like a small move, whereas in politico-philosophical terms, as we shall see, it's a huge one.

The study of the thinking of non-Western ancient cultures points to ways of thinking that have been lost, forgotten or under-explored. They beg to be recovered. Such ways of thinking are not immediately applicable as practical knowledge but they are a means by which a different world, and a different way of knowing one's being-in-the-world, can be brought to a variety of reflective relations with contemporary knowledge. Learning from this thinking is nothing to do with 'new age' spirituality or romanticization of the 'wisdom of the ancients'. Rather, it rests with relational and complex thought prior to and other than that division of knowledge which is reason.[7] Moreover, much early thought, once recovered, demonstrably brings into question assumptions about the separation between theory and practice that has so characterized many Western cultural, economic and political modes of understanding. Defined against this backdrop, pluralism is a negation of situated agency, a refusal to learn what circumstances demand, and a harbinger of dysfunction. As David Hall and Roger Ames point out:

> … we effectively tamed our ideological disputes by rejecting the notion that ideas are dispositions to act. Finally, by separating the private and the public spheres we further guaranteed that the right of each individual to think as she or he pleases would not disrupt political stability and social harmony.[8]

It should be acknowledged that the pluralism of enfranchised electorates and electoral bodies was pre-dated, accompanied and post-dated by the ever-extending trajectory of Western ethnocentricity. Is there anything more singular than the elimination of the culturally plural by the genocidal and ethnocidal force of colonial violence?[9] Here one now asks: are not the unspoken intentions and many of the consequences of 'globalization' merely an extension of the history of ethnocide? Moreover, modern democracy was built upon a foundation of economic liberalism as it 'cleared' the way for 'free trade', and mono-directional capitalist development, be it politically couched in the language of democratic pluralism (but based upon a singular theory of knowledge with the intent of creating a single ontology – modern being).

Effectively, the combined agency of the directionality, epistemology and ontology of globalization has acted on the cultures of the world so as to make 'world cultures', with all beings conforming to the laws of a liberal democratic designation of the being-*of*-the-world and particular modes of being-*in*-the-world. In doing this, not only was cultural difference reduced but, equally, political agency was gutted: politics lost its ability to direct lifeworlds and increasingly become merely gestural and aesthetic. Such ethnocentrism was not the product of some consciously mobilized 'will to dominate' but the result of a specifically embodied logic becoming elemental to operational instrumental structures (trade, aid, finance, technology transfer, etc.) and the formation of the globalized modern collective subject.

The diminishment of the plural by the globalization of pluralism means a negation of freedom. Consider these remarks from an essay on pluralism by Louise Marcil-Lacoste:

> My argument is that, despite appearances, pluralism is conceptualized within an epistemo-logical monism which—and here is the paradox—makes it inseparable from its opposite, the lack, negation, scorning or obliteration of pluralities. I shall stress that, in and through pluralism, the denial of pluralities operates in two ways, which are both problematic. The first negates the *positive* values of those pluralities we have in mind when we associate defence of pluralism with democratic extension of the principle of freedom. The second negates the *negative* value of those pluralities that we have in mind when we associate pluralism with the maintenance of inequalities.[10]

We can agree with the epistemological singularity of pluralism, yet still disagree with the thrust of the analysis. The assumption that positive plurali-ties delivered by pluralism to democracy extend 'the principle of freedom' is contestable. As our address to freedom in a later chapter will indicate, the extension of 'freedom' by democracy cannot evoke 'the principle of freedom' as if it were a consensual figure. Likewise, democracy cannot be called up without qualification – not least because of the large gap between the idea and its plural actualities. Certainly, the negative pluralities of that difference which is democracy do maintain inequalities, but, as has been argued, de-mocracy's singularity equally strives to impose 'the same' (here hegemonic 'liberal democracy' can be characterized as a key ambition of globalization). Both difference and the same here manifest the hard and soft edges of ethno-centric modernity.

Inequalities may be most extreme when viewing the difference between the ways of life of peoples of wealthy and poor nations, but they can also be seen in the conditions of the under-classes within even the richest socie-ties (graphically illustrated by the US). The fact that the dispossessed can have the right to vote does not mean they have any agency to change the status quo or that they have anyone to vote for who will work to change their circumstances.

At their most basic, those inequalities inherent to pluralism cannot be divided from the neglect, or even the obliteration, of the plural. Thus pluralist freedom is a 'freedom' whose principles rest upon upholding those 'rights' that ensure the ability to name and secure the same. Conditions that uphold fundamental difference ever remain disabled, as the history of the world's indigenous peoples confirm. Here, the finitudinal limit within the question of 'the freedom of ethnocentric being' becomes apparent, for such being is imprisoned within a condition that makes the possibility of imagining being otherwise than marginal an impossibility. The implications for design here are massive, in so far as design in such circumstances remains totally constrained.

As a result of the onward march of globalization, our the ability to re-member how 'we' were, or contemplate how we could be, as anything other than what 'we' now are as 'global producers and consumers', is under erasure. This is not a consequence of an overt politics or conspiracy. The situation results from the 'nature' of material ideological forms (images, knowledge, the designing of designed material and immaterial things)[11] to carry 'a desired pluralist world made real' and a perception of being modern as the destined essence of 'human beings and relations'.

From Plurality to Pluralism

Plurality invites an essentially diverse and a multi-perspectival point of view, whereas pluralism rests with a stasis of hyper-conformity that reduces dif-ference to equivalence. Additionally, pluralism became a relativistic norma-tive value employed by most major institutions of the late modern world (for example, universities) on which to predicate their thinking, language, policies and practices. Effectively, pluralism paralyses any ability to say or do anything beyond the pragmatic. In large part, this is because all other dis-courses are negated by a play of contradictions, with no appeal to an overall position of authority, independence or judgement. As an individual position, pluralism, to use Louise Marcil-Lacoste's designation is 'nowhere'.[12] It gath-ers incommensurate ideas, values and knowledge into a condition of mutual coexistence that leaves individual judgement indeterminate. Pluralism conserves the status quo by rendering change that is predicated on a clear direction, virtually impossible. It reduces change to continually moving elements of the same. Three options ensue: recoil into faith in the status quo; anomic resistance to prevailing circumstances; or the development of a politics that can gather the plural around a common cause based on the common good and a recreated foundation of ethics.

Pluralism – as enacted by the 'real politic' (pragmatism) of 'democratic' nation states – unambiguously demands to be critically targeted because of the defuturing consequences of its tolerated contradictions, like, for instance, a willingness to accommodate: the unsustainable along with 'sustainability'-oriented policies and practices; structural inequity while claiming a commitment to extending equity; the promotion of peace while making war; and the promotion of justice while 'turning a blind eye' to injustice. The condemnation here is not based on the notion that contradictions can be avoided, but rather that they require to be dealt with ethically rather than pragmatically (or by just being ignored).

Obviously, there is a need to more adequately situate the position just stated. The starting point is to place plurality and pluralism in a historical frame of reference. This returns us to pre-Socratic thought, in particular to Parmenides, the first monist logician. His axiom of 'the universe as one' implied that nothing required acknowledgment outside the totality that is one. His concern was taken up by Empedocles, Anaxagoras and the Atomists, Leucippus and Democritus (whose lives overlapped with Socrates, which meant they were at the end of the tradition of the 'first thinkers'). It is with these 'pre-Socratics', amid the division of thought as either monist or dualist, that we find the birth of pluralism.

For Empedocles, there was the totality of 'what is' but there was also change, as the substance of 'what is' moved in process. The sum of 'what is' is all that which comes from the elements fire, air, water and earth. The dynamic forces that move matter were said to have been 'Strife' and 'Love'. Empedocles was among the first thinkers to make a division between matter and force. We need to transpose the metaphors 'strife' and 'love' into a variety of historically changing positive and negative connotations, which would undoubtedly include the likes of good and evil, violence and kindness, friend and enemy. While the views of Anaxagoras were not identical to those of Empedocles (especially on the agency of the basic elements) he was still a 'process' thinker. He argued that all matter was an infinitely divisible continuum and no matter how often divided will always contain different elements. Both these propositions implied that everything that is encountered as plural is in fact part of the whole. The proto-materialism of the Atomists took this kind of thinking a stage further. They said that everything is reducible to elemental building blocks: indivisible atoms and voids. Thus there are just two existent conditions: the atomic assembly and nothing. Leucippus initiated this idea and Democritus refined it.

It was out of this formative moment of Western thought that 'epistemological monism' was installed. However, the idea did not gain hegemonic status. Pluralism emerged amid a plurality that had reason and deductive logic at one pole and direct knowledge from observation of 'the world' at the other, with mysticism as a free-roaming third voice. In fact, on the back of this emergence, at least as Hall and Ames argued, syntheses arrived in the thought of Plato and Aristotle whereby:

> ... Greek philosophy reached its culmination. Effectively, all of the major philosophical issues and problems, which would influence subsequent speculation, were now formulated. Of equal importance, the co-presence of the Platonic and Aristotelian visions provided distinctive strategies for the resolution of the subsequent pluralism of ideas and beliefs that would pattern the Western tradition.[13]

Clearly the plural and contested positions evident in Greek thought were not resolved prior to the arrival and domination of contemporary pluralism; rather they were accommodated to it. As Heidegger showed so clearly, this first thinking of the early Greeks was not stranded in the distant time of its creation but rather travelled within Western thought, although not as a fixed set of meanings but as a thinking always being remade by the contexts in which it arrived.[14] Continuity of presence therefore does not equate with uniformity of meaning.

The seeds of universalism were firmly planted by Greek thought. Although constituted as an assemblage of plural positions, this thinking functioned with a universal claim – structural monism's singular world view (as a source of knowledge of the world and of the being of being-in-the-world). The claim rested with the proposition of an immanent resolution of *the* difference that appeared as plural. Here then is effectively the foundation of ethnocentrism as the birth of the one that is human, with its one universe to know. While no single world-view arrived, the singularity of the culture of authority of the Western mind did come into being.

We can contrast the way a world was being viewed by the Greeks with, at almost the same time, the views of the Chinese. Again Hall and Ames give us a succinct description:

> Chinese culture is not shaped by any appeal to universal categories defining human na-
> ture and 'establishing the unity of mankind'; rather, the Chinese refer to themselves in
> more provisional locutions such as 'the people of the central states' or 'the peoples of
> the Han.' Thus, neither in their articulations of the meaning of being a human being,
> nor in their understanding of culture and history, do classical Chinese thinkers appeal to
> transcendent principles as the origin or certification of their vision. Exemplar models and
> cultural heroes from the past, such as the Sage King or Confucius, function in the place of
> transcendent structures such as the principle of Reason, or the *trintarian* God, to provide
> the understanding of what it means to be human.[15]

The shift here is from metaphysical questions and competing epistemologies claiming to explain 'what is' to a constructivist notion of world-making in difference by difference.

The first use of the term 'pluralism' is attributed to Herman Lotze, a teacher of medicine and philosophy at Leipzig in the mid-nineteenth century.[16] For Lotze, inquiry was not circumscribed by the horizon of science.[17] His position marked a particular (but obviously not unique) claim that an understanding of the complexity of the material and cultural transformation of 'the world' is beyond what science is able to explore. Lotze argued that 'a world' is constituted from a multiplicity of beings forming an 'independent' reality (that is, they do not form a singular or absolute reality). Such 'substantival pluralism' was not overarched by a singular totality, be it 'picture' or a monist conceptual construct. Pluralism, so viewed, is not seen to be linked to any schema of relationality (for example, ecology).

Epistemologically, pluralism was a key contribution to the development of the American pragmatic tradition. This is especially evident in the work of William James, who not only penned one of the major statements of pluralism – *A Pluralistic Universe* (1909) – but also acted, as psychologist and philosopher, as one of the most influential exemplars of an American liberal ontology for his age. He fused the circumstantial and experiential basis of pragmatism and the accommodation of contradiction afforded by pluralism together with a rabid individualism. He was seen not just to express the intellectual spirit of his American age – an age of the nation's burgeoning international economic power – but to be one of the strongest voices legitimizing the nation's 'God-given right' to extol democracy as the basis of 'individual freedom'. James liberated laissez-faire thought and brought it into the domain of laissez-faire economic culture. In so doing, he opened a path followed by contemporary thinkers like Richard Rorty and Jean-François Lyotard.

Pluralism's rise as a political theory and its address to a restricted set of relations, is connected to the accommodation of those differences that modernity has inflamed and proliferated (as well as to the pragmatic management of competing interests that its economies and cultures brought into close proximity with each other within the spaces of industrial society). This is very clear in a summary given by Kirstie McClure.[18] The initial expression of modern political pluralism is presented as 'Anglo-American' pluralism begun just after the First World War. Its objective was to contest the idea of a unified state sovereignty (after Hegel, Austin and English idealism under the influence of William James). Its second moment was elemental to the rise of 'empirical democratic theory', this having its greatest profile in the work of the American social scientist Robert Dahl in the 1950s and 1960s. The third moment, the plurality of positions on pluralism, in the present, includes the debate between all the current theories of democracy.

These expressions of pluralism had, however, all been predicated by the arrival of the political theory of political scientist Arthur F. Bentley. He is credited as having made a significant contribution to giving coherence to the idea with his the publication of *The Process of Government* in 1908. The later work of the economist Joseph Schumpeter is also credited with making a major contribution to advancing the idea in the 1940s.[19]

In discussing the nature and problem of pluralism what we keep coming up against, at various levels, is obviously a condition of linguistic slippage. The variable relations of pluralism, plurality, diversity, multiplicity and difference mark an instability that reasoned argument is not going to arrest. The placement of Sustainment in this setting as a naming of 'commonality in difference' does not fold into the space of pluralism – this precisely because difference is seen as being able to be gathered within the make-up of a multi-vectored process that is projected as travelling toward the same meta-diverse end. Sustainment is seen then as the imperative of the task at hand, and as such has the status of a moment of imminence driving a nascent practice. It is therefore not a question of 'when will Sustainment arrive/be attained?' but rather, by setting it as a directional goal, the impossibility of a singular direction that is intrinsic to pluralism is countered and the plural process of futuring is given its head.

Pluralism and Politics

One of the manifestations of pluralism in recent decades has been identity politics. Without opening up an entirely new argument, we can say that the rise of this kind of politics centred on an actual or claimed lack, or a refusal, of identity.[20] The exclusive 'for-itself' atavistic ontology of this politics transpires to directly design against a relationality with 'world' and 'others' that sustain. As both disposition and politics, the horizontally limited figure of identity so framed fundamentally fails to grasp the issues of diversity, ecology and the social. In its 'bid for freedom', identity politics renders the experience of freedom impossible – the very condition of being free among a multiplicity of non-identical subjects is drastically reduced by the demand for recognition.

In contrast, what is proposed here is that the demand for recognition be placed in the plural (in a social ecology of relational power) – which implies an acknowledgement of difference under a commonality that is not a unified totality. Thus the common *de facto* is constituted from a play of identity, identities of, and identifications with, that which is essential to sustain for identity and difference to be possible. Sustainment/the ability to sustain is not every-thing, but everything that we are, everything upon which we depend, and everything that depends upon us has to be sustained to be. Unless, in difference, this imperative is identified and named, there are no identities of enduring value with durable futures. It is from this perspective that the commonality of our anthropocentricity is before us as an unavoidable identification with an absolute responsibility and limit that has to be learned (including learning the error of pluralism and democracy and their current bonding to 'sustaining the unsustainable').

The pluralist notion of 'the right of others to hold and express beliefs other than one's own' inscribed in liberal-democratic society has always been a qualified right – prohibiting the right to incite racial hatred is one illustration of a constraint on the right of 'free expression'. In this context, a line needs to be drawn: *on one side* – an essential and continual questioning of what has the ability to sustain and the affirmation of what is, or has to be, sustained; *on the other side* – the imposition of constraint upon the clearly unsustainable by the curtailment of rights.

Again, at issue here is the need to recognize that without the unfreedom of the limits that secure the possibility of sustainment there is no (relative) freedom. Under sovereign Sustainment, all freedom is the unfreedom of exercised responsibilities (via delivering by design, material forms and practices which sustain, together with a culture able to learn, select, value and conserve that which must be sustained) and this marks an absolute break with any liberal notions of freedom via the imposition of the means able to control and regulate the (liberal) status quo.

The learning of Sustainment, as it translates to a making, culture and politics, is the learning, examination, adjustment and holding of the limit of an un-common humanity. Contrary to the anthropological and biological designation of the human as a single 'species' – a meaningless biologism – 'we', to repeat, are not one. The human is constructed, not found. The system of

classification of the 'species', which places particular peoples on an evolutionary line of development (legitimizing a massive amount of past and present
genocidal and ethnocidal violence), has been an enduring 'crime of humanity'.
There needs to be a recognition of difference that totally overrides the pluralism of that 'cultural difference' of the same that ethnocentrically projects
a view of the other as a superstructurally modifiable identity of habitation
resting upon an assumed essence of 'the human'. The failure to recognize just
how different difference is, profoundly undercuts the possibility of gaining
common interests across the uncommon designation of what 'we' are. Quite
clearly 'civilization' did (and continues to) negate that diversity upon which
Sustainment depends. Recognition of fundamental 'being-in-difference' needs
to break free of humanist anthropologically ordered cultural typologies, schemas and categories. Such a position implicitly refuses the simplistic either/
or, and romanticized view of, for instance, indigenous peoples remaining attached to (damaged versions of) their culture versus abandoning it in favour
of 'modern life'. Difference, in this context, is not stasis but the ability to be
otherwise by making a culture of one's own rather than having to adopt the
culture of the dominant other. While change cannot be resisted, who and
what drives change is another matter. 'We' are neither what 'we' have been
led to believe we are nor are 'we' becoming what 'we' need to be in difference.

Pluralism exposes its constraints and flaws through the racial value system
of Western humanism. Pluralist discourse ignores what is a stake. It either
negates the difference of the different (cf. the history of multiculturalism) by
not allowing it to speak on its own terms or it disregards unfamiliar forms of
uncommon intelligence.

Historically, humanism posited that its tradition of great and universal
thought 'speaks for, and touches the soul of, all humanity'. St Augustine,
Shakespeare and Goethe are obvious representatives of this tradition. Notwithstanding this, there is a propensity toward inhumanity inscribed within
pluralist humanism that designates others as inhuman and external to that
'common humanity' that it claims to represent. Such seemingly crude and
direct observations have been placed outside the remit of political discourse.
The few who confronted the inhuman – Nietzsche, Adorno, Horkheimer,

Arendt, Clastres, Lyotard and others – are effectively marginalized figures. Without doubt, and in the shadow of 'being-technological', this confrontation is still before us. The question is, who will do it?

In conformity with Schmitt's analysis, we have seen how pluralism leads to fragmentation – which now in the division of the world spatial order, flows into the ever mobile estate of corporate capitalism.[21] Under the protection of the pluralism of liberal democracies, and their notion of freedom, a globalizing (restrictive) economy is being realized by these corporations and their client states.

The Problematics of the Problem

The problem that most concerns us here is finding the language to express the impossibility of Sustainment being able to arrive democratically, while showing that, in the face of futural imperatives, the dysfunctionality of 'currently existing forms' of democracy is foundational. One can, of course, adopt a genre that tries to avoid trading in problems, or decamps to a contemporary textual preoccupation with 'the particular' that thrusts the reader into a web of micro-problems. Any attempt to fully capture all the problems a close textual reading can identify is of course fated.

It seems clear, no matter the form of expression, that democratic regimes are unaware or mute on three absolutely vital issues: the first is that defuturing is a present and absolutely critical condition; the second is that the creation of 'Sustainment' – the moment and the process – is a massive and pressing imperative; and third is the enduring blindness of 'civilized societies' to anthropocentrism. Of course, saying such things is to 'speak the unspeakable' and so invites condemnation, ridicule, the accusation of arrogance, stupidity, or any combination thereof.

The central problem of concern here is a lack of understanding of relational thought as it rides above the conceptual poverty of human centred thinking and cultural resistance to expressions of the unfamiliar. All that can be done in this situation is to offer a few openings into the needed thinking, via a *gestalt* which is lodged *in* design practice – this will be done by posing four problems.

Problem 1: Finitude – finitude is the completely singular, it cannot be divided or neutralized by pluralism. Finitudinal politics is a politics of Sustainment – that is, a politics that strives to design action towards an extension of the indeterminate temporal, but always finite, limits of being. Such action cannot be separated from the limits of knowledge, so is clearly not the action of one moment. Rather it is action that both withdraw(s) into mind, while equally being externalized and remade from learnt experience. This politics is antagonistic to the instrumentalism of currently institutionalized politics and its organizational and administrative rationalism, plus the aesthetic choreography of its gestures.

Problem 2: Essentialism – 'essentialism' is a derogatory accusation that one can expect to be laid before a commitment to Sustainment (or a commitment to anything). The case will not hold. Sustainment is not reducible to anything essential, unless one would wish to argue against the essentiality of process, change, being-in-difference and the futural. In human-created circumstances where the future ('our' future) is not assured, Sustainment is an 'essential' conjunctural, learning-to-change. Hereafter, the ability to sustain is always what has to be learnt and then commonly sustained in a specific time and place (which means striving to be constantly cognizant of the changing nature of 'what is', while 'what is' can no longer be regarded as an 'essential nature').

Again, the plural is being affirmed and pluralism rejected. We also note the necessity of, as Chantel Mouffe says, 'abandoning the reductionism and essentialism dominant in the liberal interpretations of pluralism, and acknowledging the contingency and ambiguity of every identity, as well as the constitutive character of social division and antagonism'.[22]

Problem 3: Transcendence – Hall and Ames argue that 'pragmatic philosophers, conscious of theoretical pluralism become (non-transcendental) meta-philosophers'.[23] Prior to this they claim 'the pragmatist celebrates the plurality of approaches to our central question and problems on the practical ground that the more tools we have at our disposal, the more likely we are to find the tool best suited for the task at hand.[24] A few lines later they say: 'The genius of North American society from its beginnings has been its affirmation of pluralism. This pluralism has, philosophically, been couched in aesthetic (and romantic) rather than cognitive terms and thus provided a distinctive approach to issues of inter-theoretical and inter-cultural comparison.'[25]

Hall and Ames claim here that *pragmatism plus pluralism* equals a higher philosophy liberated from transcendentalism – however, as has already been argued, the space between pluralism and monism has the ability to instantly vanish. One could also claim that what 'pragmatics plus pluralism' actually delivers is 'expedient transcendentalism' whereby resolution is delivered by whatever is pragmatically at hand. In this context, one sees 'democracy' being mobilized as a mechanism for the resolution of difference. As for the assertion that 'the more tools we have at our disposal, the more likely we are to find the tool best suited for the task at hand' – this proposition fails even within Hall and Ames' own 'logic'. If what they said were correct, it would mean that as time has passed, more and more problems would have been resolved as more 'tools' have continually arrived. However, no matter whether we are talking about philosophy or technology, irrespective of what a 'tool' solves, every new tool brings new problems. Pluralism competes, confuses and confounds, while pragmatism has the tendency to an expediency that defers an engagement with what is fundamental to 'the problem' by a temporally circumscribed perception of what is at hand and to be done (it hides problems behind the facade of meeting immediate needs via short term solutions).

More specifically, 'cashing in' on temporary and expedient solutions to 'crisis' (as Marx first showed) has been a primary driving force of capitalism. As the emergent 'carbon economy' illustrates, crisis is capital's lifeblood; but in the final analysis it is also the bringer of its terminal condition. Joseph Schumpeter characterized this crisis as 'creative destruction' in his book *Capitalism, Socialism and Democracy* (1942) whereby capitalism destroys itself in order to renew itself (as the history of technological innovation confirms). Marx, in different terms, expressed the same. But of course, now, the question of its endless renewal looks lame.

Hall and Ames' final comment above is perhaps the most worrying of all. What they have to say on the 'genius of North American society' smacks of chauvinism and surprises. As comparative philosophers, such unreflective comment would seem to be completely at odds with their project and considerable attainments. Certainly, their lack of a sense of how they undercut their own position of observation is astounding. Yet what they have done has an air of familiarity about it. Rather than simply exposing the value, complexity and relevance of the classical Chinese non-transcendental worldview and world-making, what Hall and Ames do is akin to those art historians who set out to show an affinity between modernist abstraction and 'primitive' iconography. In other words, and sub-textually, there is intent to install the impression of affinity between contemporary American 'non-transcendental' meta-philosophy and the operational functionality of the earth-bound practical thinking of much classical Chinese thought and aesthetics. Even if this is not the case in a full-blown sense, the tendency is there, and certainly it exposes two major lacks in their work: the first can be called un-negotiated logocentrism; the second is a failure to do what they themselves advocate – bringing theory and practice together. In their own hands 'strong' scholarship and theoretical rigour does not deliver a practical possibility – whereas, from the perspective of Sustainment their work can be supplemented by learning from that 'which can act towards Sustainment' as a responsive transformative praxis.

Problem 4: The same – the same, the other, identity and difference – thinking this 'problem' of relations reigns eternal.

Pluralism, in neutralizing difference, makes the same. We have already registered the violence of a paradoxical pluralism as it enforces the monism of holding difference under the same, or in its casting of excluded difference into an abysmal silence. This pluralism is: the one, the ego, the same. This same 'reveals itself in the form of the self-centred ego, who wants an autonomy to impose its laws (*nomos*) on the world in which it is at home (*oikos*)'.[26] Here is *oiko-nomia* economy: the economy of the law of the home, the economy of modernity, the economy of the ecology.

The imposition of the same, the economy of the choice is no choice (democracy). We learn from Heidegger that 'the same' so framed is our 'being here' in the world that is *Dasein* and from which 'it its self' comes to be (as a commonality of ontological designing). 'It' is both the negation and assertion of ego by identity: 'I am the same', my identity is an identification with the world and the other that moves me towards the plural 'one' that I am (the one American, Chinese, black, white, male, female, straight, gay, and so forth). The same is the resolution of oppositions; it is the erasure of that spacing that allows difference. Conversely, the absolute other is the alterity that cannot be accommodated as *the same* but equally it legitimizes the continual attempt to re-impose the subject.[27] Such is the 'nature' of dialectical 'human existence' that for 'us' now in the coming (or for many, the arrived) epoch of technological hegemony, there is another being-in-proximity in danger. This is a danger wherein the very 'nature' of that which 'comes to be' as 'the same and the other' becomes reconfigured a fundamental difference beyond sapient being.

Into this complexity arrives Nietzsche's question of the eternal return of the same (as defined by Heidegger '... the eternal chaos of necessity, is the return of the same)'.[28] We are in and of this moment of reconfigured difference – in this critical moment (which is a crucial conditions of *our* being) there is danger of non-return. We can do no more than deposit this issue (while refusing the trite evocation of the human/technology/mutation of the 'cyborg'). Noting the significance of this issue raises problems for thinking both identity and difference (as well as what Schmitt called life-indifference)[29] as they cut across determinations of the 'world totality' as the spacing between one moment of the return of the same and another. Again, the question of Sustainment arrives as the necessity of difference and change between moments of the same (change here is a space as well as a process that returns as the same). Clearly, all that has been managed so far is to open up the complexity of the problem to the extent that the very adequacy of the measure of 'problem and solution' appears to fall apart, as does a sense of continuity, crisis and human agency.

Pluralism, Design and Democracy

Defenders of pluralism proliferate – they appeal to 'common sense' 'reasonableness', 'functionality', 'proceduralism', 'consensuality', 'multiple values' and 'pragmatics' as justification and for pluralism as an essential 'operational basis' of contemporary society. These defenders extol the virtues of pluralism's practices and its theoretical armoury. In contrast, what is put forward here is a project of bringing plurality/difference to inform a theory and practice of transformative politics, economy, designing and culture centred on responding to the imperative of Sustainment. So positioned, Sustainment is seen as the measure, limit and the sovereign figure to which democracy is subordinated.

Pluralism, Liberalism and the Project of Democracy

The ideological figures of pluralism, liberalism and democracy are conjoined in the varied appearances of the political culture of the 'developed' world. The representational projection of this culture trades on theories that view its component parts (politics, race, 'the people', and so forth) in essentialist term and its manner of worldly engagement as objective. The management of appearances of party-based democratic politics conceals the fundamental, wider antagonism between (political) friends and enemies, and the complexity, dynamics and geography of power integral to its politics.[30] The conclusion that Ernesto Laclau and Chantel Mouffe come to, which many of us know and feel, is that the objectified structures of the power of operative, pluralist and 'liberal democratic' societies are hegemonic and thus totalized – pluralist democracy is a singular regime (it has in fact now become a surrogate for modernity as an instrument serving the total world order, globalizing capitalism and democracy fold into the same). Enemies are thus outcasts and either vilified or rendered invisible.

Laclau and Mouffe are among the few contemporary voices that have anything critical to say on the pluralism, liberalism and democracy nexus. Yet they speak out of the conceptual exhaustion of humanism. Their attempt to save radical democracy implicitly acknowledges that there is no viable exterior location from which to lever fundamental change. They try to radicalize 'the same' by using reason against reason. This is a doomed reformist argument, which becomes drowned in the clamour of the internal debates by 'political progressives' over pluralism and democracy. Their agenda is in fact 'haunted' by a socialist humanism that can now never be – capitalism has no recoverable other. The only way to go beyond democracy is by the creation of a new politics, acknowledging that a significant part of the new can but be a bricolage of selection, modification and reassembly of elements from the old. So while some common ground exists, there just has to be a position created beyond the failures of idealism, gesturalism and the good intentions of humanist discourse.

While establishing a marginal position toward deconstructive thought, Laclau and Mouffe retain an attachment to the very thing that they need to deconstructively undercut – democracy itself. The avoided, but in the end unavoidable, issue is totally remaking the basis of democracy rather than reforming its operational framework. As Derrida knew full well, democracy can only be recreated as futural by first being made nothing. Out of its history and towards its future, deconstruction clearly travels in two directions: first, towards the 'destruktion' of that which has to be cleared and, second, towards an undoing of foundations that renders 'the given' as matter for remaking. So the issue is not one of finding an exterior place to deconstructively engage the foundations of democracy (plural), but rather to internally render it to rubble and rebuild from the inside. Remembering pluralism as 'nowhere' suggests there is a 'game to play'. This 'move' is not aligned with Laclau and Mouffe's directional tack, which would wish to liberate pluralism from its 'facticity' and to claim it as a concept to 'celebrate and enhance'.

These comments would be pointless (and may well be taken as such) if it were not the case that (as we have been trying to show) there is a fine dividing line between plurality and pluralism that forces open a chasm of *différance*.[31]

The Place of Design in a 'Politics' of Sustainment

Reiterating – the politics of Sustainment can be summarized as being: the creation, negotiation and establishment of a commonality in difference (the plural
nature of Sustainment) and the remaking of 'the things of the world' as directionally considered (material/immaterial) objects of ontological designing – all
to make time. While every existing designed object (singular and compound)
goes on designing (often with defuturing consequences) what is being proposed,
as part of the agenda of commonality, is that such 'things' are given, by design
intent (materially, performatively and semiotically) a singular direction so that
their designing designs their own, and their users' propensity toward futuring.
While this implies a significant material change of many products, structures
and systems, it more dramatically requires the recoding and relearning of
what a vast numbers of existing things are, how they should be used, where
and how. Inseparably bonded to this is the transformation of ways of thinking and engaging questions of equity and justice. So although the ontological
designing aspect of Sustainment requires a degree of physical change, more
fundamentally, it depends on the creation of perceptual and political change.

Design and a New Political Imaginary

We are now in a position to say just a little more about the kind of things that
a new political imaginary needs to embrace – even so, the actual imaginary is
still out of reach.

The vision it projects clearly has to centre on Sustainment as the measure
and rule of all things. As continual process, and absolute authority, Sustainment clearly needs an institutional foundation ('the Sustainment' as project)
supported by a practice (redirective practice) that government (inchoately
post-democratic), the law (*terra-nomos*) and economy (general exchange)
all serve.

The perspective cannot be singular, nationalist or utopian. The vision has
to be able to be pursued by plural means, be lodged in the local and the global,

and be a regime able to deliver realizable results framed by actual needs in time rather than by pragmatics. As such, the address to change has to be reactive (identifying and responding to what needs to change), prefigurative (establishing new directions) and bonded to a new economic paradigm.

To centre power around Sustainment also implies a decentring; as such it becomes the political armature around which all activity that sustains economic, social and cultural life is wound. Its ability to generate wealth and social stability turns on an enormous re-learning, re-skilling, re-employment, all with resource re-deployment potential. As was illustrated with concepts like metrofitting, not only would the 'natural environment' be designated for major rehabilitation but so also would the city (and the naturalized artificial in general). Overwhelmingly, the task would be redirectional. How resources are managed; how community can be revitalized with new kinds of subjects and socio-ecological relations; how services can be made more social; how industry can be redirected toward an entirely new understanding of world and things; how entertainment can be reoriented to fuse pleasure and the serious – the issues, challenges and opportunities are myriad. They all demand a vast conceptual transformation of thought and action. A new visual language is needed to support design-based redirective practice as it constitutes making time, responsibility and qualitative performance as its ethos. Difference has to be seen. Likewise the presentation of power as plural and dispersed but always directly connected to the advancement of Sustainment, also requires an extraordinarily innovative representational schema.

Nothing said here has the status of a proposal. All that arrives is suggestive and merely indicative. What is actually being said is that there is a task that is huge, complex and pressing, essential to do, that can and has to be done. Moreover, design remade as a redirective practice and as a politics is an absolutely vital tool in this exercise. In the end, what has to be understood is very simple: the status quo is not an option; no matter what it delivers, it is failing, defuturing and doomed. A new social and economic order is not a matter of choice – it is an absolute necessity. The issue thus is 'what form should it take?' with the proviso that whatever form it does take must be predicated upon Sustainment.

7

Remaking Sovereignty

Everything is at stake in giving impetus to countering the unsustainable. Against this backdrop, Sustainment has to be more than just a moment and process. It has to be a normative regime: it has to be sovereign.

The vital directional changes that Sustainment demands cannot happen so long as it is overarched by liberal democracies that uphold economies predicated upon the dogma of continual growth and structural accommodation of inequity, technocentrism and the instrumentalization of culture. Even more broadly, the socio-political failure of the status quo to bring anthropocentrism to presence, as an issue that requires recognition and critical engagement, means that the ability of modern human beings to take responsibility for what they are and do (as the locus of structural unsustainability) is perpetually negated – which is not to say such being can be surmounted but it is to say that without knowledge of anthropocentrism, taking responsibility for so being is impossible.

The state of Sustainment has to become sovereign (thus the locus of ultimate power) so that politics, the economy and culture are subordinated to the meta-objective of making time – and thus act to reverse the defuturing trajectory of structural unsustainability as it diminishes the finite time of our being. So framed, Sustainment becomes empowered – as an over-determinate law of the state that imposes Sustainment as the primary responsibility of all over which the state exercises power. This thereby creates the means and the structure of an ontological designing that can transform the conduct of social subjects. By implication, the form of the state is also transformed, its agency becomes distributed – not least as it liberates the agency of designing posited in designed 'things'. Redirective change is thus not predicated solely upon changing consciousness but incrementally changing the composite nature of the world of things at large. This does not mean the change agents who design ontologically designing things do not require a transformed consciousness but it does mean that they are but transitory means.

This approach to change recognizes that appealing to and conventionally educating populations to change their minds and values is not a realizable possibility – hence the shift to the transformative power of ontologically designing things (which is to say that things already have massive power, but dominantly this power is fragmented, multi-directional and in the service of defuturing).

In evoking Sustainment as sovereign, it is understood that we are not dealing with an idea fully embedded in content and institutional agency – the union has yet to be formed. So while currently, there is no organization, infrastructure or assured destiny, the idea is imminently iconic and can be claimed to have latent force – Sustainment's victory is the only way humanity has a future. Nonetheless, making Sustainment sovereign is a vast challenge in which labour and thinking are indivisible. More specifically, there is a need for a theoretically informed redirective practice guided by a new political imaginary.

As much of what has already been said in previous chapters indicates, the project has no romantic inflection, it is not painless, and it means:

- gains arrive at the cost of losses;
- the imposition of unfreedoms to secure relative freedoms;
- the creation of a commonality carried by Sustainment to underpin all difference;
- an ontological transformation of the agency of things and what it is to 'be human'.

On this last point, it is worth recalling how Heidegger understood Nietzsche's evocation of the 'superman':

> The 'superman' does not simply carry the accustomed drives and strivings of the cus-
> tomary type of man beyond all measure and bounds. Superman is a qualitatively, not
> quantitatively, different form of existing man. The thing that the superman discards is
> precisely our boundless, purely quantitative non-stop progress. The superman is poorer,
> simpler, tenderer and tougher, quieter and more self-sacrificing and slow of decision and
> more economical of speech.[1]

Creating such a subject with an altered psychology *and* a very different understanding of politics, together with an absolutely materially grounded basis for ethics, justice and global equity, has to be what directs a new foundation of design for Sustainment as sovereign.

On Sovereignty

Sovereignty has always been fluid in form but appearing fixed in application – its nature has constantly changed except for its centralization of power. While sovereignty may appear and be enforced as singular, in actuality it is always more than this and mostly in silence. Whatever its public presence, the supreme authority of sovereign power exceeds appearances – including the power to exercise the law above the law (as the power that decides 'the state of exception').

Historically, that which is sovereign is spatially bound (to the materiality of nation, state or sacred structure). For Sustainment to be sovereign, a new mode of authority is needed that commands embodied time and unlimited space – its making has to be futural and its authority global and thus overarching. The state as we currently understand it (as a relatively new political entity) has to be subsumed by the 'dictatorship of the imperative of Sustainment' for the rule of the Sustainment to be enacted as a 'commonality in differences'. Just as freedom under the law does not reduce all law to one law, neither would the form of the state under Sustainment be one dimensional.

Sovereignty always folds into the word and the authority of command carried by utterance and text.[2] What speaks of, for and as sovereignty is not subordinate to reason. The sovereign power, be it the institutional authority of God, the monarch or the state (via the dictator, the law or the rule of military force) is ever un-reasoned. Now, in the unfolding age of unsettlement, the rational case for the sovereignty of Sustainment is overwhelming – but given the lack of recognition of this, the question is, 'how can the imperative without choice, the dictatorship of Sustainment come to be?' To progress this question we again need to critically revisit Schmitt.

(Re)turning Schmitt

Schmitt promoted sovereignty lodged in the authority of the atomized nation state. This option is flawed and fraught with danger: such a state is an entity that defines itself against its others. As such, it functions as relationally disconnected – nation states put their interest beyond the common interest. Yet positing power with an entity above the state (as has been suggested) requires compliance from states in order to transfer authority from their political processes (including the democratic liberal process) to a trans-national structure of decision that all people have to obey – for 'the sovereign *demands* to be obeyed'.[3] Can a trans-national sovereignty, in which nationally sovereign states subordinate their power of difference to the whole, be contemplated? Can the need to sustain here overwhelm what appears as idealism?

Schmitt brings the challenge into focus. In viewing the failure of the League of Nations and the United Nations to establish an international rule of law, he observed the failure of the project of the '*nomos* of the earth'. Besides recognizing that a viable framework of international law had yet to be established, he also realized that by the mid-point of the twentieth century the transformative consequences of new technologies and the increasingly globalizing order of capitalism were remaking what was taken to be the political and economic nature of the world and that, moreover, no thinking able to grasp the implications of the situation was in formation. From his perspective, even if 'the law of the land' (*nomos*) of the world were to be written and agreed to, it would not resolve the emergent problems of the transformative agency of immaterialized power. In particular, production and consumption were becoming (and now are) grounded in a powerful sign economy driving new economies of appropriation that not only assist the taking and wasting of the earth's resources, but also devour culture and knowledge.

As the structural nature of unsustainability becomes more evident and as unsettlement arrives, the feelings and perceptions of people at large will change – concern and fear will proliferate.[4] But, of course, widespread political recognition of this is still some way off – exactly how far, is a critical question and subject to political action (including by design) being taken to hasten its presence.

Schmitt points out that Hobbes emphasized 'time and time again' that on 'the question of the sovereignty of law' it is 'only the sovereignty of men who draw up and administer this law'.[5] Such a centring of authority exposes, but never fully articulates, that sovereignty rests on the rule of anthropocentric interests that actually negate the absolute law of those relations upon which all exchange depends. It follows that more is at stake in bringing anthropocentrism to presence than just a general appeal to a taking 'responsibility for what we are and do'. As is being suggested, the very nature of law has to change – as such, the relation of 'rights of the future' in need of protection have to be thought whereby Sustainment is translated into specific acts of limitation and creation.

The sovereignty of Sustainment therefore not only needs to be seen as resting on the paramount eco-nomy (*oikos nomos*: the law of dwelling) of the '*nomos* of the earth' but equally on providing the fundamental basis of those laws to which all of humankind's actions are materially accountable (in contrast to the moral accountability of 'human rights'). Here, then, is the economy and discourse of total decision, only able to be realized by re-coding all existing 'operational instruments' of those plural things deemed sovereign (be they Gods, monarchs, subjects, law, parliament, states, nations, dictators, or armies). Difference can flourish only if it is under the power of a sovereignty that is futural – making time (and always exceeding the whole and affirming the plural: it cannot be fully gathered). Nothing is without time, yet time can never be without being. It is not an object of faith.

To talk of Sustainment as sovereign and the need for a new political imaginary requires qualification. Sustainment as sovereign has to accommodate political difference. A new political imaginary needs to articulate this. Certainly, there is a need to go beyond democracy because of its limitations, but not all the world can be made post-democratic (any more than it could be made democratic).

For Sustainment to be levered into a position where it becomes truly powerful it has to be liberated by a regime of redirective design, it has to create an ontologizing force that enables commonalties in difference to be realized within a global frame. Thus it has to reconfigure 'the order of things' to subordinate human being to 'the propensity of sustaining things'. Such things have no national identity; they are not of just one culture. Authority here rests with the attainment of redirection and is the obverse of existing politics whereby promises (as policy) precede action and so often are out of joint with determinate imperatives (electoral pragmatism thereby overpowers actual need).

Can such change come about? The imperative of a future with a future demands saying yes. The appeal to a global authority here requires neither a moral nor socio-economic rationale, but rather a clear demonstration of Sustainment as an absolute common interest. Friends recognize this imperative; enemies refuse it. Change cannot depend on argument. It has to arrive with material force, with new redirective practices and committed practitioners.

Clearly the 'change community' of redirective practices – the unification of redirective practitioners – potentially can have transformative agency, but it's not enough. Besides the mobilization of any designing capability, a new kind of culture of learning begs to be embraced (what will be explored later as *Neu Bildung*). But here is the rub. None of this can happen without an exposition of all that underpins such actions and ideas – as well as a characterization of a new economic ('quality'-based) paradigm, plus a new political imaginary. Furthermore, the elaboration, development and execution of all these ideas in the end rest with and depend upon the critical mass of a change community (history tells us that cultural and intellectual volume here is more vital than base numbers). The first demand of a new politics is thus one that can form such a community able to lead via exemplary action (rather than *avant gardism* or revolution).

Framing all that has been said and informed by intellectual labour well beyond this task in hand, the imposition of the dictatorship of Sustainment globally will not arrive via force but through that demand that comes when there is no other choice. It will come or we will go. Here is the riposte to idealism and the determinate of a new internationalism of common interest.

Demands of a New Politics

It is fair to say that if pluralist democracy cannot transmute into a politics able to directly confront the structurally unsustainable, its days are numbered. The time gap between acknowledging and understanding (1) the structurally unsustainable and its locus and then (2) acting with enough vigour to slow destruction to a sufficient degree to bring creation/recreation into the future domain of Sustainment *defines* the time of absolute criticality. We have said this already; we know it.

If the time gap between acknowledging the structurally unsustainable and taking concerted action toward Sustainment is not politically recognized and immediately responded to, then politics itself will fall victim (along with so much else) to the gathering momentum of defuturing, remembering that the structurally unsustainable does not merely name biophysical conditions but the convergence of human self-centredness, conflict, inequity and environmental destruction. Unquestionably, the still-contained voice of wasteland grows by multiple means.

A breakdown of the rule of order globally, economic disruption on an unprecedented scale, cascading ecological disaster (not least in relation 'climate chaos') and, with it a redistribution of a significant segment of the human population – these situations are travelling from the future towards us. Waiting for them to arrive full-blown is madness. Scatterings of devastation are already here – yet they are ignored. Our manufactured unseeing is but one product of our anthropocentric selves. We dwell in an ecology of the image that televisually turns the devastated into the familiar. Meanwhile, instrumentalism creates the impression that every problem has a solution and that sooner or later technology will solve whatever needs to be solved. It renders the horrors of excess as temporary and accepts wars of national interest as just(ified) action. But above all, the ecology of the image keeps our eyes focused on 'our world' (materially and perceptually) at the expense of that world in which *it* is situated. Such de-relationality is at the centre of our unseeing.

Change that really changes is not the stuff of the ballot box. One does not have to be a political scientist to conclude that people who have a 'good standard of living' are unlikely to vote for the kind of major material sacrifices in their lifeworld that Sustainment demands – this is not to say, that with a significantly powerful appeal, that some level of sacrifice would not be willingly made by the majority of people – it just would not be enough. Even this prospect is far distant from the current situation wherein 'the people' are being sold a lie – they are being told that 'sustainability' (understood as green technologies, products and services) will allow them to continue to live without material loss. Without again listing the elements of structural unsustainability one can say once more: *there is no chance of viable futures without absolutely fundamental change.*

An international community of interest, a proto-change community, is in formation.[6] It is working, learning and thinking redirectively for change. As such, it can claim potential.[7]

Concluding Remarks

Unsustainability, while it has travelled with us human beings from the first moments of our existence, became evident (named, as we have seen by Nietzsche as 'the wasteland') in the late nineteenth century. Now it has arrived full blown and the long historicity of destruction has morphed into the devastating era of unsettlement. The terror of this situation is still a distant murmur, but we hear and feel it. (*As I write this, a classical music radio station is playing; the programme is interrupted to tell people in the State of Victoria to tune into their local radio station because, over the next twenty-four hours, 100 km per hour winds will fan the many huge bush fires that have been burning in parts of Victoria for almost a month. The fires indeed escalated into an inferno, destroying thousands of homes and killing nearly 200 people. But more than this, they have unsettled the nation – certainly in Australia, unsettlement is now a material condition, a fluctuating state of mind and a fact of life. Yearly the combination of drought, dry forests, extreme heat, high winds and lightning is a growing and deadly threat. Meanwhile, as the fires raged in Victoria, two thousand kilometres further north, huge tracts of land and many towns were suffering from extreme floods for many weeks.*) Recognition of the need for fundamental change hovers – it is imminent.

Faith in the ability of a conscious subject armed with reason to care and take responsibility for the world of human endeavour remains a misplaced notion, as has been the idea of emancipation predicated upon self-awareness. Either way and contrary to Hegel's dream, 'we' have neither ended up with a 'mastery of substance' nor 'in a state of absolute knowledge'. Certainly, we have not arrived at Fukuyama's (now abandoned claim) of being at the 'End of History' (with total global victory of capitalist social democracy).[8] Rather, we are in an unresolved situation of unsettlement awaiting the reclassification of our 'crisis' (and the worldly critical condition of structural unsustainability) as a crisis of our very being.

Making Sustainment sovereign as a prerequisite for a 'dictatorship of Sustainment' unavoidably implies imposed 'unfreedom' so we may be free. The issue of how this can happen rests with unfolding circumstances that will arrive in partial and unpredictable ways.

Design, not least ontological design, while not a 'magic bullet' has a crucial role to play in the creation of a future with a future, but it's likely that its ascent will emerge out of what increasingly looks and feels like an unavoidable tragedy.

Design Summary

The last thing that delivery of Sustainment and the world towards which it is directed, needs is a(nother) self-serving, bureaucratic, top-heavy institution. But prior to and within any global sovereign power, the power of design redirected has to be forged and mobilized. Unavoidably, this implies a certain level of institutionalization of a change community (without the formation of another institution) – not least in terms of design education. So said, there are four questions to frame the approach to starting to think about such an institution:

- Do we know what there is to design?
- Do we know how it can be designed?
- Do we know how design can support 'sovereignty remade?'
- To whom should this material be presented and how?

Here is one cut across these questions.

Let us provisionally call the globally overarching 'body of Sustainment' the World Council of Sustainment – in this fiction there are around 250 participant nations (from the tiny to the huge). The formation of this organization registers that structural unsustainability has become an omnipotent quality of the normal (rather being defined by aberrant events). In response to climate change induced environmental breakdowns, economic dysfunction, social instability and conflict, action to create a regime of imposed Sustainment is underway, be it 'late in the day'.

The authority of a body like the World Council of Sustainment would have to be 'real' and grounded in the sovereignty of Sustainment, rather than just moral and gestural. It could not be just another weak and hidebound global institution like the UN that leaves 'national interests' unscathed. Some kind of enforceable and futural 'nomos of the earth' constitution would have to be created to which nations (or post–nation power blocs) would have to sub-scribe and be accountable in order to function in the global order of peace, finance, trade and an ordered free movement of people. So empowered, this organization could (1) exercise decentralized economic power to regulate all fiscal and non-fiscal modes of exchange; and (2) establish non-national bod-ies to co-own resources and co-manage their renewable exploitation, trade and equitable distribution (of materials, food and wealth) – all this within frameworks of connected cooperative interests – enviro-ethical, economic and community.

An equitable global order here has to be seen not as a political and eco-nomic ideal but rather as a political necessity for which just and functional operational systems would have to be created. Relational impact evaluation (which means plotting causal patterns and possible consequence), futuring (where action in the present is based on designing back from critical and rigorous future scenarios) and quality (as reconfigured) would have to be central features of its policy and redirective practice. The norms established in all the areas would clearly have to be applied to all and every system of exchange and technology utilized. Such a 'mechanism of Sustainment' re-quires a huge amount of development in order to become the central feature of a post-nation, post-democracy model of social organization, economy and global order.

Obviously, national defence forces would become subordinate to a global regime of security. Non-compliance or hostility would no longer be viewed as nation against nation but as nation against the world. The implication is that while the continuity of nations could be expected, the power of the state would no longer be sovereign. The entire thrust of such thinking does not rest on a utopian dream of universal peace and happiness. Rather the kinds of changes sketched are not a matter of choice. They would not eliminate conflict. The primary character of national defence forces, reconfigured into a global but regionally deployed military organization, would be preventative and protective (which means intervention would be taken prior to physical conflict occurring and would be based upon protection of all that sustains).

No doubt the characterization here of such an organization is flimsy. It exists simply to claim what will become an unavoidable need to contemplate, resolve and deliver some sort of version of what has been sketched. This not least because, as will be remembered, climate change driven population movement is going to become massively destabilizing and will not be able to be managed at a national level. In fact, increasing and uncontrolled resettlement of human populations will undercut the nation state's ability to gatekeep who is allowed entry and on what terms. This will create a demand for a global resettlement authority with much more muscle than the currently UNHCR. The resettlement authority would direct where displaced people would go, their form of settlement and 'starter economy'. A universal right of resettlement would abolish the designation of people as refugees and erase the problem of 'climate refugees' not having refugee status in law.

Putting in place this type of global regime and its constitution would seem impossible. But if it cannot be done in some form or other, humanity's struggle will revert to a condition 'raw in tooth and claw' enacted with weapons of mass destruction.

Whatever the reworked and developed version of such a scheme might look like, two features have to be acknowledged as overarching – change coming from and being driven by, the development and projection of the idea of the global institution; and recognition of the arrival of a moment where there is no choice but to change radically and immediately.

Here, then, is a prefigurative context of design that supplements the development of ontological designing within the remit of redirective practice (this has already started). In other words, starting to design some of the kind of things that the creation of such a global organization would bring into being provides forms of visualization to assist its realization (new rapid construction cites – as one of the book's case studies shows – is one example of such designing). As the same time, by giving form to the institution of sovereignty remade, the potential of remaking and the efficacy of the remade are increased. There is one proviso here: whatever is designed has to be able to be realized (the grand failure to head this lesson comes from the Russian Revolution – expansive visions with no mean to deliver them). The ongoing development of redirective practice is establishing ways of undertaking such design activity. Who then would be the audience for such material? This is a key strategic question and it has many answers that lodge the activity back in the political: it needs to be the stuff of education, entertainment, art, drama, music, economic development, public debate. Essentially, it has to be the stuff to which existing institutional politics unavoidably has to respond.

While tragically, the kind of regime outlined cannot arrive until the circumstances of breakdown force its creation, its conceptualization must start now. What is presented here lays no conceptual claim but it does indicate the scope and challenge of what must be addressed and elaborated.

Part III

Design Futuring as Making Time

Unsustainability has been characterized as the concealed negation of being and a negation of the finitude of the being of human being – it diminishes our future, it defutures. Unsustainability is the compound of relational defuturing forces whose negative environmental impacts while gathered under the term 'the unsustainable' has no representational form. While climate change has come to be taken as the dominant expression of the unsustainable, even its relational complexity is hardly recognized. That climate change in turn folds into many other forms of population and resource pressures on the natural environment is even less recognized. Even if somehow and magically the problem of climate change were to be solved, the unsustainable would still exist and threaten. Currently only fragments of its symptoms are engaged, of which global warming from greenhouse gas emissions in but one. It is interesting to observe that causality here is assigned to the anthropogenic factor driving those actions that increase greenhouse gas emissions beyond a level of parts per million at which a degree of stability is possible. While causality so understood almost arrives at its essence – the unchecked anthropocentrism of that animal made human who is unable to see and act beyond its own self-centred interests – it equally remains 'oceans apart'.

So framed, this final part of the book confronts the challenge of at least trying to find a way to name and start dealing with this situation. It does this in three ways. First, it extends the argument that to have a future the 'being of our being' has to significantly change – 'we' have to become other than we

are. The agent of change is posited as cultural and more specifically education – but not in its current forms. Second, a case is made that freedom in
the future cannot exist without Sustainment being made sovereign and that
this imposition has to be by design. Finally, the last chapter reassert that for
the agency of design to be realized politically, design – understood in all its
forms – must be taken beyond its current limits. Design as politics absolutely
depends upon this.

8

Neu Bildung for a New World

Phenomenologically, we human beings exist in two kinds of worlds – both of which we depend upon. The first is the planetary world of given elements, forms and matter that constitute and supports the biosphere of our dependence. The second is the world that over the millennia we have materially fabricated by artifice and have constructed socio-culturally. These worlds are not exclusive. They affect each other and everything we are and do. Framed by these conditions of dependence this chapter will look at the relation between our world making (and unmaking), ourselves and a need to learn to be (and design) another way.

Making World/Making Selves

The world(s) we humans make for ourselves are inextricably bound to our own nature. We arrive, with our genetic inheritance, into very specific overlapping and interpenetrating environments (urban, rural, domestic, linguistic, cultural, educational, theological and so on) that determine so much of what we become (our conduct, perceptions, values, imagination, knowledge and identity). At the same time, in becoming actors in these worlds, we modify the immediate and wider environments in which we live, work and travel.

To understand our 'coming into being' requires grasping that all things (of human fabrication, institutions, social structure and form) have both design and political agency. Once we acknowledge that the world we create is directive, in large part, of what we are and become, then the nature of 'things' clearly takes on a political hue. In essence and relationally, things make ontologies – but not via a simple determinism. (For example, bad housing, bad education, bad parenting, plus poverty equal bad prospects for most people brought up in such a situation; *but* with one exception – if the parenting is good – then a different prospect can be expected. So often, the agency of the good has the ability to overcome much designated as 'bad'.)

Before going further, ontological design and its mobilization as a meta-practice (redirective practice) needs to be differentiated from two theories of determinism: historical materialism and existentialism.

Historical materialism (Marxism) postulated that history was a teleological progression of 'modes of production' divided into 'stages' (slavery, feudalism, capitalism and, eventually, communism). The 'engine of history' driving change from one stage to another was designated as class struggle. Briefly: the determinate agency of the working class was based on the proposition that once it acquired ownership of the means of production it would advance the condition of the class and thus the common good.

In contrast, existentialism posits determinist force in the transformative agency of the self whereby the self is deemed as a product of its own actions rather than of the world (as with material forces and class action). Its claim: 'we' make ourselves. In both cases the extent to which 'we' are ontologically designed was discounted. Reductively, Marxism flattened material difference, whereas Existentialism, even when associated with Marxism, retained the notion of individual action being the determinate of freedom and self (the catch cry of Existentialism being: 'man is nothing else but that which he makes of himself') which is why, for instance, that Jean-Paul Sartre, in embracing both camps, was accused of being a liberal.[1]

Ontological design and redirective practice share with Marxism and Existentialism the view that 'we' have no pre-given developmental historical destination (human nature). But, in difference, it points to the determinate designing consequences of situated 'things' – be they constructed environments, institutions, practices, objects, technologies, and so forth. Thus 'we', as agents and actors, make ourselves in the world that makes us and in so doing, contribute to the making of a world that makes others. In this relational complexity we find design working at its most fundamental as it begets forms via a process of predetermined impression (the form-giving of *Ge-stell*) – especially evidenced in the designing power of technology.

So, to reiterate: we are born into the designing of the designed. Layered onto our biology, we are the ontological product of such designing: government; constitution, laws, computer programmes, social conventions, institutions (family, education, political parties, hospitals, prisons) and the 'thinging' of material and immaterial things (buildings, tools, games, appliances, furniture ...). We are so formed in our difference by the designing specificity of all such *things* under particular conditions.

As the human-created world within the world moves through degrees of environmental devastation, wherein the structurally unsustainable increasingly threatened the future, a point arrived at which time became negated. This process, named as defuturing, recognizes the finitude of our being without laying any claim to knowledge of a quantitative limit (the existent time of our species). Here we have a negative version of ontological designing writ large. Currently, many of our created environments, institutions, materials, immaterial practices, manufactured things and ways of life are taking the future away during the very moment of their creation and ongoing operation. Against this background, it is possible to reassert that: (1) everything

directive of our future is a political agent and open to political affirmation
or contestation; and (2) ontological design, via redirective practice, has to
become a world and self-transformative force. Rather than trying to generally elaborate the implications of what has been argued, one example will be
examined in detail: institutionalized education. It has been selected because
of its subject formativeness, highly designed structures (curricula and syllabi)
and the absolute need for its redirection).

Education against Error

Very few human beings, no matter their culture or occupation, wilfully or
consciously act unsustainably. Rather, they act that way because that's how
they have learnt to be – they have been unwittingly ontologically designed
into extending the structurally unsustainable. Their informal and formal
education has been part of this process – a process not just about acquiring
intrinsically harmful occupations. While an occupation can and often does
enfold structural unsustainability, this condition is more broadly grounded
in thinking and conduct that naturalize acts of creation that fail to see what
is destroyed. In this context education marks 'our' produced anthropocentric
unknowingness. But the problem of such negation now no longer just rests
with us. We have extended it beyond ourselves as we have collectively transposed our propensity toward unconsidered destruction into the behaviour
of the things we have created. Now we are especially seeing the ontological designing of technological things turning back to act upon us. As such,
they are increasingly over-determining 'human qualities' as these qualities
become reified in the 'nature' of produced things. What is exposed here is
the *character* of 'autonomic technocentrism' wherein things take on human
characteristics while circumscribing human agency. This displacement of
human centredness is obscured by an 'ecology of the image' that conceals
via the particular 'enablements' offered by technology.[2] What this means, to
reiterate, is that a 'crisis of crisis' develops, not just because of a specific
problem lodged in particular empirical conditions but rather because these

conditions never arrive as an object of encounter (as image). Effectively, the transformative and defuturing agency of so much technology simply goes by unseen.

Bringing the critique of education to the issue of structural unsustainability, we see that research in climate science, renewable energy and 'clean' technologies and forms of 'green' design are significantly advancing in some nations, yet these developments are merely a fraction of what needs to happen to reframe education even at its most pragmatic.

In the face of structural unsustainability, even more problematic are claims that rely on experience to educate and prompt change. For instance, it is not uncommon to hear claims like 'environmentally things have to get worse before they get better'. But it is a fallacy to think that somehow affirmative change will flow from people's experience of environmental disaster and associated traumatic events. 'All hell' can be breaking out a few kilometres away – it might be a riot, an earthquake, fire, cyclone or even genocide. However, unless they are directly affected, the general tendency of people is to retreat into their normality, which frequently means being media spectators of unfolding events.

One of the structural reasons why education fails to deliver actively critical minds able to grasp and engage what needs to be known and learnt is because it has increasingly become instrumental. This instrumentalization of education now extends from pre-school to university, reaching its peak in higher education, which has predominantly become a service industry. One does not have to look beyond job advertisements in the educational press to confirm this – positions in the humanities have dramatically declined, some of the sciences have expanded, but above all, new vocation-based positions in higher education have proliferated (these include teaching for occupations in business management, tourism, leisure industries, sport, wine, food, advertising, marketing and entertainment).

What is absolutely clear is that the fundamental transformation of education towards understanding and responding to the structurally unsustainable has hardly begun. This is a direction that we will now start to outline, but to go forward we first have to go back.

Remaking: '*Neu Bildung*' and a Culture of Re-learning

Sovereign Sustainment cannot come into *being* without a culture. The creation of this culture will not occur 'organically' – it has to be made. Such making is inseparably a remaking and needs to draw on four principal agents: a change community; ontological design; cultural politics *and* education. The key question is 'how can these agents come together and bring this culture into being?' The German concept of '*Bildung*' will be used to help answer this question.

Bildung originally meant several things: cultural formation, form and foundation, cultural organization, education, knowledge, information and learning. Its relation to culture (*kulture*) was complex. Whereas the notion of *kulture* was usually defined in terms of particular social and material forms of everyday life and its aesthetic modes of expression (culture), *Bildung* fundamentally asserts *humans are made* (via cultivation/education) not born.[3] 'Cultivation' is thus deemed as a key agent in the development of humanity and human beings. The meaning of cultivation is signalled in the literal meaning of the word – *bild* denoting image or picture, with *Bildung* extending such an understanding to the idea of form/shape, forming and formation.[4] Overtly and covertly, this idea had powerful designing consequences for the form and content of modern Western education theory and practice and, as such, it occupied a significant position within humanism. Yet is also carried a clear ontological designing dimension, hence the motivation to remake it.

Bildung is not called-up here to reinstate or conserve the humanist project of which it was a part. Rather, it is being mobilized as a conceptual figure to be radically remade through a deconstructive releasement. The aim is to expose the foundational conceptual elements of *Bildung* so they can be re-created as post-humanist figures in the creation of a culture of Sustainment. Specifically, a *Neu Bildung* can form the condition for the learning of Sustainment: as reflective and applied knowledge in the realization and use of sustaining things and as conduct brought to the performative development of ontological design.

The form and formation of the *Neu Bildung* can be qualified and characterized as an acceptance of responsibility for our anthropocentric being and as a
means to contest autonomic technocentricity. It has the potential to respond
to the imperative of Sustainment through creating a culture of learning by:

- raiding the intellectual baggage of the structurally unsustainable for its
  recoverable thought;
- bringing key concepts like defuturing, change community and redirective
  practice to create historically informed educational content;
- elaborating the idea, methods and forms of application of ontological
  design.

The original intent of *Bildung* was to constitute a culture in which a more
humane and cultivated human could come into being. The aim of *Neu Bildung*
is equally to create a new human being, but the nature of this creation has to
be very different. Specifically, this being (as subject) is one who knows his/
her self-interest can only be realized by understanding that 'self' is always
relationally implicated in *the being of the world-in-being* (which, of course,
includes being with others). It recognizes that one cannot 'be' by being-for-
one's-self (for being depends on others – be they human/non-human, animate
and inanimate, material and immaterial).

Our account has moved quickly and a good deal has been claimed. Now
we need to retrace our steps, starting by revisiting the self, *Bildung* and the
history that it carries.

Re-learning: Second Pass

The Enlightenment set out to constitute the individual self as the paramount,
universal being. Niklas Luhmann observed that this objective was 'applied to
everyone without exception', then he says:

> Of course, neo-humanist thinkers up to and including Hegel and Marx could not be satis-
> fied with the statement that everyone is an individual: but they began with and therefore

had to confront the question of how this merely quantitative universality, this mere aggre-
gation, can be filled with content. The important question then became how the individual
realizes itself within the universal, humanity, the world. For Humboldt and even for Hegel,
this was a matter of *Bildung*.[5]

In writing of a post-1800 neo-humanist pedagogy, self-reference and *Bild-ung*, Luhmann notes: '*Bildung* was conceived as a methodology for developing skills and learning how to learn was an essential component. This reflexivity allowed the idea that the learning process equipped the individual for the "world," that is, for everything that he wanted to appropriate and enjoy by learning.'[6]

The claim of *Bildung* was to mediate an engagement with the universal. It aimed to overcome differences between institutions overarched by the 'cultural state' (within which culture, economy, the political and the self were sought to be unified) by learning a common meaning of culture.[7] Such integrated learning was, as Bill Readings made clear, not the stuff of liberal humanist education and cultivation but, rather, was based on the establishment of the university as a community and keeper of universal intellectual culture – a cultural organic whole (in contrast to a collection of specific disciplines) able to hold the mechanical (technology) at bay.[8] The notion had profound impacts upon and beyond, the agency of German culture. It placed culture (as an aesthetically defined quality of humanity) between 'nature (as chaos and animality in being)' and 'reason (as rule and being mechanistic)'. In so doing, *Bildung* sought to form a moral being capable of critical historical reflection and moral decision in an increasingly secular society.

This understanding of culture was taken to its most developed institutional form by Wilhelm von Humboldt with his idea of the 'University of Culture'. The intent was the creation of learning that unified 'objectified cultural knowledge' (science) with aesthetic, spiritual and moral education (cultivation).[9] Thus *Bildung* formed the armature around which the entire institution turned.

In contrast, contemporary approaches to education and culture are pluralist and academically marginal. Activities like Cultural Studies, as Readings recognized in his critical overview of the university, displayed an underdeveloped and misdirected view of the ontological and metaphysical force of 'the cultural'.[10] Reading's observations, made in the mid-1990s, now apply to the humanities in general. It is absolutely clear that the field is currently powerless in the face of de-humanizing 'autonomic technocentrism'.

Hans-Georg Gadamer, in his review of the humanist tradition in *Truth and Method,* presents *Bildung* as one of the four guiding concepts of humanism (the other three are *sensus communis*, judgement and taste).[11] Notwithstanding Gadamer's insights, the significance of *Bildung* has still not been sufficiently recognized outside Germany beyond a few members of the academy. Gadamer exposes an etymology that reaffirms *Bildung* in the company of *phusis*.[12] He sets the stage for others to take up the term, taking it from its now (unsustainable) place within humanism to a remaking for a Sustainment.

The well documented history of *Bildung* commented upon by Gadamer, cites Johann Gottfried Herder (1744–1803) as the pivotal figure in breaking the hegemony of objectified Enlightenment rationalism. Herder's projection of a subject-centred humanist force, presented as the 'concept of self-formation, education, or cultivation (*Bildung*)' was '... perhaps the greatest idea of the eighteenth century'.[13] The early use of the term was predicated upon the cultural form (and forming by) associated with *Bildung* coming from 'nature' (rather than being its opposition). As such, it named the mystery of all that nature shaped (hence the flow back to *phusis*). While this understanding fell from grace, it also returned – specifically as the agency of cultivation located with the subject's nurturing of their naturally given talents and abilities. While Kant and Hegel gave Herder's idea enormous intellectual momentum, it was von Humboldt who turned *Bildung* into a distinct and clear project. For him, whereas culture (*kulture*) was social, visible, materially manifest in the consequences of self-development and realization, *Bildung* was 'higher and more inward' and a 'disposition of mind' that powered the 'total intellectual and moral endeavour'.

The idea of *Bildung* (seen as the result of the form giving and designing that arises from the soul being inscribed with 'the image of God') was, in many ways, the bridge between the medieval, theological and the modern, secular university. In this respect, as Gadamer pointed out, it is the product, not the process, which is continually remade by a transcendent process.[14] Moreover, he observed: 'It is not accidental that in respect the word *Bildung* resembles the Greek *phusis*. Like nature, *Bildung* has no goal outside itself, the concept of *Bildung* transcends that of mere cultivation of given talents, from which the [sic] concept is derived'.[15]

Readings equally reminds us that the unified knowledge that *Bildung* aspired to create through the institution of reason, was in fact the lost unity of the integrated knowledges of the Greeks.[16] In contrast to the education of talents: '... in *Bildung* what is absorbed is not like a means that has lost its function rather in acquired *Bildung* nothing disappears, but everything is preserved'.[17]

The historical idea of *Bildung* centred on 'preservation' – what it most importantly set out to preserve was thinking.

As Hegel understood and Gadamer articulated, philosophy and, we may add, the human sciences (*Geisteswissenschaften*) 'has in *Bildung*, the condition of its existence'.[18] Later Gadamer connects the concept with *Geist* (spirit) and then makes a comment of even greater significance to our concerns: 'Man is characterised by the break with the immediate and the natural that the intellectual, rational side of his nature demands of him. "In this sphere he is not, by nature, what he should be" – and hence he needs *Bildung*.'[19]

Gadamer summarized Hegel's view of the dependence of *Bildung* on universality and then on the negation of its realization as an abstraction. He did this by continually reasserting the ego and the self as 'measure and determinate'. Effectively, individuated 'bare life' is subordinated by cultivated being (the universal) that knows its 'self' via the culture in which it comes to be (ego). Here *Bildung* becomes *telos*. The 'being-towards' the universality of *Bildung* is hereafter posited with three agents: consciousness, work and 'the thing'. Gadamer remarks:

> In the independent existence that work gives the thing, working consciousness finds itself again as an independent consciousness. Work is restrained desire. In forming the object – that is, in being selflessly active and concerned with the universal – working conscious-ness raises itself above the immediacy of its existence to universality; or, as Hegel puts it,

by forming the thing it forms itself. What he means is that in acquiring a 'capacity', a skill, man gains the sense of himself. What seemed denied him in the selflessness of serving, inasmuch as he subjected himself to a frame of mind that was alien to him, becomes part of him inasmuch as he is a working consciousness. As such he finds in himself his own frame of mind and it is quite right to say of work that it forms.[20]

This statement is a nascent registration of ontological designing. As was grasped long ago by Aristotle (and before the idea of design as we understand it arrived) – working on the making of something makes both the maker and the made. If a sense of the self is gained, it arrives obliquely and through a proximity to the 'thirdness' of the thing (the detachment that connects the maker to the making). Form-giving here (and in relation to *Bildung*) was equally self-formation. Self, world (universal) and form intersect with and in, the thing and its finitude.

What we now have before us is 'practical *Bildung*' as it was initially and generally envisioned by Hegel and as it was appropriated with a trace of his notion of 'historical spirit' and with a projected ability to: '… to reconcile itself with itself, to recognize oneself in other being'.[21] In the subsequent shift from the practical to the theoretical, *Bildung* arrives not as a leap from 'the one' to 'the other' but as a graduated process of transition. This shift could be seen in the maker's detachment from the made (*de facto* the move from the thing's 'belonging to' its 'being apart') into the thing's inscription in memory – which can be understood as an embodied futural ability to make from an ability to recall and reproduce. *Bildung* is here an opening from the practical to the theoretical, but remembering that:

… to have a theoretical stance is, as such, already alienation, namely the demand that one 'deal with some thing that is not immediate, something that is alien, with something that belongs to memory and thought'. Theoretical *Bildung* lead beyond what man knows and experiences immediately. It consists in learning to affirm what is different from oneself and to find universal viewpoints from which to grasp the thing, 'the objective thing in its freedom' without selfish interest.[22]

Remaining close to 'the spirit' of Hegel, Gadamer goes on to say: 'To recognize one's own in the alien, to become at home in it, is the basic movement of spirit, whose being consists only in returning to itself from what is other.'[23]

So while it is clear that *Bildung* fell among the ashes of German idealism, divested of its flawed foundations, it retained a resonance.

Setting the Task for '*Neu Bildung*' and Sustainment

Refracted through the lens of Gadamer and Hegel, *Bildung* now increasingly looks like the designing of a mode of 'dwelling' from which how 'to dwell' is learnt (this dwelling understood as a 'being-in-process' rather than grounded in a notion of 'fundamental ontology').

More crudely, what we are naming here is a culture that designs the designers of the vast array of things that constitute forms of dwelling that in turn significantly design modes of being in that world. Unlike modernist ideological aesthetics, the foundation of such designing would be performative. *Bildung*, so grasped in its circularity, fundamentally prefigures spaces and a time of becoming wherein the human being is forced to sustain itself and other beings via post-evolutionary 'inorganic' action.

In actuality, we all now live in a world wherein structural unsustainability has speeded change beyond the possibility of evolutionary adaptation – the 'natural' ability of processes of change simply cannot keep pace with the pace of forced circumstantial change. This means that redirection towards Sustainment by design has to respond to such a rate of change of defuturing (design thus overrides the biocentric notion of evolution). Moreover, the defuturing character of structural unsustainability means that humanity at large can now no longer be at home in that world it has historically made for itself (via denaturalization, the construction of forms of negation and outright devastation). In such making that has rendered the given world inhospitable, we and subsequent generations can only be at home in the homelessness of our loss, in our alienation. Gadamer would have it that alienation creates that distance that allows the rediscovery of oneself – as an identification of and return to, one's actualized being. In the present situation of structural unsustainability, experienced as unsettlement, the self stands before the onslaught of things that negate its fundamental being. The self is actually becoming

driven to identify its being with 'things', which, in their ontological designing, place the self under the subordination of 'autonomic-technocentricity'
(wherein the self is placed in a position of behavioural compliance to being
technological and technological things). To live in the company of ensembles
of technologically inscriptive products and modes of power cannot actually
be disarticulated from the authoring of particular kinds of identity. Here it is
important to understand that, as technology ever becomes a law unto itself,
it continually moves further beyond *nomos*. For all the instrumental forms of
compliance, standards, regulations and rationally applied science, technology
is without reason and at its most fundamental, above the law.

What we are discovering is that 'being with defuturing things' negates the
subject's ability to unify a self and normalize alienation as a precondition
for dealing with instrumentalized existence. Within late (and still emergent
in some parts of the world) modernity it is increasingly the case that there
is 'a self' who is little more than a named body of 'bare life' and designated
instrumental role. The price of refusing to play this assigned instrumental
role: economic exclusion. In what is still an unfolding age of technocentric
hegemony, a deception is perpetuated by humanism that humans are still in
the driving seat. Where there is concern about this situation one finds an idealized, ill-conceived 'resistance' that simply appeals to 'human centredness',
which is no more than an ambiguous, if nonetheless an aggressive, appeal to
anthropocentrism.

Technology does not care, it is godless. Increasingly it acts as a 'nature' and
as a law unto itself (in its 'will to will'). There is now very little correlation
between an ability to create a technology and an understanding of what it will
do, its temporality (including how it will transmute), what it will create or
what it will destroy.

Humanism uncritically embraced technology to generate its utopias. In so
doing, technology was cast as a force that would liberate us from the limitation of laws of nature. It allowed dreams of the construction of massive built
structures to be realized, once unimagined speeds to be attained, the gravi-
tational pull of the earth to be defied, biology to be manipulated and, as we
all know, much more. In so doing, humanism revealed its inherent naiveté

and exposed the complicity of metaphysics in the grandest fabrication of all: the lie of consciousness. It's clear that 'we' will never recover what we were; but to become sustainable beings with the affirmative qualities of the human, we have to find ways to recoil from what we are becoming – for what we are becoming cannot be sustained. In this frame, 'autonomic technocentrism' shows us a future from which 'we' are absent. Here we should remind ourselves of the significant changes in how the universal is being understood.

Past objections to the notion of the universal have been predicated on its projective mobilization to create what it names – in this sense, it has been simply folded into the violence of global modernization and the ethnocentric flattening of all culture to render 'them' as 'the same'. This is certain to continue but with the added element of an autonomic techno-universality. Critical debate on technology now hardly exists; it is simply, if erroneously, taken as a given along with the projection of the 'family of man' sharing the 'fruits' it delivers.

While the relation of the one (form of human being) to the others and all to technology, invites greater thought, what is being indicated is that all existing politics is predicated upon universalistic assumptions (not least about the universal human) combined with a disjunctural relation to the forces of change. Put baldly: politicians are trying to manage circumstances over which they have little control and of which they have even less comprehension. Pragmatically, they enact, at best, a combination of rationalist economics, unreconstructed humanism and the most immediate forms of crisis management.

In the bleakness of 'the structurally unsustainable present' it is crucial to develop 'another way' and to defend a memory of an otherwise – which is exactly what the remaking of *Bildung* and our project in general, aims to do.

On Futural Memory and (*Neu*) *Bildung*

Memory must be formed; for memory is not memory for anything and everything. One has memory for some things and not for others; one wants to preserve one thing in memory and banish another. It is time to rescue the phenomenon of memory from being regarded merely as a psychological faculty and to register it as an essential element of the finite historical 'being of man'.[24]

One would add three linked comments to what Gadamer says on memory. First, there is no Sustainment without memory. Next, man's finitude is the time of enabled Sustainment and this is not fixed in the future but in the past as it passes from the present. Finally, 'man' does not have one time. Remembering what *Bildung* was, we ask 'what can "*Neu Bildung*" really be?'

Certainly, *Neu Bildung* should not be the voice of a new humanist subject or renewed humanism. Neither should it project a utopian vision of a culture of the future. Rather it would start by acknowledging the alienation triggered by 'our' fall from *phusis*. In this forgotten moment is the beginning of the 'denaturalization' of our being that constituted 'human nature' and its other worldly fabrication. 'Now' the unnatural nature of human worldly occupation is itself becoming 'denaturalized' – experienced as unsettlement – this moment marks the arrival of both alienation and homelessness.

The task, then, although enormously complex, is quite clear. It is to think and design Sustainment from the soul of an almost-lost culture (that is from the recovered memory of the Idea of *phusis*) in order to create a culture that learns how to develop mental and material practices that can produce forms that sustain. What has to be sought is neither another utopia nor the positing of 'nature' as the foundation of politics but rather the discovery of and attachment to, all that fundamentally sustains – here is what has to be learnt and thus what a *Neu Bildung* has to advance.

Again recalling Hobbes (and remembering all that has arrived on the back of his confrontation between 'nature and the political') one can say that the institutional foundations of the politics of humanism inchoately erased recognition that a biophysical (reductive) *model* of sustainability was as problematic. The idea of 'nature' was simply taken as the given foundation of being. That this 'crude' condition has not been evident is not surprising because liberal humanism imposed what has became an almost impenetrable super-structural skin of sophistication, hyperbole and aesthetically honed appearances over (as Bruno Latour has pointed out) a constructed naturalism.[25] Historically, critical thought knew this, but contemporary 'critical' culture refuses it, as the biocentric characterization of 'sustainability' affirms. *Neu Bildung* has to learn to speak the unspeakable – it cannot tolerate the good manners of terminal humanism as it stands on the edge of the abyss. Rather than serving the 'human' it has to help shatter it and thereafter remake our 'being here' within a politics of absolute care. While our inability to overcome anthropocentrism can be named, it can be taken responsibility for. Unquestionably, such action can and should commence.

We are neither a cultural singularity nor the universal being that humanism claims 'us' to be (the classification 'the human' was and is an ethnocentric imposition).[26] As we are, we cannot save what needs to be saved. And we ourselves should not be saved. Unevenly, as defuturing entities, as destroyers, 'we' cannot 'save the world'. Rather there is a need to mobilize 'our' destructiveness against the structural unsustainability that is within ourselves and the world we have created. In bringing ontological design and *Neu Bildung* into being, we have to become other than we are. Notwithstanding that from our very beginning our 'tool making' made us technological beings, this in no ways means we become technological mutants (like Donna Haraway's notion of cyborg).[27]

The trace of memory of what once we were is all but lost. Erasure here, as Bernard Stiegler makes very clear, is indivisible from the industrialization of memory as it accelerates forgetting.[28] But equally, we exist without any real sense of what 'we' are becoming. However, Sustainment offers an identity and demands a remaking that brings our being technological and our becoming futural together.

Clearly, the activity of remaking *Bildung* has to impose itself on the dysfunctional edifice of democracy while contributing to the formation of a culture of sacrifice – a non-heroic culture able to confront Western metaphysic's realization and degeneration of knowledge into 'autonomic technocentrism'. Making the political as a culture of Sustainment, via a *Neu Bildung,* demands the learning of forms of redirection specific to particular situations, the material content that underpins them, as well as the practices from which they were fabricated. To do this requires going beyond the limits of existing configurations of design, design education, design practice and relations with clients – all directed with a clear understanding of what design futuring is and can do. It equally requires openness to remaking, especially in the context of the opportunities disclosed in the disclosure of crisis.

At the very core of the 'culture of learning' that begs to be created via *Neu Bildung* is not only learning against the error of past education but also the learning of a new range of *things*, including:

- recognition of responsibility for our anthropocentrism;
- critical engagement with 'autonomic technocentrism';
- how to make 'things' that care (their ontological designing) as a basis for a viable general economy within a 'care structure' for 'being-after-the-human';
- how to prevent conflict prefiguratively beyond past and failed diplomatic mechanisms and the discourse of peace;
- how to establish Sustainment as a foundation of redistributive justice;
- a new politics beyond democracy as it is;
- a learning to sacrifice for the new common good.

Obviously, such learning is extremely hard, verging on the impossible. In response to the tendency to recoil against even contemplating such a prospect that might be expected from vast numbers of people there is but one answer. There is no choice! This is the magnitude of the challenge that is the future with a future. The only other options are the dystopic fragmentation of 'humanity' or a complete biophysical as well metaphysical giving over to technological being. The open question is how many will survive the process of non-adaptive change?

Everything posed by this book, everything said of 'politics as design', goes to the attempt to make an affirmative future in the time available, no matter how difficult. For this to happen, the liberal underscoring of social democracy has to fall, because, in addition to all the reasons given, as Wolfgang Palvers points out, 'liberalism can be characterized by its rejection of sacrifice'.[29]

Design and Learning

After this general introduction to *Neu Bildung*, let's now deposit the idea in the realm of design as politics.

Lexicographically, as already indicated, *Bildung* is an interesting word. *Bild* literally means picture, image; whereas *Bildung* can mean form, formation, shape, foundation, organization. Bringing the old concept together with the literal meaning and remaking it in the service of Sustainment allows us to define *Neu Bildung* as a way to name the new cultural foundation and how it is made to appear. As such, and placed in the frames of design and learning, it is futural knowledge embedded in forms of futuring practice. It is futuring directed towards the creation of a new foundation of design education for schools and universities. It demands the extension and development of two kinds of knowledge: prefigurative and applied.

Prefigurative Knowledge

'Prefigurative knowledge' provides the theoretical ground for thinking redirective design action – it is that knowledge which guides design (not least, politically). It draws on old concepts to fashion new ones driven by the imperative of Sustainment.

Prefigurative knowledge does not rest upon truth claims. It is concerned with probability, potentiality and redirection. It is about learning how to project the consequences of design action onto a future already partly filled with what the past and present have thrown into it. Mobilizing this knowledge means being able to read a situation as a designing environment and the consequences of this designing, plus having an educated historical sensibility and the ability to deploy it. More specifically, it requires having a developed grasp of 'memory' as a condition of being that is well beyond mere recall.

Historical sensibility and memory are negated by autonomic technocentrism (its operative moment being the 'continuous present').

Notwithstanding a trajectory of diminishment, memory has a material presence in practices in which it is embodied and directive. This is seen, for instance, in the hand of skill in action, be it the hand of the wood-carver, pianist or machinist. Likewise, memory rests in the voice that sings, in the skyward eye of the farmer and in the ear of the mother as she hears the cry of her baby. Memory is equally carried by material things that show the traces of all the iterations before them – the cup, the chair, the bicycle, the cooker, the power drill. But more than this: memory, as carried in language, is also elemental to sight – it arrives before what is seen as the already known. Memory is carried by our taste, the way we walk, vocabulary, gestures and disposition toward all whom we know. Memory is the sense we have of our self, our identity and the foundation of our future actions. Memory is that which puts our being before itself. And memory is the resistance to the forgetting that the structurally unsustainable manufactures and then trades upon (as it strives to displace attachment to the old by a desire for the new) – as such memory is a primary locus of conflict.

In contrast, historical sensibility rests with recognition of the past as a repository of recoverable potentialities. It is that disposition and knowledge that knows the value of the historical as a domain of investigation and inquiry – which is to say that what is discovered is always the product of an interpretative encounter, where the perspectives of the present transform the historical material engaged. Essentially, a historical sensibility recognizes the value of such an undertaking, not least as a means to counter a propensity toward forgetting that underscores 'cultures of the present' and the continual progression of memory's industrialization.

Drawing from the already known, prefigurative thought gathers to constitute a whole new environment of thinking (the new always stands on, emerges out of, fragments of the old). Take, for example, the idea of quality – a familiar word that demands to be re-thought. To bring the notion of Sustainment to some 'thing' is to bring it to qualitative evaluation. Here quality may be material, immaterial, aesthetic or performative, but in all cases it expressively and operatively gives forms of enrichment that are immediate and futural (and thus sustaining). The idea of quality re-learnt is an important element of the agenda of *Neu Bildung*.

Likewise, community is another familiar figure that begs to be reanimated as a prefigurative means of sustaining a future. This remaking would be contrary to the vacuous way that 'community' is now mostly deployed as an emptied out idea and gestural reference standing in for commonality, belief, solidarity, belonging and all those other constituents from which communities were formed. Moreover, appeals to 'community' have become part of an ideological language of illusion. As such, community has been rendered inoperative – 'that which binds' has been caught up and eroded by the devastation of structural unsustainability.[30] 'Community' now dominantly exists as an asserted figure marking its own absence. Yet there can be no Sustainment without community. In myriad ways, people need strengthened bonds to each other in order to survive. In the context of re-thinking community and seeing the transformation of learning inherent in *Neu Bildung*, the idea of the common good is another foundational proposition that requires being dragged out of the realm of idealism, utopianism and political gesturalism and into the space of necessity.

The kind of radical reappraisal, remaking and redeployment needing to be brought to quality, community and the common good obviously applies to many other familiar concepts that underpin our worldly actions and everyday life. Certainly the meaning of care, ethics, responsibility, need, health and sacrifice are numbered among them.

The relation between *Neu Bildung* and the complexity of ontological designing – notwithstanding an existing underscoring by prefigurative thought – needs to embody a sustaining capability animated by use that acts on the user and the environment. Subject, object, world and worlding all turn in relation to each other in that relational play of design(ing) that ontological design names and enacts.

Contrary to the existing approach to sustainability, with its dominance on instrumental/technological action, prefigurative knowledge and ontological designing combine to serve the advancement of *Neu Bildung*, the formation of a new economic paradigm and its advancement of Sustainment. It equally folds into the agency of design as politics giving directional impetus to Sustainment as a process and a continuous transformative moment.

A Note on Care

One can view the ontological character of 'care' within design as politics as it merges with *Neu Bildung*. 'Care' here means an inscribed performative quality of the being of all human beings: it is both that care of the self that intuitively anticipates danger and acts; and it is also the intrinsic performative qualities of things (that care).

Understanding care as *performative* means understanding that our well-being and the well-being of all beings is indivisible. Thus care for and by 'the environment' is care for 'life in general' as it un-differentially cares for the life of humans. So, for instance, in caring for the quality of air, soil and fresh water, we are equally caring for ourselves and for the quality of food 'naturally' produced. While this is absolutely obvious, unknowing still reigns. Likewise, the imposition of unfreedoms to secure the environment as *an extended care structure* is, again, an absolute, but negated imperative. It marks a clash between the law of unknowing politics and the law of Sustainment. The former law protects companies that fill supermarket shelves with huge amounts of tested 'safe' foods with almost zero nutritional value; it supports the inequity of global food production; at the same time, it neglects to adequately protect the essential quality of the atmosphere, rivers, oceans and agricultural soils (the intrinsic crime of pollution is divided into the legal and the illegal).

Unambiguously, care as outlined here has nothing to do with charity or emotional disposition. But it has everything to do with a new kind of economy and an ideology of enacted Sustainment as an integral feature in the being of everyday life. Care can be an explicitly materialized example of design as politics. For instance, it could redirect specific domains of 'the provision of care' (like social services and health) towards substantial designed means of prefigurative care (amplified prevention).

A Note on Craft

In 'making with care', craft (traditional and remade) constitutes care as practice.

Craft could have a pivotal role in the creation of a 'quality economy' as it folds into the new economic paradigm. As said earlier, craft is not reducible to past and current (dominantly handicraft) understandings. For Sustainment, craft demands to be dramatically expanded to bridge: individual and industrially applied skills; the head and the hand; the material and the immaterial. Craft, rethought and remade marks a re-engagement with artifice and artefacts that enfolds an investment in things (what they are, what they do, for whom and why) based on care as a sustaining quality. Craft means better rather than more, a recovery and generalization of pleasure in production. Above all, it means recognition of making the self in the act of making.

Craft can be common to all redirective practices as they redirect almost all that is – built, manufactured, institutionally delivered, produced by creative practices or communicated by designed media. It also links to the redirection of education. It is a form of action able to evidence relationality as a key economic driver of a quality based economy (and counter force to productivity). Like most of what has gone before, what is being attempted is an agenda-setting exercise of the massively ambitious project of design as politics. *Neu Bildung,* ontological design, care and craft are all specific objects of thought and labour that materially ground this agenda in a potential program of work.

9

On Freedom by Design

Our exploration of freedom will start by interrogating how it has been understood. Thereafter, the relation between freedom and liberalism will be examined, followed by Schmitt's critique of liberalism. His remarks will lead us to a discussion of the links between nature, rights and violence. Finally, the focus will fall directly back on freedom, closing by an engagement with design.

Increasingly, in the unfolding and defuturing epoch of unsettlement, and in so far as we belong to the world rather than being merely in it, freedom cannot be without Sustainment. As a condition of potentiality, freedom rests with dependence rather than with liberation.

Maurice Merleau-Ponty tells us that 'my actual freedom is not on hither side of my being, but before me, in things'.[1] To this one can add, that 'intention, prefiguration, design and things bring freedom or destroy it'. In actuality, all design is directional: it does not arrive without a posited causality (imposition). Thus whatever design can free, comes out of the unfreedom of what it delimits.

Freedom from oppression, hunger, harassment and political interference. It's a free country. Freedom of speech. Free and fair elections. The free market; free love; freedom of choice. The language of freedom comes at us from all directions. Its meaning is assumed as self-evident but this is not so – in fact few things are as hard to grasp as freedom. Several millennia of philosophy support this assertion. At base, freedom is beyond measure. By its very nature, freedom embraces the free, which means that it is beyond thought, constraint and definition.[2]

Unsurprisingly, nowhere does design as politics become so intellectually challenged as when it faces the question of freedom (from perspectives of thinking, understanding, experience and appearance). And nowhere are the political demands as great as when conditions of limitation (unfreedoms) are imposed by design in order to secure freedom as elementally futural.

Freedom in the Picture

Unambiguously, structural unsustainability and responses to it, brings the issue of freedom into question. At the extreme, we see conflict folding into this condition – especially evident in the asymmetrical wars of the Middle East, Asia and Africa, as well as the West's employment of the 'state of exception' to curtail freedoms in response to the fear of terrorism.

In the popular, up-market and even the political media of the West, democracy and freedom are presented as synonymous. This coupling can be contested in two ways: first the nature of freedom is taken (erroneously) to be firmly lodged in common sense and, second, democracy is projected as coherent, which demonstrably it is not. Freedom is interior to the individual and community; it is a spatial and communicative condition of the world; it is the having been freed in order to be free; it is beyond any and all political ideologies (including democracy).

To get into the picture we are going to oscillate between two poles: the political and the existential. The starkness of the question of freedom, politically, is evident in the following four propositions that will shortly be traversed.

- Within modern democracy, based upon pluralism and liberalism, the question of freedom is defined by what it ideologically serves (rather than the claim to deliver freedom itself).
- Market freedom, the freedom to consume, has increasingly become a negation of futural time by being at the fore of the advancement of structural unsustainability (as disposition and practice).
- There is no liberation from anthropocentrism, but equally there is no freedom without it. (The questions of 'the human', being and freedom are unified – freedom is a human construct.)[3]
- The dictatorship of Sustainment is a dictatorship of the relative freedom of futuring limits.

The existential pole centres on the tension between the condition of delimitation (subjectivity) and freedom to be.

The subject produces an inversion: being becomes a projected representation of the subject's ontology, whereas it is the pre-existence of the being to become subject that makes subjectivity possible. So while being is not freedom, there can be no freedom without being. In this situation being withdraws in order to 'free freedom'.[4] Of course, the relation between the subject, being and freedom does not occur in the abstract but upon a metaphysical ground, which means the subject is always a historical (ontologically designed) figure.[5]

Notwithstanding our unutterable and instinctual knowledge of experienced freedom, or its loss, there is almost nothing that can be said about freedom that does not either fall between banality (which is to say, almost all political rhetoric) and a moment of profundity (mostly, a rare philosophical insight).[6]

So, What Is Freedom?

While freedom has been a preoccupation, a cause to defend and an oft-made demand in the modern world, there is no simple answer to this question.

Its pursuit, according to Jean-Luc Nancy, one of France's most significant contemporary philosophers, has marginalized or simply enfolded the struggle for equality, fraternity and community.[7] The reason, he suggests, rests with a division between: a rationalistic 'ethico-juridico-political' engagement with freedom in law and politics; and a more considered philosophical inquiry. The former resulted in the rise of institutionally taken-for-granted notions of freedom; the latter meant, for instance, that critically considering freedom as spirit, the good and collectivist became marginalized. In this frame, a mode of reasoning ruled that became destructive of freedom. Max Weber recognized this and postulated that the creation of modern 'rational society' marked a general loss of freedom.[8] Effectively, freedom became a gestural figure centring on notions of individual liberty and consumer choice. Our immediate aim here is to undermine such unthinking in its overt and mild forms. The promotion of such an 'experience of freedom' has to be (and slowly is becoming) displaced by the necessity of 'freedom by delimitation'. At its most basic, neither rationalized freedom under the law, nor the expressive acts of individuals, have the ability to secure the very ground that freedom is claimed to stand upon.[9]

Philosophy has been engaged in trying to comprehend and communicate the essence of freedom from time immemorial. Not only, for instance, did both Plato and Aristotle engage the issue, but they did so while exploring the ideal of the possibility and limits of democracy. Likewise, the question of freedom was a major preoccupation of the Enlightenment philosophers. For instance, in his *Ethics,* Benedict de Spinoza (1632–77) set out to show a fundamental division between freedom and will (to choose or create). Spinoza's views were heavily influenced by his life as an optical-lens grinder (mediated observation) and his persecution by the Catholic Church for his pantheist views, which brought received notions of the power of God and causality into question (these views led to a contract being taken out on his life).

Immanuel Kant (1724–1804) shared Spinoza's 'faith' in reason, elevating it and positing it with transcendental authority. In so doing, he placed freedom firmly in the realm of the intelligible – thus the idea always travelled ahead of claims of the experience of freedom (or lack of it). Conversely, Friedrich Schelling (1775–1854), who shared Spinoza's naturalistic disposition, posited knowledge (including the knowledge of freedom) in objects/objectivism. He sought to define the concept of freedom in relation to good and evil (one cannot be without the other: thus to designate and pursue freedom, as the good, is to dialectically acknowledge evil). While Schelling positioned his analysis within an emergent scientific worldview, G. W. F. Hegel (1770–1831) partly broke with the received philosophical discussion and situated his address to freedom within his philosophy of history (via the agency of 'the state' – the means of freedom's actualization – a force taking 'man' beyond nature[10]). Hegel thus repositioned freedom within a politico-philosophical frame.

In the closing decades of the Enlightenment, we find the iconoclastic idealism of Friedrich Nietzsche (1844–1900) who put forward a notion of freedom that admitted the possibility of evil being a 'most fearful and fundamental' drive for power that only ethics could hold in check. For him, freedom not only implies thinking the unthinkable but it emanated from thinking itself – freedom goes before thinking. It is a gift from thought.[11] Obviously, the converse is true – a loss of the ability to think is a loss of freedom.

Over the history of the project of thinking freedom – which we have but touched upon – a number of conclusions become apparent. Certainly, it can be said that freedom is not reducible to a singularity: it is not some particular thing.[12] Neither is it captured by a singular idea, or held by any tangible form. Likewise, it is not something we can own – it does not and cannot, belong to us. The reverse is true: we belong to it.[13] And as said, the recognition of freedom depends on our being anthropocentric.[14] Jean-Luc Nancy tells us that 'human beings are not born free in the same way as they are born with a brain; yet they are born, infinitely, to freedom.'[15] Prior to this, Martin Heidegger (1889–1976) pointed out: 'the sole, adequate relation to freedom in man is the self-freedom in man'.[16] Therefore freedom is that which we realize for ourselves as a condition of possibility for our being in action in our world. While our liberty can be taken away, our freedom is not actually ready-to-hand. Nelson Mandela did not suddenly gain his freedom when he was released from Robben Island; it was vested in his ontology rather than material conditions. He had lost his liberty but not his freedom. Of course freedom is not purely a subjective condition. As perhaps the paramount philosopher of 'the Other', Emmanuel Levinas (1906–95) tells us that freedom is directly implicated in a relation of 'responsibility for an Other', which is a commitment prior to 'human fraternity itself'.[17]

Levinas argued that what we ourselves are, as a subject with an identity, depends on an Other – our becoming depended upon acts of appropriation and recognition. In so far as we gain freedom 'to be', our being gains this possibility from an Other. This takes the condition of freedom beyond the subjective and bonds it to an objective relation wherein its meaning requires an Other's recognition.

This argument is clearly illustrated by what Levinas says about the face: 'in his face the Other appears to me not as an obstacle, nor as a menace I evaluate, but as what measures me.'[18] In other words 'I' cannot have a measure of myself without 'an Other'. 'I' cannot see myself (the image in the mirror is simply that: an image) and recognize myself, without being recognized. 'I' therefore exist in an ethical obligation to 'Others' and thus from among all that 'I' am given, I am given the possibility of freedom: it can never be just a springing forth from 'me.'

So, at a basic level, the potentiality of freedom is fundamentally political (socially dependent) and of the common good (ethical). As such, it bleeds between the self and its world. By implication, liberalism, with its absolute commitment to individualism (notwithstanding its bond to pluralism), is a negation of the common good (as a precondition of freedom) and thus an enemy of freedom.[19]

In so far as freedom is not a thing, it cannot but be perspectival. This was made especially clear in Kant's characterization of freedom in his controversial regime of causality: negative freedom as independence from nature, world and God – thus 'freedom from' in contrast to positive freedom as the ability to lay down conditions of self-direction. Overarching both is practical freedom, as the nature of action in the moment of decision.[20]

No matter how we try to place freedom before us, it remains out of reach. By its very nature, it exceeds thought and the measure of definition. Yet the act of striving to think freedom is absolutely necessary, for the loss of the ability to think is the loss of freedom. The 'fact' of thinking equates with 'the fact of freedom'.[21] But freedom is more than a condition of mind: it is of the body, knowledge, the world and it is ontologically lodged. It's equally a quality of being-in-common – as such, it can even be taken to be ecological (relationally: it is of mind, dependent upon others and 'vital nourishment').

Freedom, Limitation, Unfreedom, Design

We learn something we instinctively know from Theodor Adorno's *Negative Dialectics* – in so far as the subject is a subject (has been subjectified) who exercises 'free will' s/he is always held within unfree worldly circumstances.[22] 'Free will' does not own freedom. From at least Spinoza onward (as in his *Ethics*) there has been a major philosophical enterprise aimed at totally breaking the claimed connection between freedom and will.[23]

Whatever the experience of freedom, it is always experienced in a condition of unfreedom. Philosophically, unfreedom has been posed in relation to evil – freedom's other. But as we have seen, 'humanity' is now in a situation where 'the common good' and 'environmental commons' can only exist in a 'workable' relation to each other by imposing limits on human actions – the experience of freedom thus now rests on newly created, specific unfreedoms. Such action, as Levinas would say, 'can seem to be violent' but is justified by 'being not for itself'.[24] Elsewhere he observes that 'we must impose commands on ourselves in order to be free'.[25]

The theme of freedom coming from unfreedom (as imposed limits) is well rehearsed. Adorno powerfully argued against German idealism's claim that thoughts are free by showing the coercive nature of thinking.[26] Likewise he pointed out that 'men are unfree because they are beholden to externality' yet he also recognized (with the help of Hegel) that there can be no notion of freedom without a sense of unfreedom.[27] Nancy, echoing Adorno, affirms the unfreedom of the subject's ontology.[28] The more the thinking of freedom is explored, the more contradictions are amassed – yet the dialectical relation between freedom and unfreedom remains constant.

Nancy identifies with the still-growing resonance of Adorno's words on Enlightenment philosophy's fated quest for the essence of freedom by its investment in the 'freedom-undercutting agency of rationality and the subject'. One of Adorno's utterances delivers a sentiment to be emblazoned above the pillars of pluralism and liberalism: 'The alliance of libertarian doctrine and repressive practice removes philosophy farther and farther from genuine insight into the freedom and unfreedom of the living.'[29] There is another matter accompanying the question of freedom and unfreedom that Adorno confronted (which stands alongside Heidegger's work on Schelling's *Treatise on the Essence of Human Freedom* and prefigures Nancy's concern). This is the matter of the abysmal nature of evil.[30] Adorno writes: 'The trouble is not that free men do radical evil ... the trouble is that as yet there is no world in which ... men no longer need to be evil. Evil therefore comes from the world's own unfreedom. Whatever evil is done comes from the world.'[31] Of course this world within 'the world' was constituted by anthropocentric interests.

In this defuturing age of unsettlement it becomes more apparent that regulatory delimitations (like 'freedom under the law') are insufficient to deliver those unfreedoms upon which future freedoms depend. Design comes into the picture as embedded in the nature of externality – it holds sway over the propensity of external things. So many designed things have a major dispositional consequence in forming a subject's ontology, including the character of their unfreedom (enabling or disabling the subject's exercise of freedom). The design of unfreedoms for freedom can be directly posed against the humanitarian idealism of the privileged acting for the underprivileged. This is because unfreedoms (the rule of law and political institutions) can be the mechanism of redistributive justice. The words of Levinas cited earlier, now gain a new resonance: 'we must impose commands on ourselves in order to be free'.[32]

Politics Boxed

The efficacy of 'the exercise of democratic freedom' (the vote for a choice that often is no choice) depends upon educated decision. Unfortunately, the dominant instrument of 'political education' in the contemporary world has become the media (especially the televisual). The power and excess of the televisual, as it enfolds all digital visual media, exceeds definition. It is a primary agent of the aestheticization of everyday life – via the televisual, politics is first diminished to image and then to entertainment, thereafter it is rendered a-political.[33]

Adorno and Horkheimer were concerned with the mediation of mass media. We are now beyond mediation and dwell within an 'ecology of the image' – object and agency constituted out of the exchange relations between language, word, picture, sign and world. Initially, Marshall McLuhan and later Jean Baudrillard exposed television as a 'reality' rather than as reality's representational instrument and mode of appearance.

While formal political discourse realizes that television has changed political life, it does not get past thinking of it as an instrumental medium for marketing messages, constructing personas and influencing public opinion. Mainstream political parties constantly demonstrate their failure to grasp the televisual environment and its transformation of form, space, time and the political. In this respect, televisual politics, as the site of the political, is located at 'the end of the politics'. The televisual has fractured the structures of sovereignty. Nation, state, church, parliament and monarch have all become refracted through the spectacle of the designed, edited and managed image (as has war). The televisual, after the fall of the sacred, the sovereign and the political, becomes an environment of shrinking utopias (the most expressive forms being 'the dream' of appearing on television and the commodified 'good life' promised by advertised products).

Liberalism, Democracy and the Free Subject

The emancipatory ambition of the Enlightenment delivered the notion of the free, independent, individuated subject who became the primary figure of concern for liberal democracy: freedom of the individual over the mass and freedom of the market – which transpired to be a 'freedom' that negated the 'common good' and liberated defuturing. Ambiguity reigned.

As argued earlier, liberalism goes hand-in-hand with pluralism and parliamentary democracy in blocking how to think Sustainment. In its commitment to capital and wealth creation, liberalism is effectively committed to defuturing. Liberals speak the language of concern but take actions that sustain the unsustainable (by upholding practices underpinned by ideologically inscribed 'core values' antithetical to futuring). It is important to understand that liberalism's ideology exists in gradualist forms: it is an intellectual position and, equally, it is an ontology. Thus to be a liberal does not necessarily mean espousing liberal ideology. Such is its pervasiveness, that it simply constitutes a worldview.

Schmitt, acknowledged to be '… probably the twentieth century's most profound critic of liberalism', spent much of his life prefiguring liberalism's inevitable demise – yet he did not break free from it.[34] Tracy Strong, as a reader of Leo Strauss (Schmitt's interlocutor), notes that Schmitt's critique of liberalism rested on a humanist morality that folded back into its object of confrontation.[35] In the last instance, the political, for Schmitt, is the human moralized (his defence of the political while not exonerating his failings, firmly contradicts the claim that he was inherently evil). Schmitt did not attain, via his critique, what he intended. But he did create a thinking that beckoned others to follow (not least because he viewed liberalism as far more than just a political philosophy or ideology). For him, liberalism was a historical event with destructive agency. Strong writes: 'To see liberalism as a historical event means that one understands it as the inheritor and bearer not only of rights and freedoms but also of structures of power and domination, of colonial and class exploitation, of hatred of, rather than opposition to, the other.'[36]

Democracy became united with liberalism so it could appropriate its ability to co-opt, coerce and dominate. The relation between the two, as Schmitt realized, was corrosive. This structurally unsustainable relation, as we will explore later, was mediated by pluralism.

Liberalism travelled with pluralism while managing to retain an appearance of having a singular character. There are many examples, like the projection of the 'free world' by the United Nations wherein members exercise their rights to represent their interests within *the authority of the democratic process, the institution's autonomy and in the company of the 'freedom' of modern market capitalism.*[37] So while different member nations came to the organization with their own rhetoric, needs, political ideologies and agendas, in the end, their only available option was to comply with the conduct vested in the institution's liberal foundations.

In Contradiction

Wherever liberalism asserts its presence there is an inherent contradiction. Liberalism carries a trace of the utopian notion of universal freedom, deemed as personal liberty, predicated upon the elimination of conflict and the rule of consensus. But because of its political associations, liberalism retreats into a rationalization of freedom based on a requirement to protect particular interests. Within this condition, it will not tolerate that which poses a threat to those interests. Thereby it exposes and shares, the sham tolerance of its fellow traveller: pluralism. The idealism of the Hobbesian notion of 'freedom under the law' was exposed by Marx's dictum that 'all law is class law'. In this context, liberalism regards any difference that is fundamentally *other* as absolutely 'unreasonable', uncivilized or 'ideological'.

Liberalism effectively accepts all difference that does not make a difference while imposing conformity to its rule (hence its disposition to sustain the unsustainable). All non-conformity that is thought to be able to threaten 'the same' is eliminated. Depending on the nature of threat, neutralization arrives (1) as commodification (the disarming of counter cultures, sub-cultures and avant-gardes), (2) by exclusion from economic, social and cultural exchange (thereby driving its others toward total assimilation or complete *anomie*), or (3) if difference really asserts itself, by violence (justified by, for example, the containment of deviance, the criminalization of political resistance or maintenance of national security).

Liberalism holds the appearances of a 'well ordered rational society' in place. But the thinness of this façade and the ease with which it can slip is constantly exposed. There are numerous examples: the use of troops against striking workers or 'racial minorities' struggling for 'civil rights'; the treatment of homeless people as a criminal class; pre-emptive strikes against potential terrorists; the erasure of 'human rights' in the name of protecting freedom; hard and soft political censorship and so on. The violence of the enforced 'consensus' of liberalism is, *de facto*, a fundamental negation of the democratic claimed by its fellow traveller (democracy). In this respect, liberalism generates and represses its own dysfunctionality.

Again we point out that Sustainment, as freedom's foundation, can only be established under the rule of new limits. Currently, neither the existing institutions of law or politics (anywhere) have recognized this. 'Environmental laws' come nowhere near what is urgently needed – they are weak, partial and partitioned. Sustainment, it should be understood, is not a matter of a specific area of concern, policy, the particular responsibility of a specific arm of government or the remit of a particular discipline. Rather it has to 'infect' all policy and undergird the practices of every arm of government, the conduct of the private sector and everyday life.

Foundations

Liberalism, in its various guises, has not only permeated social democratic politics but has also considerably shaped the Western psyche. However, before further elaboration, we need to say a little about liberalism's foundations.

Emerging out of the pluralism of the Reformation and thereafter, the political philosophy of the Enlightenment; inspired by the extraordinarily influential political philosophy of Thomas Hobbes (1588–1679) and articulated by the pre-eminent English empiricist philosopher John Locke (1632–1704) ('coercive institutions are necessary to secure the freedom of individuals'), political liberalism arrived and converged with the wider project of modernity. Its assumptions are expressed in a contemporary form by one of its staunchest advocates, American liberal pragmatist philosopher John Rawls, as: rationality as the basis of human conduct; pluralism; free institutions; and the inscribed rights of citizens who are abstracted as 'being free and equal.'[38] In its pluralism, political liberalism overlapped with economic liberalism – the longstanding ground of globalization – based upon enduring notions of free trade between (un)equal partners (terms laid down by the economically powerful).

Modernity emerged from independent philosophic, scientific, cultural, political and economic projects initiated in different times and places. These projects became inter-related conceptually and in directional intent. This directionality is retrospectively named 'modernity'. Although there were competing intellectual traditions within modernity (as well as different cultural paradigms), the liberal model became hegemonic. This produced a seismic shift in the world of human occupation including: the formation of the modern subject; the supremacy of property rights; and safeguarding the rights of individual citizens. The nation state, the institutions of civil society and parliamentary democracy all came out of this moment. So too, did the elevation of the arts and the modern university as the flagship of reason and science. Under the influence of the spirit of modernity, the form of the Western world changed, most visibly by the rise of industrial society and the modern city. Yet the project – a world made one and modern – remained unfinished. This is the unresolved world we occupy.

One can be amazed by the attainments of the Enlightenment while also being horrified by its failures, not least its entrenchment of a condition of anthropocentric myopia. Herein lie the shortcomings and virtues of the human species – worldly making and unmaking, including the practices and psychology of structural unsustainability fused with the being of 'bourgeois man'. Cuttingly, Schmitt writes, in the shadow of Hegel, of this 'man' as a man …

… who does not want to leave the sphere of the unpolitical, risk-free private, who in possession and in the justice of private possession behaves as an individual against the whole, who 'finds' the substitute for his political nonentity in the fruits of peace and acquisition and, above all, 'in the perfect security of the enjoyment of things,' who consequently wants to remain exempt from courage and removed from the danger of a violent death.[39]

This prefigures the character of 'defuturing man' (the modern consumer) – an individual who acts 'against the whole' and sacrifices the future for the 'enjoyment of things' in the present. Schmitt devoted much of his life's work to analysing the 'nature' of 'bourgeois man' as extant 'human nature'. A great deal of his political thinking was an extrapolation from this position. His preoccupation, again, led him back to a major engagement with Hobbes.[40]

To claim Hobbes as a founding figure of liberalism implied that the ideology came from his reaction to the 'un-liberal nature of man' (as man emerged as the 'bourgeois subject') and that the ground of modern civilization and humanity centred on this subject.[41] Schmitt took Hobbes' argument further, viewing liberalism as an attack on religion and 'the sacred', as both an ideological and theological enemy of freedom. At liberalism's core, he claimed, was a new secular faith aiming to establish a 'victory of economy, industry and technology over state, war, politics'.[42]

In his writings of the 1950s, Schmitt pre-empts the postmodern 'end-of-man' thesis and observes, via a perverse evolutionary twist, that the perfection of technology has become indivisible from human perfection, as well as becoming a force of (human) 'neutralization' rather than enablement. Through technology 'man' now creates a 'new world' in 'which he is the strongest, indeed the *sole* being'.[43] In this world even consumption has become a 'pure' form – 'grazing'.[44]

Attacks on liberal utopianism and its moral impositions are never far away in Schmitt's writing. He exposes a problematic naturalism underpinning politics linked to the violence of Hobbes' politics (an enforced overcoming of man as an un-liberal 'natural' being subordinated to the whims of a 'nature' who needs to be liberated by order and its structures). Hobbes saw the state as the mechanism of such order and structure. For him, the state demanded conditional obedience (which is obedience minus the risking of one's life – Hobbes rejected such risk along with the notion of courage as a virtue).[45] Schmitt's commentator, Heinrich Meier recalls that the state demands (in seeming contradiction – differences were ignored by liberalism and society was viewed as if it were autonomous) that: '… the people defend it from its external enemies, to preserve its internal peace, while allowing the individual to work to gain enrichment and enjoy "innocuous freedoms"'. Moreover 'as soon as "humanity" became the subject or object of planning, these principles have lead to the ideal of civilization, that is, to demand for rational social relations of humanity as *one* in 'partnership in consumption and production'.[46]

While Hobbes claimed order as an essential function of the state, he also asserted the inalienable human right of the individual above this function.[47] Thus the *contracted* rights of the sovereign individual were asserted as the basis of an ideal civilization (and liberalism). This move to fuse the sovereign subject with the 'structure and order' of the state was intended as the means to overcome the brute being of nature while, at the same time, fabricated rights were claimed as 'natural'. The 'modern ethical move' Hobbes made was the major reason why his ideas gained agency within the aegis of modernity. He presented 'the good' as a constructed imposition rather than either a secular or theological transcendental figure (for example, the agency of Plato's ideal forms or the gift of God's creation). Notwithstanding a nature/politics/metaphysics problematic, the continuing value of Schmitt's re-reading of Hobbes is evident in Meier's account:

> If it is true that the final self-awareness of liberalism is the philosophy of culture, we may say in summary that liberalism, sheltered by and engrossed in a world of culture, forgets the foundation of culture, the state of nature, that is, human nature in its dangerousness and endangeredness. Schmitt returns, contrary to liberalism, to its author, Hobbes, in order to strike at the roots of liberalism in Hobbes's expressed negation of the state of nature. Whereas Hobbes in an illiberal world accomplishes the founding of liberalism, Schmitt in a liberal world undertakes a critique of liberalism.[48]

Here we are reminded of Bruno Latour's assertion that there has never been '… any other politics than the politics of nature, and there has never been any other nature but the nature of politics'. In the context of the discussion above, one can say that politics fundamentally centres on engaging the futural relation between human beings, non-human beings and the worlds they all occupy. In this respect, politics, as a category of practice, is not delimited by a metaphysical categorization of 'nature' – or the attempted realignment of this relation by biopolitics. This issue begs a brief review.

Nature, Rights and Violence

Nature as 'purely natural' has been refused. What is ontically extant as biota is, of course, acknowledged, but such phenomena can no longer able to be presented by a metaphysical presencing named 'nature'. The idea of nature can no longer rest upon (if it ever could) divisions between the organic and the inorganic, the natural and the artificial, biology and technology, the animate and the inanimate. 'Nature' is steeped in fabricated, romantic and biocentric visions that conceal its denaturalization. The more it has become defined by science and aesthetically reified, the more remote it has become from any sense of its foundation as *phusis*.[49] Nature has in fact become a representational trope, an image, a narrative of entertainment, a televisual genre and above all, an unthinking. At the same time, that ontic condition (named 'nature'), which 'man' was claimed to have overcome, is refused. 'Natural man' was never 'denaturalized' as Hobbes would have it by the arrival of (political) covenants underpinned by force. Neither was there any inherent evolutionary dynamic within 'man' whereby 'he' advanced automatically to overcome 'nature'. Whatever the 'advancement', it has been partial, instrumental and at the cost of the creation of 'the wasteland'.

In the process of 'man' becoming 'denaturalized' – which actually meant becoming ecologically de-relationalized and fundamentally homeless (completely estranged from the given world) – what commenced unevenly was what Marx called a 'second nature' (being in the world within the world). 'Man's' plural social realization occurred in this condition of difference. Varied relational ruptures from the given world and multiple constructed forms of worldly occupation, militated against a single mode of 'being-in-the-world'.

The discourse of humanism has acted to obscure such fundamental differences (as well as commonalities) – effectively for millennia 'the West' has been striving to 'accommodate' 'the Rest' under the rubric of 'the human'.

The biological reductionism of evolutionism became indivisible from ethnocentrism and the concealment of the differences of 'man' (as a 'plurality' rather than 'species-being'). More crudely and historically, the genocidal, ethnocidal and ecocidal violence of the notion of a single evolutionary line (with peoples of varied levels of development arranged along it) is incalculable.

For Hobbes, 'natural rights' were rights of humans to antagonistically engage and exploit 'nature'. Now, while some qualification of what this exactly means is needed, the most significant point is that such a view became foundational to modern politics. Effectively, it amplified the proposition of 'mankind's' transcendence over nature. Politics was thus effectively the institutionalization of anthropocentrism and as such, deemed as an instrument of progress to mobilize against the ground of 'mere nature' – seen as 'Anarchy, and the Condition of Warre'.[50]

'Natural rights' were obviously not founded in the 'rights of nature' but rather in divine law. For Hobbes 'natural rights' were based on a God giving free exercise to the right of man to: '... use his own power, as he will himselfe, for the preservation of his own Nature' for 'Every man has a Right to every thing; even to one another's body'. He then emphasized *'That every man, ought to endeavour Peace, as farre as he has hope of obtaining it; and when he cannot obtain it, that he may seek, and use, all helps, and advantages of Warre.'*[51] The very basis of these rights was the right to life itself, notwithstanding any 'impediment' put in 'his' path. Moreover, here is a moment when life was contested in an arena shifting away from the sovereign power of the (aristocratic) few to the emergent individuality of 'bourgeois man'. The 'nature' of 'natural rights' therefore is exposed as not only *'human* nature' in general but equally centred on 'the nature' of a particular kind of human (one who is driven by self-interests and 'their own vain glories').

Let's be clear, there are no connections between the 'nature' called up by Hobbes and the 'nature' summoned by contemporary environmental ethics (especially when claiming 'intrinsic value' and an essentialist foundation of 'nature'). Moreover, Hobbes' view of 'human nature' was a 'nature' as an onto-political formation.

His project was not to describe '*human* nature' but rather to present ideas to help shape it in a particular form – anthropocentric, self-interested, cultivated – all announced as 'modern man'. It can be argued that the work of Hobbes and the subsequent development of a liberal metaphysic, demonstrates how a generalized psychological condition of repression was prefigured by the imposition of political values (these values acting to determine the socio-political environments in which the psychological dispositions of modern subjects were formed). In significant part, modern 'being-in-the-world' (being 'civilized') concealed (repressed) an immediate 'being-of-the-world'. The price of being a modern individual was loss of engagement with and 'alienation' from, the relational ground of beings (the arrival of the idea of 'nature observed' and therefore externalized, simply reinforced this distancing).[52] The simple division of 'bare life' and 'social life' conceals this complexity.

Partly predating both Kant and Hegel and in contrast to Hobbes, Locke posited 'natural rights' as given rights that begged a mutual recognition of each other predicated upon reason (which was both inherent in and materially realized as law). Locke's focus on rights centred upon a relationship between 'nature', liberty and property. He viewed 'nature' simply as a 'God given' resource that existed for the exploitation of 'man' and in this respect his understanding overlapped with Hobbes. He regarded the right to exploit nature as one of the defining qualities of liberty. He argued that liberty also carried the assumption that all members of the human species are given an equal freedom to exercise their own will under the 'laws of nature' (an underscoring of natural law) and are free from the will of others. His characterization of the relation between 'man' and property was based on the notion that politics (as government) addresses deficiencies in (human) nature, including tendencies of human beings to transgress the property of others.

Although these quick sketches are an inadequate presentation of the true complexity and influence of Hobbes' and Locke's ideas, they nevertheless reveal the crucial place occupied by 'nature' in the emergence of a liberal politics and the way that unsustainability was structurally inscribed into its very foundations.

Heidegger's naming of 'nature' as a 'standing reserve' able to be plundered without constraint as a natural right, was framed by this history as it predated any modern technological ability to appropriate resources on a huge scale. The naming echoes and then inverts how Hobbes and Locke, as proto-liberal political theorists, viewed 'the natural'. As Macpherson put it, 'both Hobbes and Locke read back into the nature of man a contentious, competitive behaviour they drew from their emergent model of bourgeois society. Each thinker's theory of natural rights was determined by postulates about the "nature of man".'[53]

The more one investigates the relation between 'the human, the natural and rights' the more that the history of human rights seems to fold back into liberal and absolutely anthropocentric foundations, wherein the 'human' is an ethnocentric universalistic fabrication. This problematic history certainly poses critical questions to the essentialism carried by the contemporary evocation of 'human rights'.

From Now to 'Now'

Thinking about *the politics of the redesign of politics for Sustainment*, the substance of what has been discussed above begs to be put more sharply.

Notwithstanding a validation of the rule of law, liberalism has never realized the structural imperative of establishing unfreedoms to guarantee realizable freedoms. Inevitably, this inability is lodged in a flawed thinking of modernity and its failure to grasp the defuturing dynamic that it itself unleashed. The complicity of design, technology, science, politics and economy in that unmaking, which unfolded as structural unsustainability, still goes unseen. Faith in 'progress' lingers. Liberalism still does not have any sense of the dialectic of Sustainment (the indivisibility of creation and destruction) as it demands ethical decisions.

To recognize that 'Sustainment' is not stasis, an endpoint, but process and project, means grasping the 'nature' of this process as a precondition of freedom. Without Sustainment as a work, we will have nothing – as such, it is the exercise of taking responsibility for being anthropocentric and the condition of 'structural unsustainability' this mode of being has delivered. Inseparably, a politics of Sustainment is a politics of freedom.

Historically, liberalism legitimized taking freely that which was not free. Futurally (from individual, corporate and government levels) liberalism supports environmental and economic action that sustains the unsustainable. As indicated, such action is writ large in the very project of globalization.

One does not have to undertake a full review of the political and economic theory of liberalism[54] to conclude that (1) the issue and imperative of Sustainment has little presence in this literature; and (2) a massive historical revision of the consequences of liberalism is required. Having made these observations there are still a few more pertinent points to make.

Certainly the difference between liberality and liberalism (the latter as both an economic and political ideology) suggest a complexity at least equal to, as well as being implicated in, the relation between plurality and pluralism. The historical force of liberalism is embedded in the archaeology of ideas that underpin the designing of governmentality, laws, forms of public education, together with systems of economic exchange and modes of operation of public institutions. Likewise, liberalism is pervasive in how national and personal security and the 'function of technology' are addressed and publicly perceived. Such is the breath of liberalism that it bleeds into other 'isms' (like egoism, subjectivism, romanticism, humanism and idealism). As a particular 'ecology of mind' it inflects how an enormous range of issues are thought and debated (from the power of art to the use of 'morally justified' violence). Like anthropocentrism, it cannot simply be cast off. But it can be named as an enemy and confronted (this runs completely counter to what John McCormick identifies as the 'tired course' of political theory of liberalism since the 1990s).

Critiquing liberalism's longstanding defuturing impetus is not a matter of finding new crimes but of exposing the consequences of old ones. It means acknowledging that, for instance, liberalism constantly expels and renders silent its human surplus – it is generative of the unfree (the current extreme example is that while globalization has expanded the middle classes of newly industrializing nations, the poor are more entrenched in their condition than ever). Rights posited by liberalism are always vested in the centrality of *its* system of dispersed power, thus those who most need the protection of these rights get the least (or even no) protection. Equally, whereas liberal society is deemed to function by persuasion rather than by force, it is always persuasion underwritten by the order of law, which in turn is always underwritten by force (civil and military). As Schmitt pointed out, again in the shadow of Hobbes, 'authority not truth makes the law.' Clearly, irrespective of the quality of the law, its mode of imposition or the degree of justice of its administration, politics rests on the rule of law. And there has been a long-standing consensual view that bad laws are bad, but no law is worse.[55]

For liberalism, Sustainment – as an emergent radical moment and process of transformation of how worlds are viewed, engaged, constituted and inhabited – is held in check. This is because it is deemed to carry the greatest threat to what is traditionally most feared by liberalism: economic breakdown of the status quo leading to chaos or violence. Historically, liberalism has addressed this threat with politically directed force. It does this specifically by using orthodox legislative and 'special executive powers' to mobilize instruments of the state against 'internal' and external enemies (seen in national security legislation – linked to the 'State of Exception' – allowing virtually unlimited surveillance capability to national security agencies and the holding of 'suspected terrorists' without charge for extended periods *plus* engaging in pre-emptive combat in foreign lands, justified as being in 'the national interest' to defeat the spread of terrorism).[56] In the face of conflict, liberalism claims the 'moral high ground' and the 'neutral' forces of reason, technology and law as instruments it can rightfully deploy in the 'defence of freedom' (as defined in its own interests).[57] Increasingly, in a contemporary setting (and not least with the prospect of millions of environmental refugees), we see these instruments folding into normalized technocratic and dangerous (unsustainable) structures of control.

Making liberalism critically present is not a matter of choice but necessity. As is the creation of a political alternative: a politics of Sustainment.

Prefigurations: The Universal and the Individual

Francis Fukuyama announced in 1992 that with the universalization of liberal democracy (after the end of the 'Cold War') the final form of human government had been reached and that this marked the 'end of history'.[58] In the Hegelian sense, the project was complete – the 'end-state' had arrived. There is, of course, quite a different way to read the consensual neutralization and technocracy of this 'last politics'. While the substance of the criticisms levelled at his view diminished its authority and while his own position has radically shifted, what nevertheless is clear is that when one looks at the defuturing trajectory of structural unsustainability, liberal democracy will not be able to hold its ground. Neither its directional force, nor the destination toward which liberal democracy is directed (towards a world of affluent individuals 'consuming' without constraint) provides a basis for viable futures. The universalization of liberal democracy's freedom, the reaching of its goals, would literally be 'the end' of a lot more than just its politics. The currently dominant democratic processes can neither halt the onward march of the structurally unsustainable nor deliver an economic paradigm shift to secure those conditions that are prerequisite for viable futures. Moreover, liberal democratic consumer sovereignty has been a prime contributor to the excision of the political from politics and thus has stymied the essential discursive means to discuss, explore and create vital change.

Effectively, liberalism is so entrenched in the restrictive economy (capital's de-relational mode of exchange) that it has no ability to grasp the interconnectedness upon which Sustainment as process depends – this failure of understanding exchange at its most basic is longstanding. For example, here (as we saw in Chapter 5) is what Hegel had to say on connectedness in 1807:

> Air, water, earth, zones and climate are universal elements of this sort, which constitute the indeterminate simple essence of [natural] individualities and in which these are at the same time reflected into themselves. Neither the individuality, nor universal element, is absolutely in and for itself: on the contrary, though they appear to observation as free and independent, they behave at the same time as *essentially connected,* but in such a way that their independence and mutual indifference are the predominant feature and only

in part become abstractions. Here, then, we have law as the connection of a [universal] element with the formative process of the organism which, on the one hand, has the elementary being over against it and on the other hand, exhibits it within its organic reflection.[59]

Dominantly, modernized 'human beings' view themselves as monadic (changing singularities), while at the same time being absolutely dependent upon a complexity of relational connections (which, as demonstrated by Hegel, require critically reflective knowledge to make present).

Hegel's thinking on a 'single individual [human] being' actually dismembers the liberal notion of individual freedom and a polarization of the singular in relation to the collective. In so doing, Hegel affirmed: singularity, the universalized and connectedness as the key features of the determinate essence of all members of the species. This essence continually returns with each generation.[60] It is possible, from a contemporary position – one less based on a biocentric view of the organic, nature and the human species – to criticize Hegel's analysis but it is nevertheless remarkable that what he was saying at the opening of the nineteenth century remains in advance of the thinking of most environmentalists and liberals today. Specifically, what he points out is that difference exists by virtue of 'the same'.

The general framework of relational connectedness and the 'universal particular' is common to every 'being in being'. The universal is an ontic configuration that needs to be affirmed as an essential determinate in understanding the same and the different (which are always operative and immanent). Conversely, the universal claim of modernity needs to be 'destructed' – not least because of its logocentric and ethnocentric disposition. This 'destruction' is fundamental to futuring and needs to be replaced by the universal claim of 'Sustainment in difference'.

Recasting

Let's be clear – there are no intrinsic rights (or values). All rights are created out of a metaphysical construct projected upon particular circumstances or recipients. All rights stand or fall on the ethical claims of human invention. Nobody has the 'right' to exploit, pollute, waste resources, wage war, seriously damage the planet's atmosphere, turn desire into an insatiable hunger for commodities, act to eliminate plant and animal species. There is absolutely nothing 'we' do by right other than the right we have given ourselves. All 'our' actions, even the most philanthropic or seemingly benign, turn on individual or collective interests. Both the positing and the negation of rights (be they harmful or for good, directed at ourselves or towards other species) are un-ambiguous expressions of anthropocentrism (all rights, even animal rights, are human posited). None of this is to say that 'rights' should not be created but it is to say that the anthropocentric interests that they stand upon have to be made explicit.

Being anthropocentric confronts us with our selves and others equally as enemy. Schmitt showed how this relation to the enemy forces seriousness into our life and how being-in-danger forces the conservation of life as such and the valuing of the friend (who is affirmed via solidarity in confronting an enemy). But more than this, the rule of agreement (consensus) is the loss of the ability to ask what is right and to identify the vital tension between freedom and the unfree. The greatest danger is neutralization (the efficacy of liberal democratic politics in relation to 'the people') and the loss of serious-ness (which, as Schmitt warned, is the consequence of the now ubiquitous world of 'entertainment').

Schmitt, in his book on Hobbes *Leviathan,* identifies the 'decisive first step' towards the danger of neutralization 'that culminates in technologizing'. Meier translates a key passage from Schmitt as follows: 'But the idea of the state of technologically perfected *magnum artificium* created by man, as a machine that has its "right" and its "truth" only in itself, that is, in perform-ance and function, was first grasped and systematically developed as a clear concept by Hobbes.'[61]

Schmitt clearly displayed both an affinity with and hostility towards, Hobbes. He treats him as both friend and enemy. Although less overtly brutal than Hobbes, Schmitt, from his inner darkness, equally embraces a 'rationali-zation of violence'.[62]

Unfreedom has a lineage that ranges from the 'necessity' of repression of the 'id' – which underpins the conventions of any collective culture – through to the regulation of social order and the rule of law. The relative freedom of humans is given by imposition upon human animality. The confrontation with the unfree, that always remains unfree, rests with anthropocentrism as it works to conceal this essence of our bare life from our selves. The confrontation with animality casts human being into constant conflict. The attempt to neutralize this conflict by technology, via human being becoming technological (an instrumentalized ontology), presents a great danger. Not only does it portend negating the possibility of responsibility, decision and ethical questioning but a 'handing over' of contestation between the structurally unsustainable and sustain-ability to technology. However, technology, including 'sustainable technology' does not 'care' what it sustains (and it certainly is not bonded to the project of Sustainment).[63] Technologies (from energy infrastructure to the internet) ontologically design dependencies that 'naturalize' existing systems of power. Universally, once mega-techno systems are established, they cannot be taken away – they are serviced, upgraded and sometimes subject to local attack, but overall, they take on a life of their own (so nothing, except wholesale devastation, can take them away).

In such a context, giving war over to technology (the trend of warring) is its neutralization, for while war is (or at least was), as Carl von Clausewitz put it, politics 'by other means' it is also a fight for life (for Hobbes this fight was a 'natural condition').[64] This does not mean that war is 'neutral' but that it is removed from direct inter-human exchange, while killing ever more non-combatants. Enemies cease to directly confront each other, but more engage remotely, on the basis of technical assessment. The more war is waged on screens (be they head-up images on helmet visors, projections onto walls of central command centres, or televisual images) the more 'enemies' are abstracted and technologies take on a 'directive life force' of their own. No longer is war identified by formal sets of signs or contained within a specific location – the 'battlefield' is now in-place, displaced and electronic. War now gains a permanent presence in our lives – we are increasingly emotionally and politically neutralized by the omnipresence of its imagery. At the same time, 'the image' also interpolates potential combatants (who have no grasp of what they are doing politically or what they are fighting for).

Those weaknesses posited as material movers by Hobbes: vanity, glory, self-interest, fear (to which we would now add egoism) are neutralized by the neutralization of war by technology. But equally, in this neutralization, 'man' is also eliminated. That 'man' shows scant ability to transcend 'his' limitations is why Schmitt posited such great store in God and faith. In doing so, he rejected the evolutionary spirit, the vitalism of Nietzsche and all science. In closing, it is worth citing the opening of Hobbes *Leviathan*:

> Nature (the Art whereby God hath made and governs the World) is by the *Art* of man, as in many things, so in this also imitated, that it can make an Artificial Animal. For seeing life is but a motion of limbs, the beginning whereof is some principall part within; why may we not say, that all *Automata* (Engines that move themselves by springs and wheels as doth a watch) have an artificial life? For what is the *Heart*, but a *Spring*; and the *Nerves*, but so many *Strings*; and the *Joynts,* but so many *Wheels,* giving motion to the whole Body, such as was intended by the Artificer? *Art* yet further, imitating the Rationall and most excellent worke of Nature, Man.[65]

Design (Re)placed

Design is integral to the 'nature' of the world of our existence – it holds sway over the properties of external things as they bring, or take away, our freedom and future. As such, design is antithetical to freedom, while equally being a precondition. This is to say it delivers the specificity of the unfreedoms upon which all future freedoms stand.

Design as worlding (world-making) is ecologically and ontologically transformative. In this respect it has causality, which affirms it as political. Design as politics not only fundamentally acknowledges this situation but also takes responsibility for it – which means that it returns the political into the realm of politics. Immediately, an agenda arrives whereby the designing nature of things – their ontological designing – becomes a matter of political decision (without the comfort of certainty). Likewise, design is implicated in biopolitics, both as a mechanism of mitigation and/or as a means by which to constitute resistance and alternatives (not least in the exploration of new modes of being-in-common). Inescapably and instrumentally, design is implicated in the management and use of material resources – as a means of conservation, a basis of metabolic process innovation (full cycling), impact reduction and materials innovation. In all these examples, the aim of the freedom to use rests with impositions that prefigure what can be used and how (unfreedoms) so that the resource remains.

As the impetus towards the technologization of everyday life continues and as the physical environment alters dramatically from climate change (and from other environmental forces in the future) it is certain that there will be technological responses. The designing consequences of these responses upon our very 'nature' could be substantial and in fact significantly change the very being of human being. Certainly it is already clear that how 'the human' is understood is in question (and under threat and part of what design as politics, predicated on futuring, would contest). But also in question, is the very mode of being of 'our' being (in relation to being *per se*). In fact, the technological transformation of our being is occurring at a much faster rate than incremental biological changes.

It is certain that losses are going to be experienced as 'the wasteland' without and within, continues to grow. Some of these could be positive – the propensity toward devastation and the current general human passivity (of those who are aware) in the face of it might diminish. Likewise, global inequity could be reduced. Yet such changes would be remarkable! Of course much would be gained, some new responsibilities would be deemed a burden (like the massive task of redirection and a vast increase in the responsibility of being human). But then there would be new pleasures from the rise of a 'quality-based economy' such as more rewarding work from a mass and reinvented model of craft and the rewards of new knowledge. Above all there would be the cultural revitalization from *Neu Bildung,* with its reclaiming and remaking of culture. In such a framing, so much exists to offer up to remaking. Some of these possibilities have been mentioned, others have not. Most significantly, all converge on making time – craft, care, community, memory, meaning, value, self and much more all beg subordination to remaking to make time, to futuring.

10

Design Beyond the Limits

As has been indicated, taking design beyond current limits means another kind of design thinking and practice.[1] Three moves are elemental to this action. The first two have already taken place in earlier chapters; the third is what will focus our concerns here.

Move one was to extend the scope of design beyond the remit of existing design discourse, practice and practitioners – as such, design names all futural prefigurative actions of makers (material and immaterial) and the made. Move two was to acknowledge that humanity at large is entering a third moment of worldly habitation: the age of unsettlement (this being preceded by the extensive age of nomadic non-settlement and the briefer, familiar age of settlement). Move three comes from the way a line has been drawn under existing institutional politics. This sets a limit point that design reconfigured has to transgress. Before going further, the very idea of limit requires qualification.

The Greeks understood limit not just as the point at which something terminates but rather, and equally, as a condition that marks a beginning, an unfolding.[2] So framed, the argument presented by design as politics has designated a limit of design, but in so doing it has also marked a beginning from which design starts to be re-created, but other than it was. Thus re-created, design can return with a major increase in its efficacy when mobilized against structural unsustainability. As we shall see, design beyond the limit implies reasserting the need, once again, to confront anthropocentrism. That, in turn, means exceeding the horizon of 'the human'.

The Same and Difference

In countering a claim to a common humanity (a plurality misread as a unity) there is a question to ask: 'what do 'we' share in our difference and with whom?'

There are a whole range of commonalities and 'commons' that all human beings share.

A Body in the Flesh of the World

Contrary to the history and politically framed ideology of individuality, we are not autonomous entities but rather organisms within an organic complexity.

The Elements

With other beings we share our constitution and life by virtue of common dependencies (on water, air, light and earth – for the minerals and food it brings forth).

A Dependence upon Others

We cannot be and become human without others – without the social fabric that constitutes our sociality.

The Need for Sustenance (Nourishment, An Ecology of Mind, A Culture)

In common with all other humans, our minds need interconnection with the minds of others and the creation of a world of meaning.

A World (Biophysical/Naturalized Artificial)

Human beings depend not just on the given world but also the world they make via material and socio-cultural practices. In making this world, 'we' are all creators and destroyers.

These commonalities of Sustainment represent the basis of what has to be fundamentally valued for 'our' difference and futures to be possible. A question now travels with us: how do we get these commonalities acknowledged politically and practically?

Although Sustainment is a need above all others – for without it we have nothing – it desperately struggles for recognition amid the noise of economic demands (including, for sustainable development). As it folds into structural unsustainability, the defuturing collateral damage caused by this assault is massive and threatens our very existence. Even when problems (like climate change) are recognized as serious, their inter-relational complexity is refused – focus remains fixed on symptomatic manifestations and inward reflection upon anthropocentric causality is overlooked.

Although maybe sounding strange, we still really do not know what we are. Most of us live in a culture wherein we are told we are humans who have evolved (albeit now into technological beings). Equally, we have remained the same (as we learn from Nietzsche): we remain animals (as we remain linked to 'bare life'), yet we're also social beings. While surrounded by the trappings of civilization and thinking ourselves civilized, 'we' (not just the few) can revert to barbarism with so little effort. Civilization is such a thin veneer. As such, it conceals the continuity of our inhumanity (as it has been continually remade in new forms, with ever increasing destructive potential). Our auto-destructiveness, structural unsustainability and inter-species violence are but one un-named totality of our being – the commonality 'we' repress and refuse.

Sustainment is not just a matter of sustaining what we need but it also means overcoming what (in our difference) we are.

A Culture of Capital

The rise of capitalist culture flowed out of a radical transformation in the labour process whereby workers traded control over their skills for higher wages and a working day that afforded leisure time. There were two consequences. First, the domestic sphere became a far more significant commodity domain and combined with increased disposable incomes, prompted the arrival of 'a culture of consumption'. Second, 'culture' itself became incorporated into the commodity sphere (as affordable products to populate the making of a modern way of life). The result: a capitalist commodity sphere constituted as a 'world of desire'.

For millennia, culture was in large part a practical and symbolic consequence of communities adapting to their climate, available natural resources and the development of agricultural practices. But with the rise of extended systems of trade, industrialization and the modern urban environment, culture increasingly became constituted through the purchase of commodities, including cultural commodities that influenced dreams and desired ways of life. Although this complex history has only been glossed, what needs to be drawn out from it is that political ideology became more and more embedded in and directive of, culture. Moreover, the more culture became 'inorganic' (economically manufactured) the more the politics, as we shall see, become dependent upon support from humanism.

The Human and Humanism

Humanism, as a product of the Enlightenment, became a ground upon which to create the rhetorics, metaphorics and semiological elaborations of a modern lifeworld. John Dewey provided one of the most direct statements of this.

Dewey asserted that the humanist view needed to 'infuse' every aspect of society and culture including 'science, art, education, morals and religion, as well as politics and economics'. Humanism was viewed as a bonding agent holding the modern world together. It functioned in association with the notion of 'the human' not merely to name and define the species but to mark a specific condition of 'civilized and cultivated' being able to be mobilized morally to coerce difference into the same.[3] Humanism thus operated (and still operates) as a cultural ideology to underscore not just the fusion of different cultures but cultural conduct itself. In so doing, it is complicit with an evolutionist and ethnocentric classification of cultures on a graded scale of 'development'. Schmitt made apparent the underside and dangers of humanism in two senses.

First, and existentially, was that Schmitt's passing proximity to fascism brought him 'face to face' with the danger of 'an other' within humanism and himself. Here is a history that is viewed as aberrant but which, in fact, has touched the lives of millions of people (as transgressors, the transgressed, or as passive/neutralized observers of dehumanization). Rather than being of a single moment, this history recedes back into the ethnocidal character of Western global colonization and forward into ongoing forms of 'ethnic cleansing' and cultural imposition – it thus ever retains an ability to set the stage for future conflict.

The second sense goes to the dangers of humanism expressed through Schmitt's writing. Late in his life (at the age of eighty-nine – he died seven years later in 1985) he wrote a substantial article on law and revolution in which he addressed 'humanity as a political subject', in which he said:

Humanity as such and as a whole has no enemies. Everyone belongs to humanity. Even the murderer, at least as long as he lives, must be treated as a human being. If he is as dead as is his victim, then he no longer exists. However, until then he remains good or evil, a human being, i.e., a bearer of human rights. 'Humanity' thus becomes an asymmetrical counter-concept. If one discriminates with humanity and thereby denies the quality of being human to a disturber or destroyer, then the negatively-valued person becomes an unperson and his life is no longer the highest value: it becomes worthless and must be destroyed. Concepts such as 'human being' thus contain the possibility of the deepest inequality and become thereby 'asymmetrical'.[4]

Forty-five years earlier he had written:

> Humanity as such cannot wage war because it has no enemy, at least on this planet. The concept of humanity excludes the concept of the enemy, because the enemy does not cease to be a human being – hence there is no specific differentiation in that concept ... To confiscate the word humanity, to invoke and monopolize such a term probably has certain incalculable effects, such as denying the enemy the quality of being human and declaring him to be an outlaw of humanity; and a war can thereby be driven to the most extreme inhumanity.[5]

Historically, humanism has travelled in the company of 'plural, expedient and experimental methods' while being supported by advancements in the social sciences, education and aesthetic expression, especially in those forms that socialized the exercise of intelligence and 'civilizing' powers.[6] In this context, it is worth drawing attention to the inchoate ontological designing at work in Dewey's positioning of technology in relation to humanism. He argued that technology, through its subordination as an instrument of human endeavour, could be made a structurally inscribed tool of human emancipation.[7] Clearly the question that remains open is: 'was technology ever available to be subordinated by human beings?' This question does not imply that technology could never be, or was never, subordinated as a specific instrument of equipmentality. Rather, it draws attention to technology's ontological designing of (what is a) human being. Post this observation, another question arrives: is the binary 'the human' and 'the technological' illusory? Is it not the case that, over time, the human being and the being of the technological have designed each other *with the result that there is no being that can call upon technology from outside the technological?*

In 1932 Schmitt expressed a particular fear, asking ... 'upon whom will fall the frightening power implied in a world-embracing economic and technical organisation?' We clearly know which regime seized the power evoked in this utterance.[8] The ironic contradiction of the Nazi's embrace of technology was that it was based on using instrumental means to realize a romantic, utopian, pre-technological fantasy (recapturing the halcyon days of ancient Greece).[9] The fear expressed by Schmitt has now, of course, been amplified many times over, not least by 'humanity' creating sufficient technological power to wipe out the entire human species and much else besides.

The lifeworld of technological operability can be seen in capital and democracy's partnership in continuing the project of bringing the universal human into being. Human 'rights', democratic free expression, consumer choice, modern media, advanced technologies – all these familiar elements of globalized modernity are in fact part of the face of the singularity of disaggregated neo-modernity (inadequately named as globalization and projected as global postmodern culture).

Notwithstanding talk of the undecidability of universal rights, the challenges to reason's designation of 'the universal' and the problem of claiming democracy as a politics of global freedom, the questioning of the 'nature' of the human and anthropocentrism still remains un-confronted.[10] Humanism has become the dominant means to transport the idea of being human from one epoch to another. Yet this centring of 'human interests' (from the limited horizon of the 'species' self-interests) has its hubris in the manner in which the question of Sustainment and what is to be sustained, arrives. Across cultural and technologically induced difference, as a circumscribed singularity and a monistic being, 'the human' acts as if it were possible to be independent from all else in being. Its 'nature' remains, *in summa,* the will to *anthropos* – a condition putting our being and much else, at risk.

Revisiting the Anthropocentric

Notwithstanding the discourse of humanism carrying the anthropocentric intent of transferring human over-determining interests into the future (so that the future follows directions) anthropocentrism now travels with a contradiction, for as we have acknowledged, while bonded to the human, it is no longer totally lodged in the 'human'. A displacement has occurred: by default, via technological innovation, human existence is becoming independent of human control. The values posited with technology have become self-replicating

and generative of auto-mutating forms assisted by uncritical human technologically inflected agency (autonomic technocentrism). Although this observation has been made before, what begs particular emphasis is the arrival of
the 'Frankenstein syndrome as system'. 'We' are not, for instance, in control
of what we have brought into being (information technology, the televisual,
genetic engineering, nanotechnology, and so forth). These technologies have
become independent 'tectonics'. No individual, group, corporation or nation
can control them or their onward designing (of biophysical ecologies and
ecologies of mind). The subjects who work in their orbit are equally, at least
in significant part, mental and genetic objects of their creation.

Here we revisit and recast Dewey's employment of technology as an instrument in the service of humanism. Certainly technology is not 'ready-to-hand'
in the manner Dewey assumed it to be, even with his expanded notion of the
nature of technology. Nor is technology grasped as an instrument of anthropocentric extension that has taken on a (autonomic) world-transforming life
of its own. The issue can no longer be redirecting or stopping technology, for
it has become unstoppable as a world structuring and ontologically designing
force. Rather the challenge is to find *ways to know it and reposition one's self
toward it within the rise of an epoch of Sustainment.*

The grounds of being human are shifting and the anthropocentric dynamic
retains enormous directional force within globally inequitable contexts. This
force is structurally and profoundly undemocratic. Its vociferous but unde-
monstrative appetite takes without regard for time, consequences or others
in the processes of creation and destruction implicit in human world-making
and unmaking. Without a general and situated recognition of this condition
infecting 'our' being', Sustainment at a fundamental level is impossible to
realize – this in large part because so much that is absolutely critical in securing viable futures would go unseen.

From the perspectives just outlined, not only can we see defuturing being
deeply inscribed but also that the very theoretical and practical foundations
claimed for democracy actually lack firm ground (reiterating: democracy is
deficient in the ability to secure the conditions of vital exchange upon which
'being' depends). The market-based freedom(s) of democratic societies (the

freedom to consume) increasingly defuture and thus precipitate conditions of absolute unfreedom.

To strive for Sustainment demands being: post-humanist – going beyond humanism's limit(ations). This means being hyper-critical of 'being techno-logical' and being willing to accept responsibility for being anthropocentric. The exposure of humanism as the handmaiden of anthropocentrism is clearly a supra-deconstructive task. Moreover, the task of advancing a post-humanist agenda means undoing all that humanism takes for granted, while also tak-ing responsibility for the 'yet-to-be-created' (a primary function of design futuring).

These remarks must not be thrown back into the old frame of human endeavour, like the desire to overcome scarcity, gaining emancipation from 'nature', while romantically elevating 'the natural'.

What is actually being called for here is a clean break with the Enlightenment tradition. This is seen, for instance, in breaking with: Locke's assertion of 'unlimited desire' as rational and thus always constitutive of scarcity (taking always more than is available); Kant's positing of 'man's social and economic advancement' inscribed in overcoming the hardships delivered by 'the cun-ning of nature' (self-overcoming of animality) as the motor of history; Marx's positioning (in the *Economic and Philosophic Manuscripts*) of the drive towards 'nature external to being' as the lack, the force and the 'hunger', that propels man's being forward (again scarcity being the directive force) and finally, Baudrillard's critique of the way Marx understood 'the transformation of nature according to one's needs'.

Few contemporary presentations of the social complex connect to the relational complexity of being in which being human being is implicated. This adds up to overlooking the foundational ground of the human and its interdependencies. The omission means both difference and commonalities are overlooked, with the result that the ethnocentric character of such analy-sis goes unseen. The poverty of this kind of thinking exposes, among other things, a distorted theory of justice that misdirects moral philosophy – as evident in the 'influential' work of John Rawls and his commitment to 'fair-ness'.[11] In stark contrast to Rawls, one can consider Heidegger's reading of

Nietzsche on justice (explicated in Heidegger's reading of Nietzsche's literary notes).[12]

For Nietzsche, freedom and justice were one, with the very basis of justice coming from the estimation of value itself, which was the 'supreme representative of life itself'.[13] In the setting of contemporary concerns and in relation to the argument unfolding here, justice cannot be without Sustainment and vice versa – which is to say that it cannot be without the freedom of the unfreedom of Sustainment. Here, liberation from anthropocentrism is never an option, but acceptance of responsibility for its omnipresence. In turn, this indivisibly connects to design, via finding artificial means of controlling the defuturing agency of extant ontologically designed modes of human being – which includes the redirection of 'what (already) is'. Design (as a redirective practice) and ethics (in materialized and performative embodied forms)[14] merge and constitute a counter ontological designing of the status quo.

Now what presses, is a giving way to Sustainment and the establishment of its sovereignty, as foundational to the imposition of those limits that all ethical and sustaining practices depend upon (to proliferate, to become secured and to gain efficacy). The imposition of the means to regulate the status quo marks an absolute break with any liberal notions of freedom and its ideological underpinnings.

Sustainment (as a historico-futural moment) has to be able to deliver material forms and practices which constitute the project of a *Neu-Bildung*, while eliminating, conserving and remaking the materially present – its culture, economy, politics, law, science, materials, products, systems, infrastructure and technologies. Offsetting the seemingly impossible task has to be the realization that, to a very great extent, the means to Sustainment are already available but are currently overwhelmed by the structurally unsustainable. In other words, the real efficacy of redirection stands upon recognizing that so much can be redirected. Establishing and developing such critical actions lies at the core of the creation of the constitutive forms of design as politics. This enterprise requires gaining a deep understanding of the nature and form of dispersed power and then learning how to comprehensively reconfigure how 'we' view what we are and the consequences of what 'we' do (the question of

impacts and ethics) and then how 'we' treat each other (the question of global economic equity and justice). It means shattering illusions of democracy
while making new political practices (to fold into a new political imaginary).
In this context, Fred Dallmayr makes a statement that begs a reply. He says:

> I am troubled by Heidegger's continuous self-distancing from modern democracy, al-
> though on this score one can speculate more readily about reasons for his reticence. From
> Heidegger's vantage, democracy or 'popular rule' very likely signified a collective type of
> anthropocentrism or a collective will to power along humanist-metaphysical lines. Perhaps
> his scruples would have been eased by non-foundational or post-metaphysical conceptions
> of democracy such as have been advanced in recent times from various quarters. Clearly,
> the issue of anthropocentrism was at the heart of Heidegger's complaint about planetary
> technology, which he probably construed in too all-embracive or monolithic terms.[15]

It could be counter argued that Heidegger's distancing from modern democracy was warranted (as to whether it was done for the right reasons is
another matter).

To act with an awareness of anthropocentrism and a critique of humanism
is, as indicated, to act in the recognition that democracy is unable to deliver
the conditions of freedom (the unfreedom of Sustainment). In the light of the
events that have unfolded since Heidegger's death in 1976, one could suggest
that his views would have both hardened and become more sharply focused
as the untenable nature of democracy has become ever more apparent (for
a general 'will to power' now read the 'will to will of the techno-sphere' combined with the momentum of 'the unstoppable desire to consume'). As for the
academicism of 'progressive' post-foundational theories of democracy, they
hardly recognize, let alone offer the means to erase, the ongoing defuturing
that constitutes the negation of the relational interdependencies of being in
which our being is embedded.

The pluralism of 'democratic radicals' simply accommodates that which
it claims to rise above, in the faint hope that a 'superior' democratic position will gain mass support. Besides this kind of thinking displaying a lack of
understanding of just how power now (ab)uses power, it also smacks of utopianism. If technology is viewed as the techno-sphere's structuring of product, mechanism, operation, system, employed perception and occupation of

'world' as instrumentalized, Heidegger's position of more than half a century ago now seems like a high point, as critical positions increasingly seem to dissolve. The tendency to moderate his position and characterize it as over-general, is misplaced.

If Heidegger is open to criticism and modification, it is not because his view was too bleak, but rather that it was under-developed. He was expectant of a liberatory potential arriving through the formation of 'informed' ontologies with an ability to secure being in the path of an inherently auto-destructive technology (with its embodied anthropocentrism). A close reading of Heidegger's 1938 essay 'The Age of the World Picture' and especially its fifteen appendices (which, while written at the same time, were not made public until published with the essay in the *Holzwege* in 1952) supports this view.[16] Of particular importance is Appendix 9 which concludes with 'being after the subject', defined as 'imperialism of technologically organized man'.[17] The concern of Sustainment, in this framing, is not the meaningless 'survival of Earth', but the survival of what 'man' has and is becoming, as the giver and the taker of meaning and value. Anthropocentrism embraces both good and evil. The task of responsibility before this Janus-faced monster is to ensure a giving way to an ethics that can act. Recall Nietzsche: 'Man first implanted values into things to maintain himself – he created the meaning of things, a human meaning! Therefore he calls himself: "Man", that is the evaluator.' Evaluation is creation: hear it, you creative men! Valuating is itself the value and the jewel of all valued things.[18]

Redirective Design and Everything Designed

While it is impossible to redesign everything that is already designed, within the project of the redirection of 'what (already) is' it is possible to disrupt the identity of a thing dramatically to transform what it means (and in doing so, effectively redirect its status, value and use).[19] Placed in the context of futuring such action fuses phenomenology with the political. Here the activity of 'recoding', as a significant form of redirective practice, clearly evidences the immediate possibility of situating such a fusion. In the context of design as politics, recoding and the public perception of democracy, structural unsustainability and the future, it is worth giving some consideration to 'the media' in relation to the need to 'see the world another way'.

On the Media

As should now be apparent, to gain an adequately critical view of democracy means acknowledging it as fractured and problematically framed by pluralism and liberalism. In addition, this critical view also requires grasping how the 'the fifth estate' – 'the media' – is a 'para-political' force.

There has, of course, been a longstanding notion of democracy being formed and animated by a community of communication. As pointed out, the Greek idea of democracy and the *polis* was predicated on the restricted constituency of a few thousand people who could all be directly addressed and expected to reply. Obviously, in large, modern, complex societies, the democratic process became increasingly dependent upon mechanisms of mediation, with the mass media becoming the key actor. Initially, mass media acquired the power and exercised it as political 'bias' in the reporting of politics so as to shape public opinion – the most strident examples being newspapers from the mid-nineteenth to the mid-twentieth century.

Once television established itself, not only did it become the primary tool in shaping public opinion but also it profoundly changed the nature of politics. Politicians had to be performers and compete with the charisma of movie stars. Votes increasingly came to be decided by the media appearances and performances of these 'star performers' (their looks, rhetoric, the political 'goodies' they put on offer and the style of their packaging). The media both designs and delivers the political persona as commodity. But even more than this, the media also designs so many 'burning' issues: for they also have to be visualized and made saleable in the electronic public sphere in order to become matters of concern and policy (which, presented in any detail, is the key absence of televisual politics).

Free choice never arrives in freedom of appearances. There is a vast literature around this topic (surprisingly little of which seems to have made a mark on political philosophy). Much of that literature explores 'the problem' in terms of the construction of an ideological screen between 'the public' and 'reality' or 'the truth'.[20] The constructed ground of the image of such exchange is rational debate, when in actuality the media appearance of the political continually 'degenerates' into pure, mostly not very entertaining, entertainment.

The media always makes democracy dysfunctional and any 'liberal talk' that claims a 'free media' or 'media democracy' displays almost total failure to understand its designing power. This designing has, as many media theorists for many years have been telling us, gone well beyond 'distortion' of 'the truth'. While these arguments flow along both straight and complex paths they all converge on the absolute transformation of the 'public sphere' and 'public opinion'. Now as Derrida noted, these changes have changed '... the very concept of "event". The relation between deliberation and decision, the very functioning of government has changed, not only in its technical conditions, its time, its space and speed, but without anyone having realizing it, in its concept.'[21]

Again in concurrence with Derrida, the destabilization this transformation turns on has precipitated a crisis on several counts: the illusory claim of representative democracy is undone; the imaged politician is no longer a 'respected' figure whereas the space of political activity is diminished by the primacy of the media. At the same time, the socio-cultural, economic, environmental, international, military, technical bureaucratic machine of government grows by the day.[22] This machine feigns accountability and acts totally undemocratically, while claiming to be an instrument of representatives of the will of the people.

For most people, the condition of structural unsustainability is but another media appearance and event – one in which worlds are refracted. The crisis that is structural unsustainability is made a crisis by the inability of the representational machine to represent crisis as anything but reported events to attract, hold and entertain an audience. Here is the 'crisis of crisis' – concealment in disclosure. Here is a crisis of entertainment filling (in)time. It is not as if there were us, world and media; for the media is a world, it is an environment. We do not watch crisis; we are crisis as watchers. We are technologically spaced and anthropocentrically in-formed in our being put in place and in-formed by the 'eventing' picture. The 'we' is, of course, inclusive of the politicians who are expected to understand, engage and solve the problems, which themselves often get reduced to problems of the momentary credibility of appearances. So not only is democracy unable to face that which Sustainment demands but because of the world picturing (the knowing of the world) that is the media, it does not even hear or see the demand. In this silence, democracy is as one in its hyper-conformist plurality and un-uttered fear.

The counter view, that somehow the blog-sphere is an alternative to sound-bite dominated media monopoly, is at best contestable. At worst, it simply amplifies pluralism. Polarization between a monopoly mainstream view and a proliferation of opinion is not a viable option in the face of the structurally unsustainable. A real alternative would take the notion of 'commonality in difference' and 'quality remade' as a basis for media under the 'imperative of Sustainment'. Thus media freedom, as with other freedoms, arrives as a result of unfreedom, of limitation.

Living Otherwise

Alternative lifestyles, sustainable culture, green consumerism – such characterizations of 'change' exist within (and often as extensions of) the status quo. In contrast, 'living another way, living otherwise' means exactly what it says. It is an imperative for everyone everywhere, not just 'environmentally aware' subcultures. In difference, it means living with the losses of what has to be eliminated, it means lower economic standards of living for the privileged, it means that status-related conspicuous consumption, commodity desires and aspirational consumerism are all fated and will die. Elimination here is not just a matter of defuturing things (and institutions) that are present and to hand, but also dealing with those future-negating things that have been thrown into the future as unconsidered bequests. It means that sacrifice becomes a crucial pragmatic of futuring that equally opens a pathway for possible gains. Positioned within a *Neu Bildung* and contextualized by a 'quality' based economy, living otherwise implies a new kind of active life that is highly social and very much orientated toward cultural production and a material culture that is smaller but enriched. The pain of elimination and the harshness of the environment in which everyday life is lived, means that whatever the gains they do not equate to a utopian existence: the mantra 'to live is to suffer' reigns eternal.

Economic and cultural production begs to be elaborated as the creation of things that are gifts to the future. Living with this other kind of culture, as said, is not going to be easy. Certainly the working day will be shorter but other life-supporting activities will increase. Notwithstanding a propensity for people to dream, the reality of unsettlement and the demands of futuring will mean that romantic visions of the future will look increasingly untenable. Yet a new political imaginary has to be created, to counter and compensate for loss suffered – it needs to be a radical, affirmative and continuous making of *a home in the world* (and as such, the reverse of creating 'another world within the world'). This move does not imply any kind of 'return to nature' but rather recognition and engagement with relationality and the naturalized artificial that now infuses 'the world'.

In the kind of world that has been characterized throughout this text, one vital message should be clear – radical change is essential and unavoidable and it demands a process of decision and directive action that brings the two imperatives of freedom and futuring together to form an unbreakable unity. Design as politics not only gives this process a name, but makes 'being political' a form and force available and potentially present at almost every level of cultural, social and economic life. Such a post-institutional politics does not presume political institutions as we know them will cease to exist, but rather that politics and the political become elemental to the everyday life of 'supermen and superwomen' in the struggle to remediate, redirect and remake the wasteland.

Notes

Preface

1. Martin Heidegger, *What is Called Thinking?* (trans. J. Glenn Gray), New York: Harper & Row, 1968, p. 76.

Introduction

1. Martin Heidegger, *What is Called Thinking?* (trans. J. Glenn Gray), New York: Harper & Row, 1968, p. 69.
2. Anthropocentrism – 'we' or 'our' is used throughout this book as an invitation to identify with a sharing of values of the coming community of sustain-ability rather than as a designation of an identity that arrives with an anthropocentric imposition of all as the same.
3. Martin Heidegger, *Contributions to Philosophy (From Enowning)* (translation of the *Beiträge* by Parvis Emad and Kenneth Maly), Bloomington: Indiana University Press, 1999, p. 76.
4. Claude Lefort, *Democracy and Political Theory* (trans. David Macey), Cambridge: Polity Press, 1988, pp. 100–11.
5. Michel Foucault, *Discipline and Punish* (trans. Alan Sheridan), London: Allen Lane, 1977.

6. Obviously 'consumerism' is not a 'natural condition', but rather an inculcated economic practice linked to a constructed ontology. C. B. Macpherson, *The Life and Times of Liberal Democracy,* Oxford: Oxford University Press, 1977, p. 79. Macpherson's argument is that consumer sovereignty is a commodity domain whereby what is put on offer politically is judged as if it were goods. The packaging of politicians, their manufactured appearance, the form of their rhetoric, their television manner and the consumer rating of policies, including their ability to deliver more purchasing power, all fold into this characterization.

7. To make greater sense of the relation between politics and religion it is worth considering Carl Schmitt's thoughts on political theology, specifically the way he understands it as a fusion of belief and decision. See Carl Schmitt, *Political Theology* (trans. George Schwab), Chicago: University of Chicago Press, 1922/1985.

8. The theocratic Islamic state, while making political decisions, does so via 'men of God', and in 'God's name'. It is important to understand that a movement to liberalize such a regime is not seen as supplementary to religious life; rather democratic secularism is viewed as a pagan society that threatens the very being of the religious subject. The original meaning of a *jihad* was a war on pagans. Thus any Muslim construction of modern pagans links to this past view and action. Until the Crusades (1096–1270), Muslims, Christians and Jews had harmonious relations and pagans were other.

9. Tony Fry, *Design Futuring: Sustainability, Ethics and New Practice,* Oxford: Berg, 2009.

10. For a full discussion of this complex topic see Joan Stambaugh, *The Finitude of Being,* New York: SUNY Press, 1992.

Chapter 1: Facing Finitude

1. Tony Fry, *A New Design Philosophy: An Introduction to Defuturing* (Sydney: UNSW Press, 1999).

2. Distinguishing between affluence and liberation from poverty is a topic in its own right that begs substantial debate.

3. From the melting of polar ice, rising sea levels, extreme weather events, to the loss of biodiversity, rates of change are increasingly outstripping the reporting of peak organizations, including the Intergovernmental Panel on Climate Change (IPPC).

4. This condition being the fundamental condition of (*hyle*) all matter.

5. At the time of writing, carbon capture technology is unproven on a commercial/economic scale.

6. See UNDP, *Human Development Report* (Oxford: Oxford University Press, 2005).

7. While an imprecise category, slums have been defined by the United Nations as the fastest growing housing type in the world. More positively, although living conditions are appalling, slums can also manifest the seeds of social sustainment, seen, for example, in the social viability of low-rise, high-density living and communities that function well – more effectively than many in planned, well-serviced cities. See Mike Davis, *Planet of Slums,* London: Verso, 2006.

8. Inequality is both long standing and structural. See, for example, Samir Amin, *Unequal Development* (trans. Brian Pearce), Hassocks: Harvester, 1976.

9. People relocating due to feared or actual sea level rises; the breakdown of agricultural systems; heat islanding making some cities inhospitable – this all adds up to a massive redistribution of the human population. One of the earliest and most influential publications was the 'Environmental Exodus' Report by Professor Norman Myers for the Washington-based Climate Institute in 1995. The IPCC Forth Assessment Report of 2007 projected 150 million by 2050 but subsequent data on the rate and impact of global warming suggests the figure is now nearer Myers' original projection. Clearly, as the situation gets worse the figure rises.

10. This was the United Nations Commission on Refugees (UNCR) figure in their Report of 2009.

11. Reported in the *New York Times*, ClimateWire, 11 March 2009. The Climate Congress was an activity of the Intergovernmental Panel on Climate Change (IPCC).

12. The prospect of conflict is overtly confronted in, for instance, Gwynne Dyer, *Climate Wars,* Melbourne: Scribe, 2009, and in documents like the Australian government's *Defence White Paper 2030,* Canberra, 2009.

13. It has been estimated that only 1 per cent of all materials flowing through the US economy end up in products still being used six months after manufacture. P. Hawken, A. Lovins and H. Lovins, *Natural Capitalism: Creating the Next Industrial Revolution,* New York: Little Brown & Co., 1999, p. 10.

14. Bruno Latour, *Politics of Nature* (trans. Catherine Porter), Cambridge, MA: Harvard University Press, 2004, p. 28.

15. For example, Confucian philosophy addresses nature as process. See David L. Hall and Roger T. Ames, *Thinking Through Confucius,* New York: SUNY Press, 1987.

16. A crucial stake in the conflict between the 'West and the rest' is how the nature of (our) being is defined, who defines it and why – obviously this directly links to how the human is understood.

17. His early work, circa 1954, engaged questions of mental illness culminating in *Madness and Civilization* (1961). His exploration of biopolitics extends through to his final work on the *History of Sexuality* vol. 1 (1981). Of the numerous interviews with Foucault, the one that gives an excellent snapshot of his oeuvre is S. Lotringer (ed.), *Foucault Live* (interviews 1966–84, trans. J. Johnson) (New York: Semiotext(e), 1989).

18. See Paul Patton, 'Agamben and Foucault on Biopower and Biopolitics' in Matthew Calarco and Steven DeCaroli (eds), *Giorgio Agamben: Sovereignty A Life,* Stanford: Stanford University Press, 2007, pp. 201–18.

19. Giorgio Agamben, *Homo Sacer* (trans. Daniel Heller-Roazen), Stanford: Stanford University Press, 1998, p. 119.

20. Ibid., pp. 120 and 169.

21. Agamben, *Homo Sacer,* p. 131.

22. Ibid., p. 188.

23. Prompted, for example, by regional food crises; tens of millions of climate-displaced persons on the move, as the vanguard of a massive redistribution of human populations crossing borders uninvited; plus aggressive competition for the command of finite resources.

24. Agamben, *Homo Sacer,* p. 142.

25. In particular, the issue of scale begs review (for many years, the Greek model has been dismissed as unworkable for large populations – an argument that falls in the 'electronic age'). Existing referenda-based democratic models also beg examination.

26. On the issue of 'the people' see Fred Dallmayr, 'Post-metaphysical Politics: Heidegger and Democracy' in *The Other Heidegger,* Ithaca: Cornell University Press, 1993.

27. On this history see Christopher Hill, *The World Turned Upside Down,* Harmondsworth: Penguin Books, 1975.

28. C.B. Macpherson, *The Life and Times of Liberal Democracy,* Oxford: Oxford University Press, 1977, pp. 20–1.

29. Alain de Benoist, 'On Politics', *Telos* 125 (2002), p. 33.

30. Claude Lefort, *Democracy and Political Theory* (trans. David Macey), Cambridge: Polity Press, 1988, pp. 232–3. Fred Dallmayr in *The Other Heidegger* provides insightful commentary on Lefort's position.

31. For example see Neil Levi, 'Carl Schmitt and the Question of the Aesthetic', *New German Critique* 101, 34 (2) (2007), pp. 36–7.

32. Carl Schmitt, *The Crisis of Parliamentary Democracy* (trans. Ellen Kennedy), Cambridge, MA: MIT Press, 1988, p. 11.

33. See for example: Larry Diamond and Marc Plattner (eds), *Democracy: A Reader,* Baltimore: John Hopkins University Press, 2009; Robert Terchek and Thomas Conte (eds), *Democratic Political Theory: A Reader,* Lanham: Rowman & Littlefield, 2001. For a broad sample of more specialist writing see for example, Seyla Benhabib (ed.), *Democracy and Difference,* Princeton: Princeton University Press, 1996; Jürgen Habermas, *Theory of Communicative Action,* trans. Thomas McCarty, Boston: Beacon Press, 1981; Ernesto Laclau, *Emancipation(s),* London: Verso, 1996; Jan-Werner Müller, *A Dangerous Mind,* New Haven: Yale University Press, 2003; C.B. Macpherson, *The Life and Times of Liberal Democracy,* 1977; Alain de Benoist, 'On Politics'; Chantal Mouffe, *Dimensions of Radical Democracy,* London: Verso, 1995; Jacques Derrida, *Spectres of Marx,* New York: Routledge, 1994.

34. Seyla Benhabib (ed.), *Democracy and Difference.*

35. John Medearis, *Joseph Schumpeter's Two Theories of Democracy,* Cambridge, MA: Harvard University Press, 2001.

36. Ibid p. 5. While Medearis comprehensively and rigorously reviewed Schumpeter's entire oeuvre, it is his most influential book *Capitalism, Socialism and Democracy* (1942) that provided the armature around which the complexities of his project are most discernibly evident.

37. Ibid., p. 106.

38. Ibid., pp. 87–90.

39. Ibid.

40. Ibid., p. 88.

41. Ibid., p. 83.

42. Ibid., p. 9.

43. Tony Fry, *Design Futuring: Sustainability, Ethics and New Practice,* Oxford: Berg, 2009, pp. 126–7.

44. This is a key topic in Fry, *Design Futuring.*

45. Georges Bataille, 'Hegel, Death and Sacrifice' (trans. Jonathan Strauss), *Yale French Studies* 78 (1990), pp. 14–15.
46. Jenny Elkins, 'Whatever Politics', in Matthew Calarco and Steven DeCaroli (eds), *Giorgio Agamben: Sovereignty and Life,* Stanford: Stanford University Press, 2007, p. 89. In the same volume see also Matthew Calarco, 'Jamming the Anthropological Machine', pp. 163–79.
47. See John L. Esposito, *The Islamic Threat,* Oxford: Oxford University Press, 1999.
48. Ibid., p. 87.
49. On futuring see note 43.

Chapter 2: Inadequate Solutions of Now

1. Antonio Gramsci, *Selections from Prison Notebooks* (trans. Quintin Hoare and Geoffrey Nowell Smith), London: Lawrence & Wishart, 1971, pp. 325–34. Gramsci was transferred to a sanatorium in 1935 with a series of serious illnesses. He died early in 1937.
2. Joseph Marie Jacquard (1752–1834) was a French textile manufacturer. His loom is recognized as a significant technology in the pre-history of computing.
3. This was pointed out by Martin Heidegger in his 1949 essay 'The Question Concerning Technology' (trans. William Lovitt) in Martin Heidegger, *The Question Concerning Technology and Other Essays*, New York: Harper Torchbooks, 1977, pp. 3–35.
4. The convergence between Schmitt and Heidegger on the question of technology is noted in John McCormick, *Carl Schmitt's Critique of Liberalism,* Cambridge: Cambridge University Press, 1997, p. 45. We should note that this convergence was not mere chance but the result of their both being in the same cultural environment of the radical right, where a concern with technology was a major preoccupation. They also both shared a friendship with one of the most influential thinkers of this culture: Ernst Jünger (see note 6 below).
5. One of the earliest and most powerful expositions of the self-making by the made can be found in the work of André Leroi-Gourhan in the 1940s, revisited and advanced more recently by Bernard Stiegler in *Technics and Time 1* (trans. Richard Beardsworth and George Collins), Stanford: Stanford University Press, 1998.

6. Schmitt was writing on the dangers of technology from the early 1920s. The point about neutralization was made in 1929, in an essay where he makes connections between the mastery of nature, neutralization and the extension of modernity, see 'The Age of Neutralisation and Technology' (trans. Matthias Konzett and John McCormick), *Telos 96*, Summer (1993), pp. 130–42. Schmitt was writing some twenty years before Heidegger's influential essay 'The Question Concerning Technology' which was first presented as a lecture in Bremen in 1949. Heidegger said his own essay 'Concerning "The Line", dedicated to Jünger on his sixtieth birthday 'owes enduring advancement' to Ernst Jünger's *Der Arbeiter* published in 1932. During this period, Jünger and Schmitt were close friends (see Jeffrey Herf, *Reactionary Modernism: Technology, Culture and Politics in Weimer and the Third Reich,* Cambridge: Cambridge University Press, 1984, pp. 115–16. These observations give some sense of Schmitt having played a significant part in the formation of an intellectual culture that was critical of technology; furthermore, this was at a level of sophistication that in many respects has still not fully arrived (in fact the technophillia of the current moment considerably reduces the prospect of the moment's arrival). That the reactionary, non-democratic right had a more critical perspective than the progressive left is another reason for the delay. It should also be added that this intellectual culture had a significant literature and notable figures in addition to those named – such as Oswald Spengler, Hans Freyer, Werner Sombart, Manfred Schroter, Carl Weile and Friedrich Dessauer.
7. In my youth, many older people still feared technologies like the telephone, X-Ray machine and escalator, while a few generations earlier photography, trains, and then motor cars, all induced widespread fear in the population.
8. The term 'double bind' indicates being locked into 'solutions' for which no problem has been defined; it was coined by Gregory Bateson, *Steps to an Ecology of Mind,* St Albans: Granada/Paladin, 1969, pp. 242–8. As an example of transfer of one 'nature' to another the Marxian term 'dead labour' is of interest here. 'Dead labour' refers to the transfer of embodied knowledge into disembodied, economically employable, accumulative forms – initially machines, now machines directed by software, that 'learn' by the feedback of performance data.
9. McCormick, *Carl Schmitt's Critique of Liberalism,* p. 253.
10. Ibid.
11. Fred Dallmayr, 'Rethinking the Political' in *The Review of Politics*, Fall (1990), p. 541.

12. The claim that leadership in this activity has been lacking, and could be expected to come from the philosophy of technology, begs to be tested.
13. How to name the diversity of human beings is increasingly an issue that the very notion of humanity conceals. Current ways of naming are both underdeveloped (failing to recognize diversity) and inappropriately technophillic (such as taking up science fiction's notion of a cyborg).
14. Heidegger, *The Question Concerning Technology,* p. 32.
15. This is what Schmitt says on this topic: 'The masses have a religion of technicity, and every technological progress appears to them to be at the same time a perfection of man himself, a direct step to the earthly paradise of the one world.' Cited in Heinrich Meier, *Carl Schmitt and Leo Strauss: The Hidden Dialogue*, Chicago, IL: University of Chicago Press, 1995, p. 73, n. 86.
16. Ibid.
17. Cited by Heinrich Meier, *Carl Schmitt and Leo Strauss: The Hidden Dialogue,* p. 114.
18. Schmitt actually took up and radicalized the influential ideas of Max Weber on the mechanistic 'nature' of the modern world and its institutions.
19. On Metrofitting see the booklet by Tony Fry, Nora Kinnunen, Petra Perolini and William Odom, *Metrofitting: Adaptation, the City and Impacts of the Coming Climate,* Brisbane: Griffith University, Queensland College of Art, 2009.
20. The City Move project was supported by: the European Union Regional Development Fund; the Swedish Ministry of Enterprise, Energy and Communication; the Municipality of Gellivare; the County Administrative Board of Norrbotten; the Swedish Industrial Design Foundation; and the International Council of Societies of Industrial Design.
21. The information given here draws on LKAB, *A Historic Journey,* LKAB Communication, 2006 and Brigitta Svensson and Ola Wetterberg (eds), *Malmberget: Structural Change and Cultural Heritage Processes – A Case Study,* Stockholm: The Swedish National Heritage Board, 2009.
22. 'Climate change and our coast', *Future Tense* (presented by Antony Funnell), ABC Radio National, 19 November 2009.

Chapter 3: Redirection, Design and Things

1. Redirective practice is presented at length in Tony Fry, *Design Futuring: Sustainability, Ethics, New Practice,* Oxford: Berg, 2009.
2. See note 19 of chapter 2.
3. A crude but powerful illustration of instrumentalism can be seen in the dramatic shift in university education of most nations since the 1960s, away from traditional academic disciplines to vocational education directly serving the economy (the proliferation of courses in business, tourism, management, accountancy, marketing, information technology, contract administration, and so forth).
4. It's worth noting what Heidegger says here: 'philosophising proper is a questioning concerning *phusis* in this dual sense: questioning concerning beings as a whole, and together with this, questioning concerning being. This is how things stand for Aristotle. At the same time Aristotle says nothing, or we have nothing handed down, about how he thinks these two orientations of questioning in their unity, to what extent precisely this questioning in its dual orientation constitutes philosophising proper. While this quest remains open to this day, it is *de facto* no longer even posed. Martin Heidegger, *The Fundamental Concepts of Metaphysics: World, Finitude, Solitude* (trans. William McNeill and Nicholas Walker) (Bloomington: Indiana University Press, 1995), p. 33. Note that the term *phusis* is a transliteration of the Greek in the actual quotation cited – it is often translated as 'nature' but it is far more. It, in fact, designates everything that 'is'; the term was diminished in the Roman translation to *natura* (bursting forth from, giving birth to or in German *ursprung*); this, in turn, was further reduced by the English 'nature'.
5. For all the efforts of anthropology and sociology, culture is far more complex than these disciplines recognized. What has to be rejected is a conservative (liberal) reduction of culture to a 'culture of nature' that rests with cultivation (of being, soil, soul and sensibilities) within a 'natural' process wherein nature is inscribed with an impetus toward its own overcoming – the product of this overcoming being 'culture'. This was extolled by Leo Strauss in his 'radicalizing' of Schmitt's view of culture, which was posed against a universal culture that Schmitt saw as a means, along with technology, of serving 'neutralization and depoliticization'. See Heinrich Meier, *Carl Schmitt and Leo Strauss*, pp. 30–3, 41, 94–8. On the 'political economy of the sign' see Jean Baudrillard, *For a Critique of the Political Economy of the Sign* (trans. Charles Levin) (St Louis: Telos Press, 1981).

6. At the time of writing, to give one very basic example, the rate of unemployment in Timor-Leste is over 70 per cent. For people without an income, the only cooking fuel is wood. This has led to large-scale environmental damage as the countryside is stripped bare of timber and soil erosion sets in.

7. This is a 'quality-based economic paradigm.' See Fry, *Design Futuring* pp. 217–21.

8. David Hall and Roger Ames, *Anticipating China*, New York: SUNY Press, 1995, p.104.

9. Martin Heidegger, *Aristotle's Metaphysics* Θ *1-3 On the Essence of Force* (trans. Walter Brogan and Peter Warnek), Bloomington: Indiana University Press, 1995, see especially pp. 64–98.

10. François Jullien, *The Propensity of Things* (trans. Janet Lloyd), New York: Zone Books, 1995.

11. François Jullien, *A Treatise on Efficacy* (trans. Janet Lloyd), Honolulu: University of Hawaii, 2004, p. 45.

12. Ibid., p. 51.

13. Ibid., p. 45.

14. Ibid., p. 222.

15. The first physician sees and removes the spirit of sickness before it takes shape, and his name does not get out of the house; the second cures sickness in its early stages, and his name does not get out of the neighbourhood; and the third physician punctures veins, prescribes potions and massages the body, and his name is known among the lords. Of this story a Ming commentator wrote: 'What is essential for leaders, generals and ministers in running countries is no more than this.' Sun Tzu, *The Art of War* (trans. Thomas Cleary), Boston: Shambhala, 1988, p. 1.

16. François Jullien, *A Treatise on Efficacy,* pp. 86–91.

17. Heidegger, *Aristotle's Metaphysics*, p. 72.

18. Jullien, *The Propensity of Things* pp. 219–58.

19. Ibid., pp. 220–1.

20. Jullien, *The Propensity of Things*, p. 221. For the reference to Leibnitz see n. 3, p. 301.

21. Robert A. Scalapino and George T. Yu, *Modern China and Its Revolutionary Process*, Berkeley: University of California Press, 1985, pp. 11–39.

22. Australian Government, *Defence White Paper*, Canberra, 2009, para 4.37.

23. Ibid., see especially paras 1.9, 4.5, 4.7, 4.35, 4.60 and 4.61.

24. This project started in April 2009, directed by Tony Fry from Griffith University in Brisbane with two researchers based in Dili.
25. For more detailed discussion of a specific example of indigenous cash economies see Tony Fry and Anne-Marie Willis, 'Aboriginal Art: Symptom or Success?' *Art in America*, July (1989), pp. 108–16 and 160–3.

Part II: Re-framing the Political

1. Jean-François Lyotard, *The Inhuman* (trans. Geoffrey Bennington and Rachael Bowlby), Stanford: Stanford University Press, 1988, p. 2.

Chapter 4: The Political, Sovereignty and Design

1. The potential conflict and social destabilization that climate change might bring is given significant attention in, for example, the priorities outlined in the Australian Government's 2009 White Paper on Defence.
2. Besides the prospect of more nations acquiring nuclear arms, the more nuclear power stations, the more nuclear targets and sources of 'dirty bombs'.
3. Carl Schmitt, *Political Theology: Four Chapters on the Concept of Sovereignty* (trans. George Schwab), Chicago: Chicago University Press, 2005.
4. On 'ban' and an elaboration of this discussion see Giorgio Agamben, *Homo Sacer* (trans. Daniel Heller-Roazen), Stanford: Stanford University Press, 1998, pp. 28–31.
5. Ibid, p. 28.
6. Ibid, pp. 39–40.
7. Alain de Benoist, 'What is Sovereignty?' *Telos* 116 (1999), pp. 98–118.
8. Giorgio Agamben, *State of Exception* (trans. Kevin Attell), Chicago: Chicago University Press, 2005, p. 15.
9. Giorgio Agamben, *Homo Sacer,* p. 181.
10. Carl Schmitt, *Political Theology*, p. 1.
11. Ibid, p. 59.
12. White settlers and the security forces killed thousands of Mau Mau; many were tortured and then killed while 'attempting to escape'. By the end of 1954 more

than 80,000 people who survived were sent to concentration camps in which they were subjected to such levels of brutality and savagery that many of them died. Additionally, about 100,000 Kikuyu squatters were deported back to the reserves. In the camps not even the most basics of life were available. Detainees were kept short of rations, overworked, subjected to brutality and humiliated. Their treatment was in total violation of the United Nations Universal Declaration on Human Rights. The situation was not exposed until 1959, when eleven Mau Mau were murdered at the remote concentration camp at Hola; nobody was ever punished for this crime. Joseph Ndecha, the Mau Mau chairman, spent fifteen years gathering evidence on behalf of the tens of thousands of Kenyans detained in concentration camps and many others who had been deprived of their land and property by the British. See, for example, Brian Lapping, *End of Empire,* London: Granada Publishing Ltd, 1985; Robert Edgerton, *Mau Mau: An African Crucible,* London: I. B. Tauris & Co, 1990.

13. Agamben, *State of Exception,* p. 3.

14. Agamben, *Home Sacer,* p. 52.

15. The idea of subsidiarity was originally proposed by Johannes Althusius (1557–1638) and is outlined in de Benoist, 'What is Sovereignty?' Its basic principle is that the local level retains, rather than delegates, power. All those things it cannot do, it delegates upwards (or outward).

16. The term 'law' is used here in a broad sense. This means it embraces judicial powers to prohibit and punish certain kinds of unsustainable actions, but equally acts to establish an ethical regime, codes of moral and economic conduct while also recognizing the need to comply with the laws of 'sustaining materiality' (*phusus*) re-conceptualized to reverse its reduction to nature.

17. The life-work of Joseph Needham in recovering the lost material history of Ancient China is an interesting example of a project that begs re-reading – not in terms of what it tells us about the past but rather what it contains that is relevant to the future. See the many extraordinary volumes of his *Science and Civilisation in China* published by Cambridge University Press over more than four decades.

18. Martin Heidegger, 'The Thing' in *Poetry, Language, Thought* (trans. Albert Hofstadter), New York: Harper & Row, 1971, pp. 163–86.

Chapter 5: In the Shadow of Carl Schmitt's Politics

1. While the concept of relationality has its roots in pre-Socratic thought, its modern expression rests with Leibniz and his notion of the indivisibility and the relational connection between the fragment and the universe – his thinking on this topic is discussed by Ernst Cassirer, *The Philosophy of the Enlightenment* (trans. Fritz C. A. Koelln and James P. Pettegrove), Princeton: Princeton University Press, 2009 (revised edition), pp. 32–3.

2. Specifically, Derrida addressed an emergent transformation of international law, its concepts and modes of intervention in the face of the inadequacy of the discourse of human rights. Jacques Derrida, *Spectres of Marx: The State of the Debt, the Work of Mourning and the New International* (trans. Peggy Kamuf), London: Routledge, 1994, p. 85. In the context of our concerns, Derrida's confrontation with the ghost of Marx invites confrontation with another materialism, another determinism, that has no idealized destination, no 'end of' but, rather, a continuation of that which change sustains.

3. Ibid., p. 85.

4. Ibid., p. 87.

5. As discussed in relation to Kafka's novel, *The Enemy*, see Jan-Werner Muller, *A Dangerous Mind*, New Haven: Yale University Press, 2003, pp. 55–6.

6. Paul Hirst, 'Carl Schmitt's Decisionism' *Telos* 72 (1987), p. 23.

7. See Chapter 1 in Tony Fry, *Design Futuring: Sustainability, Ethics and New Practice,* Oxford: Berg, 2009.

8. Carl Schmitt (trans. George Schwab), *The Concept of the Political*, Chicago: Chicago University Press, 1996, pp. 62–3.

9. Ibid., p. 63.

10. See Heinrich Meier, *Carl Schmitt and Leo Strauss: The Hidden Dialogue* (trans. J. Harvey Lomax, Foreword by Joseph Cropsey), Chicago: University of Chicago Press, 1995, p. 104–5. We can note that Schmitt offered only one route to overcoming the political: a 'war against war' for the humanity of the humane is always negated in the inhumanity that is war in its making of the other, the enemy, as an inhuman other.

11. Martin Heidegger (1927), *Being and Time* (trans. John Macquarrie and Edward Robinson), London: Blackwell, 1962, pp. 396–400. See also Tony Fry (ed.), *RUATV? Heidegger and the Televisual*, Sydney: Power Publications, 1993.

12. Cultural Studies in its passage from Marxism to social democracy deployed its theoretical resources to claim popular culture as politically 'serious'. But in so doing, 'the serious' (as political, popular and entertaining) appeared to be taken seriously, as opposed to being recognized as inherently serious.

13. Paul Hirst, 'Carl Schmitt's Decisionism', pp. 21–2.

14. This was well before either Schmitt's or Heidegger's analysis of technology and its relation to the erasure of the political by the instrumental. See, for example, Carl Schmitt, *Political Theology* (trans. George Schwab), Chicago: University of Chicago Press, 1985 (first published in German 1922), p. 65.

15. Heinrich Meier, *Carl Schmitt and Leo Strauss: The Hidden Dialogue,* n. 40, p. 43.

16. Carl Schmitt, *The Crisis of Parliamentary Democracy* (trans. Ellen Kennedy), Cambridge (Mass): MIT Press, 1996, p. 24.

17. For one version of this situation see Michael Hardt and Antonio Negri, *Empire,* Cambridge (Mass): Harvard University Press, 2000.

18. Take for example Sheldon Wolin's consensual and diminished definition of the political as: ... 'an expression of the idea that a free society composed of diversities can nonetheless enjoy moments of commonality when, through public deliberation, collective power is used to promote or protect the well-being of the collectivity. Politics refers to the legitimisation and public contestation, primarily by organised and unequal social powers, over access to resources available to the public authorities of the collectivity.' Seyla Benhabib (ed.), *Democracy and Difference: Contesting the Boundaries of the Political,* Princeton: Princeton University Press, 1996, p. 31.

19. Cited by John McCormick, *Carl Schmitt's Critique of Liberalism,* Cambridge: Cambridge University Press, 1997, p. 42. The work cited by Schmitt was *Theodor Däubler (1916) 'Nordlicht': Drei Studien über die Elemente, den Geist und die Aktualität des Werkes,* Berlin.

20. These views were expressed in Leo Strauss's notes on Carl Schmitt in *The Concept of the Political*, archived in 1932 and published by Strauss in the 1960s – these notes are cited by Heinrich Meier *Carl Schmitt and Leo Strauss: The Hidden Dialogue* (see editorial note, p.120 and pp. 111–12).

21. Ibid., p. 45–6.

22. Ibid., p. 46.

23. See Tony Fry, *A New Design Philosophy: An Introduction to Defuturing,* Sydney: UNSW Press, 1999, pp. 227–51.

24. While the passage towards such a level of commodification was clearly signalled by Schmitt it was overtly designated by Heidegger as a major phenomenon of the modern age. The fact of human activity being 'consummated as culture' fed and formed 'the essence of a culture' that was to become 'the politics of culture'. Martin Heidegger 'The Age of the World Picture' in *The Question Concerning Technology and Other Essays* (trans. William Lovitt), New York: Harper & Row, 1977, p. 116.

25. C.B. Macpherson, *The Life and Times of Liberal Democracy*, Oxford: Oxford Univesity Press, 1977, pp. 79–82.

26. Ernesto Laclau says, for example, that 'radically democratic society' is plurality in which difference is the basis of identity. He also says as a 'socialist I am prepared to fight against capitalism for the hegemony of liberal institutions . . .' As there is no outside of capitalism, as its hegemony is predicated on there being only one mode of production (capitalism), what is there to fight? What does it mean to call oneself a socialist in this context (especially as the 'struggle' for social justice is a contest now within capitalism)? And, if what is being fought for are liberal institutions, why does he not call himself a liberal, for certainly there is a long history of this cause with liberalism? Ernesto Laclau, *Emancipation(s),* London: Verso, 1996, p. 121. Laclau's long-time collaborator, Chantal Mouffe, in her closing essay of an edited collection, describes radical democracy in this way: 'Its aim is to use the symbolic resources of the liberal democratic tradition to struggle for the deepening of the democratic revolution, knowing it's a never-ending process.' Chantal Mouffe (ed.), *Dimensions of Radical Democracy,* London: Verso, 1992, p. 238. In this context, one returns to Laclau and asks if, after all, the liberal cause is but a ploy?

27. Jacques Derrida, *Spectres of Marx,* p. 92.

28. Hegel, *Phenomenology of Spirit,* para 255, pp. 154–5.

29. On this history see Walter Kaufmann, *Hegel*, London: Weidenfield & Nicolson, 1966, and the introduction to Hegel's *Philosophy of Nature* (ed. and trans. M.J. Petry,) London: George, Allen & Unwin, 1970.

30. The connection between Nazism, biology and ecology was evident in both its eugenic theory of race and its 'blood-and-earth' centred ecology. Nazi ecology was especially theorized by Walther Schoenichen – the Nazi Chair for the Protection of Nature at the University of Berlin in his publications of the 1930s and 1940s. While Luc Ferry gives a useful account of this history, he mischievously employs

it to try to discredit ecological thought in general. See Luc Ferry, *The New Ecological Order* (trans. Carol Volk), Chicago: University of Chicago Press, 1995.

31. See Fry, *Design Futuring,* 2009.

32. These prospects, and more, are detailed at length in Gwynne Dyer, *Climate Wars,* Scribe: Melbourne, 2008. He references, for instance: a report by the 'Development Concepts and Doctrine Centre' of the British Ministry of Defence, *Global Strategic Trends Programme 2007–2036*; and a CNA Corporation report, *National Security and Climate Change,* 2007, funded by the US Department of the Navy.

33. See note 19 of Chapter 2.

Chapter 6: Pluralism Is a Political Problem

1. Heraclitus *Fragments* (trans. T.M. Robinson), Toronto: University of Toronto Press, 1987. See Fragments 12 and 91a in relation to rivers (his most memorable statement being that 'it is not possible to step into the same river twice', Fragment 91a); as for change, this is the focus of Fragments 30, 30a and 31b. His metaphors are powerful, loaded in a contemporary sense, and go to the 'fundamental world' (the actuality of the planetary qualities of 'the Earth'), which, as 'the same for all', is presented as an 'ever living fire, being kindled in measure and being put out in measure'.

2. Hannah Arendt, *The Life of the Mind*, New York: Harcourt, Brace & Co., 1978, p. 74.

3. A non-dualist relation of self and other underpins much of what Levinas argues in *Totality and Infinity* (trans. Alphonso Lingis), Pittsburgh: Duquesne University Press, 1969 and other works.

4. Maurice Merleau-Ponty, *The Visible and the Invisible* (trans. Alphonso Lingis), Evanston: Northwestern University Press, 1968, p. 248.

5. Ibid., p. 19. In certain respects, this notion of the plural owes a debt to, and is a criticism of, Heidegger. Dasein's being-in-the-world was for Heidegger a being-with (mitsein). However, it's claimed that Heidegger's exposition of Dasein's 'being there' is always a 'being-with-others'. This was the key to Arendt's notion of the significance of plurality. That Heidegger directed his concerns to the temporality and finitude of being, rather than towards 'being-with' is claimed as a major political and ethical delimitation of his work. On this, see Seyla Benhabib, *The Reluctant Modernism of Hannah Arendt*, London: Sage Publications, 1996, pp. 51–61 and 104 ff.

6. This criticism has a late work of Arendt as its focus – Hannah Arendt, *On Violence*, New York Harcourt Brace & Co., 1969. For examples of critical comments, see John McGowan and Stephan Leonard in Craig Calhoun and John McGowan (eds), *Hannah Arendt and the Meaning of Politics*, Minneapolis: University of Minnesota Press, 1997.

7. The work of David L. Hall and Roger T. Ames has been of note in establishing this understanding, see especially *Thinking Through Confucius*, New York: SUNY Press, 1987 and *Anticipating China*, New York: SUNY Press, 1995.

8. Hall and Ames, *Anticipating China*, p. 156.

9. The concept of ethnocide is drawn from Pierre Clastres 'Of ethnocide', in *Archaeology of Violence* (trans. Jeanine Herman), New York: Semiotext(e), 1994, pp. 43–52.

10. Louise Marcil-Lacoste, 'The Paradoxes of Pluralism', in Chantal Mouffe (ed.), *Dimensions of Radical Democracy*, London: Verso, 1992, p. 132.

11. For a full discussion of the disposition of things again see François Jullien, *The Propensity of Things* (trans. Janet Lloyd), New York: Zone Books, 1995.

12. Louise Marcil-Lacoste, 'The Paradoxes of Pluralism' in Mouffe (ed.), *Dimensions of Radical Democracy*, p. 136.

13. Hall and Ames, *Anticipating China*, p. 81.

14. Martin Heidegger, *Early Greek Thinking* (trans. David Farrell Krell and Frank A. Capuzzi), San Francisco: Harper & Row, 1975.

15. Hall and Ames, *Anticipating China*, pp. 90–1.

16. Lotze attempted to unify a modernized Cartesian view of the body as machine (publishing his *Metaphysik* in 1841 and then a *General Pathology and Therapy: As Mechanical Sciences* in 1842).

17. This comment, and the elaboration of the significance of Lotze is indebted to, if in some disagreement with, the opening of Louise Marcil-Lacoste's essay in Mouffe (ed.), *Dimensions of Radical Democracy* and the manner in which she uses the agency of William James to stand for a broader tendency of thought and contestation over the 'nature' of science from at least Kant onward.

18. Kirstie McClure, 'Pluralism and Political Identity' in Mouffe (ed.), *Dimensions of Radical Democracy*, pp. 113–15.

19. These observations are again drawn from an excellent survey by Louise Marcil-Lacoste in Mouffe (ed.), *Dimensions of Radical Democracy*, pp. 129–30.

20. The refusal or lack of identity is, of course, underpinned by a fundamental lack of recognition by the self and an other in a profoundly Hegelian sense:

'Self-consciousness exists in and for itself when, and by the fact that, it so exists for another: that is, it exists only in being acknowledged.' See the opening to 'Lordship and Bondage' in G.W.F. Hegel, *Phenomenology of Spirit* (trans. A.V. Miller), Oxford: Oxford University Press, 1977, p. 111.

21. As discussed by McCormick, Schmitt wrote at length in 1930 of an economy wherein pluralism reinvented feudalism. The power of trans-national corporations to influence governments, economies, labour movements, patterns of development and the movement of capital confirms this – see John McCormick, *Carl Schmitt's Critique of Liberalism,* Cambridge: Cambridge University Press, 1997, pp. 201.

22. Chantel Mouffe, *Dimensions of Radical Democracy,* p. 10.

23. Hall and Ames, *Anticipating China,* p. 173.

24. Ibid., p. 171. The central question to which they refer goes to the relation of reason and relativism – their position goes like this: The last desperate defence of the transcendentalists facing the inexorable pluralism of late-modern cultures is to level the charge of 'relativism' against any who would abandon the Enlightenment project. But, truth be told, struggles over relativism are in fact family quarrels among two sorts of transcendentalists.

25. Ibid., pp. 173–4. At this point Hall and Ames make reference to Jonathan Edwards' work on 'aesthetic pluralism' in America. In this context we should also recall Schmitt's major critique of the rise of aesthetics, via the guiding hand of cultural modernity and its most overt expression, romanticism, and its latter subset, modernism. This argument is presented in one of his most strident books, Carl Schmitt, *Political Romanticism* (trans. Guy Oaks), Cambridge, MA: MIT Press, 1986 (first published in Berlin in 1919). At the centre of Schmitt's polemic was the view that the world, the subject and a romantic spirit had been unified as a totalizing aesthetic force by which '. . . the romantic subject treats the world as an occasion and an opportunity for his romantic productivity.' This argument can be linked to unsustainability, for if Schmitt is correct, then the romantically produced aestheticized appearance of the world is directly connected to its operational concealment. Thus, for example, the image of a 'green and pleasant land' becomes a basis of judgement that negates recognition of the ecological consequences of how it was made and how it is kept green.

26. Adriaan Peperzak, *To The Other: An Introduction to the Philosophy of Emmanuel Levinas*, West Lafayette: Purdue University Press, 1993, p. 120. One can also note that equality is constituted as a 'threat of the same' within the debate on

pluralism within pluralism – again see Louise Marcil-Lacoste's essay in Mouffe (ed.), *Dimensions of Radical Democracy,* pp. 137–41. Also note that the meaning of *nomos* and the relation between it and *oikos* (which can be shorthanded as the relation between law and ecology) is an issue that begs serious exploration elsewhere. According to Schmitt, 'all human *nomoi* are "nourished by" a Godlike *nomos,* whatever it may be, meaning any *nomos* can grow like plans or property.' *Telos* 95, Spring (1993), pp. 39–51. See also G.L. Ulmen 'American Imperialism and International Law: Carl Schmitt on the US in World Affairs', *Telos* 72, Summer (1987), pp. 43–72 and Carl Schmitt, 'The Land of Appropriation of a New World' (trans. Gary Ulmen and Kizer Walker), *Telos* 109 (1996), pp. 29–80.

27. It is in the space between the other and the same that, for Levinas, ethics becomes possible. See Simon Critchley, *The Ethics of Deconstruction,* Oxford: Blackwell, 1992.

28. Martin Heidegger, *Nietzsche Vol. 2* (trans. David Farrell Krell), New York: Harper Collins, 1991, p. 109.

29. In 1923 in *Roman Catholicism and Political Form,* Schmitt prophetically writes: 'Modern technology easily becomes the servant of this or that want or need. In modern economy a completely irrational consumption conforms to a totally rationalized production. A marvellously rational mechanism serves one or another demand, always with the same earnestness and precision, be it for a silk blouse or poison gas or anything whatsoever.' Cited by McCormick, *Carl Schmitt's Critique of Liberalism,* p. 43.

30. This is argued by Ernesto Laclau and Chantel Mouffe, *Hegemony and Social Strategy,* London: Verso, 1985 and reiterated by Mouffe in Seyla Benhabib (ed.), *Democracy and Difference: Contesting the Boundaries of the Political,* Princeton: Princeton University Press, 1996, p. 247.

31. See Chantel Mouffe in Benhabib, *Democracy and Difference,* p. 246.

Chapter 7: Remaking Sovereignty

1. Martin Heidegger (trans. J. Glenn Gray), *What is Called Thinking,* New York: Harper & Row, 1968, p. 69. The term is equally translated as 'overman'.

2. As Georges Bataille knew well, and as Derrida reminded us, writing de-relationalizes (and so severs and subordinates); one would now have to add that in the shadow of the electronic word, the power of writing is at best in danger. See Jacques Derrida,

'From a Restricted to a General Economy' in *Writing and Difference* (trans. Alan Bass), Chicago: University of Chicago Press, 1978, pp. 251–77.

3. As we now know full well, the complexity of his moment was that a non-democratic political party was on the scene, with a strong intent to be the absolute power. In his gross error of judgement, compromised, pragmatic and misguided egoism, Schmitt believed he could appropriate, influence and inform the Nazi Party to posit the state as its primary instrument on which to build the Third Reich.

4. And with it the 'drummed up' debate on fear of the past decade will evaporate.

5. Carl Schmitt (trans. George Schwab), *The Concept of the Political,* Chicago: Chicago University Press, 1996, p. 67.

6. See Tony Fry, 'The Sustainment and its Dialectic', *Design Philosophy Papers One* (ed., Anne-Marie Willis) Ravensbourne: Team D/E/S Publications, 2004 and other related articles and discussions in the online version (www.desphilosophy.com) of this journal.

7. To cite two examples: 'Fundamental Sounds' was a hybrid performance presented at Queensland Conservatorium of Music in Brisbane in December 2007. It brought together jazz, the indigenous music of Australia, traditional Indonesian dance and graphical design in a dynamic live and electronic event that set out to ask and answer the question of what is actually fundamental, while demonstrating that making music is a 'commonality in difference' that all cultures share. The event was supported by the performers, a Brisbane university, a development corporation, an architectural practice, a design studio and a new media artist. Example two (discussed in more detail in Chapter 3) is more ambitious – the creation of an art and design school in Timor-Leste based on local culture, knowledge, need and sustainment. At the time of writing, the nation has no formal institution of this kind. In circumstances where there has been a great deal of violence, poverty and hardship such an institution provides the potential to form a very significant change community.

8. On Fukuyama, see Chapter 9.

Chapter 8: *Neu Bildung* for a New World

1. See the concluding discussion of Jean-Paul Sartre *Existentialism and Humanism* (trans. Philip Mairet), London: Eyre Methuen, 1948, p. 60.

2. Both 'autonomic technocentrism' and the 'ecology of the image' are interrogated in detail in Tony Fry, *A New Design Philosophy: An Introduction to Defuturing*, Sydney: UNSW Press, 1999.

3. The word '*Bildung*' has its origins in medieval mysticism, with echoes of the thinking in Hobbes; it ended up, via Herder, meaning the emergence and formation of humanity via cultivation. *Bildung* was given enormous momentum by Goethe. Essentially, the idea has its origins in the Greek notion of *phusis* – an 'emergence', a springing forth that was simplified by the Roman notions of *natura* and *cultus*, which, in turn, were diluted by the modern understanding of nature. Perhaps more astutely than anyone else, Wilheim von Humboldt, one of the dominant German intellectuals of the nineteenth century, drew out the difference between *Kulture* and *Bildung*.

4. There is also a much more complex relation between development, cultivation and culture which directs us back to the idea of culture in agriculture. See Raymond Williams, *Keywords,* London: Penguin, 1976.

5. Niklas Luhmann, *Social Systems* (trans. John Bednarz Jr. with Dirk Baecker) Stanford: Stanford University Press, 1995, p. 259. Luhmann quotes William von Humboldt, 'Theorie der Bildung des Menschen' *Werke* vol. 1, second edn, Darmstatt, 1969, p. 235 as follows: 'The ultimate task of our existence: to give as great as possible a content to the concept of humanity in our person, both during our lifetime and beyond it [there is no word of indestructibility] through the traces left behind by our life's work; this task can be fulfilled only by linking our ego with the world for the most universal, vivid, and freest reciprocal action.'

6. Ibid., p. 465.

7. Luhmann importantly deals with the afterlife of this 'development' as it had a profound impact upon identity, difference, self-reflection, self-reference and how the world is viewed. Ibid., pp. 464–7.

8. Bill Readings, *The University in Ruins*, Cambridge, MA: Harvard University Press, 1999, pp.74–5. It is clear from Readings that the concept of *Bildung* still has considerable significance for living and working in the ruins of the humanist university. The ability of the university, in its ruined state, to be able to generate new, major cultural formations has to be seriously doubted. This suggests that change has to come from an external force. Sustain-ability, and its proto-redirectional practices, has to arrive in the university – it cannot come from the university.

9. Ibid., pp. 63–7.

10. Ibid.
11. Hans-Georg Gadamer, *Truth and Method* (trans. Joel Weinsheimer and Donald G. Marshall), New York: Continuum/Crossroads Publishing, 1990, p. 11.
12. Its basic definition is attributed to Herder's notion of 'rising up the humanity through culture'. In this respect, *Bildung* is the agency within culture that cultivates humanizing potential. Ibid., p. 10.
13. Ibid., p. 9.
14. Ibid., p. 11.
15. Ibid.
16. Bill Readings, *The University in Ruins,* p. 65. The relation between German and Greek culture is not only complex but also tragic (evidenced by the history of fascism).
17. Gadamer, *Truth and Method,* p. 12.
18. Ibid., p. 12.
19. Ibid. We can also note that the connection to spirit begs a project of thinking the relation between *Bildung* and Aristotle's fusion of knowledge, life, soul and desire in his notion of *De Anima*.
20. Ibid., p. 13.
21. Ibid.
22. Ibid., p. 14.
23. Ibid.
24. Ibid., p. 16.
25. Bruno Latour, *Politics of Nature* (trans. Catherine Porter), Cambridge, MA: Harvard University Press, 2004.
26. See the debate between Tony Fry and Samer Akkach in *Design Philosophy Papers Collection Two* (ed. Anne-Marie Willis), Ravensbourne: Team D/E/S Publications, 2005 arising from Fry's article 'Design and the Question of Eurocentrism', in *Design Philosophy Papers* no. 6, 2003/4, www.desphilosophy.com.
27. See Donna Haraway, 'A Manifesto for Cyborgs' *Socialist Review* 15(2) (1986), pp. 65–108.
28. Bernard Stiegler, *Technics and Time 2* (trans. Stephen Barker), Stanford: Stanford University Press, 2009, pp. 87–197.
29. Wolfgang Palaver, 'Schmitt's Critique of Liberalism' *Telos* 102 (1995), p. 43. Let's say that from Hobbes onwards, it would be possible to show liberalism's implication in moving the anthropocentric 'nature' of Western human being into overt economic self-interest and thereafter, into complete and myopic selfishness.

30. Jean-Luc Nancy, *The Inoperative Community* (trans. Peter Conner *et al*), Minneapolis: University of Minnesota Press, 1992.

Chapter 9: On Freedom by Design

1. Maurice Merleau-Ponty, *Phenomenology of Perception* (trans. Colin Smith), London: Routledge, 1962, p. 452.
2. Jean-Luc Nancy, *The Experience of Freedom* (trans. Bridget McDonald), Stanford: Stanford University Press, 1993, p. 53.
3. Ibid., p. 32. See also Martin Heidegger, *Kant and the Problem of Metaphysics* (trans. Richard Taft), Bloomington, IA: University of Indiana Press, 1990.
4. Ibid., p. 4–5 and p. 68–9.
5. Michael Haar, *Heidegger and the Essence of Man* (trans. William McNeill), New York: SUNY Press, 1993.
6. Ibid., note this example as it forces a thinking of freedom that breaks free from received ideas.
7. Nancy, *The Experience of Freedom*, p. 1.
8. This view is rehearsed at length by David Ingram 'Habermas on Aesthetics and Rationality: Completing the Project of the Enlightenment', in *New German Critique*. 53 Spring/Summer (1991), pp. 67–103.
9. Nancy, *The Experience of Freedom,* p. 3.
10. Schelling published his treatise *On Human Freedom* as part of his *Philosophical Writings* in 1809. Central to this work was the 'Metaphysics of Evil as the Foundation of a System of Freedom', which Heidegger interprets at length in Martin Heidegger, *Schelling's Treatise on the Essence of Human Freedom* (trans. Joan Stambaugh), Athens, OH: Ohio University Press, 1985.
11. Nancy, *The Experience of Freedom,* p. 51.
12. Martin Heidegger, *The Essence of Human Freedom* (trans. Ted Sadler), London: Continuum, 2005, p. 94.
13. Ibid., pp. 94–5.
14. Ibid., pp. 19–20.
15. Nancy, *The Experience of Freedom*, p. 32.
16. Heidegger, *Kant and the Problem of Metaphysics*, p. 178.
17. Emmanuel Levinas, *Otherwise than Being or Beyond Essence* (trans. Alphonso Lingis), Dordrecht: Kluwer Academic, 1991, p. 116.

18. Emmanuel Levinas, *Collected Philosophical Papers* (trans. Alphonso Lingis), Dordrecht: Martinus Nijhoff Publishers, 1987, pp. 57–8.
19. Levinas, *Otherwise than Being,* p.116 and Theodor Adorno, *Negative Dialectics,* London: Routledge, 1973, p. 8.
20. Kant's causal model is discussed at length in Heidegger, *The Essence of Human Freedom,* pp. 15–22.
21. Ibid., pp. 62–6.
22. Adorno, *Negative Dialectics,* p. 213.
23. On this break see Gilles Deleuze, *Spinoza: Practical Philosophy* (trans. Robert Hurley), City Lights: San Francisco, 1988, pp. 69–71.
24. Levinas, *Otherwise than Being,* p. 116.
25. Emmanuel Levinas, 'Freedom and Command' *Collected Philosophical Papers* (trans. Alphonso Lingis), Dordrecht: Martinus Nijhoff, 1987, p. 17. Lest it should be thought that Levinas is being 'proto-fascist' here, it can be noted that he designated the first imposition on 'ourselves' (as opposed to others) and more poignantly, apart from his wife and daughters, all other members of his (Jewish) family died at the hands of the Nazis.
26. Adorno, *Negative Dialectics,* p. 233.
27. Ibid., p. 219.
28. Nancy, *The Experience of Freedom,* pp. 4–5.
29. Ibid., p. 104. These words come from Adorno's important chapter on freedom in *Negative Dialectics*, London: Routledge, 1973, pp. 214–15.
30. Heidegger, *Schelling's Treatise on the Essence of Human Freedom.*
31. Adorno, *Negative Dialectics* pp. 218–19.
32. Levinas, 'Freedom and Command', *Collected Philosophical Papers,* p. 17.
33. The most overt example is the theatre of the 'great TV debate' between the incumbent leader and challenger that has become a 'democratic election' fixity.
34. Paul Piccone, Gary Ulmen and Paul Gottfried, 'Ostracizing Carl Schmitt: Letters to the New York Review of Books', *Telos* 109 (1996), p. 87.
35. Tracy Strong, Foreword to Carl Schmitt, *Concept of the Political* (trans. George Schwab), Chicago: University of Chicago Press, 1996, p. xix. This view is confirmed by Jan-Werner Müller's reassessment of Schmitt's critique in *A Dangerous Mind*, New Haven: Yale University Press, 2003.
36. Ibid.

37. One can note here the dominance of the US in the formation of the United Nations, its rhetoric and liberal political foundation. *De facto*, the UN was, and in many respects still is, an instrument of modernity.

38. See John Rawls, *Political Liberalism,* New York: Columbia University Press, 1993 (generally regarded as the most influential work of its age).

39. Schmitt cited by Heinrich Meier, *Carl Schmitt and Leo Strauss: The Hidden Dialogue,* p. 38.

40. Schmitt's critical calling upon Hobbes is central the argument that Meier develops in *Carl Schmitt and Leo Strauss: The Hidden Dialogue*, pp. 30–8. The same claim of agency has been made of Locke, who brought liberalism and governmentality into closer articulation with his essay of political philosophy 'Two Treatise of Government' (1689–90) and his major statement on empiricism 'Concerning Human Understanding' (1690). Yet Leo Strauss's notes on Schmitt's concept of the political, turned in large part on his reading of Hobbes.

41. Cited by Macpherson, *Democratic Theory* (from Hobbes *English Works*, p. 3 first published in 1651), p. 240.

42. Cited by Meier, p. 73

43. Ibid p.73 n. 86.

44. Ibid.

45. Ibid., p. 100.

46. Ibid. The reference here to "partnership in consumption and production" is from Schmitt's 1932 treatise on the 'order of human things' cited by Meier, *Carl Schmitt and Leo Strauss: The Hidden Dialogue* p. 91. Equally Schmitt writes: 'That production and consumption, price formation and market have their own sphere and can neither be directed by ethics nor aesthetics, nor by religion, nor, least of all by politics was considered one of the few truly unquestionable dogmas of the liberal age.' *Concept of the Political,* p. 72.

47. We note here that Schmitt was far more ambivalent about the state than Hobbes, he writes: 'Although liberalism has not radically denied the state, it has, on the other hand, neither advanced a positive theory of the state nor on its own discovered how to reform the state, but has attempted only to tie the political to the ethical and to subjugate it to the economic. It has produced a doctrine of the separation and balance of powers, i.e., systems of checks and controls of state and government. This cannot be characterised as either a theory of state or a basic political principle.' *Concept of the Political*, p. 61.

48. Ibid., pp. 101–2.

49. As already registered, *Phusus* names the original Greek idea of the relationality of all things, from which the idea of nature, via the Roman *natura*, arrives as a degeneration.

50. Thomas Hobbes, *Leviathan,* (ed. Richard Tuck), Cambridge: Cambridge University Press, 1996, Chapter 31, p. 245.

51. Hobbes *Leviathan,* Chapter 14, pp. 91–2. Echoing Aristotle's notion of life force, he asserted that man is self-moving matter in motion. See Macpherson, *Democratic Theory* on Natural Rights in Hobbes and Locke, p. 226. Ulmen noted that Schmitt was fully aware that world disorder, the history of the concept of war and the history of international law were all intimately linked to each other, G.L. Ulmen, 'American Imperialism and International Law: Carl Schmitt on the US in World Affairs', *Telos* 72 (1987), pp.61–2. Schmitt provides a sobering word on the matter in *Concept of the Political*: 'A war waged to protect or expand economic power must, with the aid of propaganda, turn into a crusade and into the last war of humanity' (p.79).

52. What has been said clearly resonates with some of the conclusions of the early 1940s project of Theodor Adorno and Max Horkheimer, *Dialectic of Enlightenment* (trans. John Cummings), London: Verso, 1969. We note, however, the historicity of unsustainability (that is just starting to become 'visible' and arrive as a narrated history) suggests that the forces of destruction recognized by Adorno and Horkheimer were seriously underestimated when viewed from the present; even when they open on the concept of the Enlightenment by saying: 'In the most general sense of progressive thought, the Enlightenment has always aimed at liberating men from fear and establishing their sovereignty. Yet the fully enlightened earth radiates disaster triumphant. The program of the Enlightenment was the disenchantment of the world; the dissolution of myths and the substitution of knowledge for fancy' (p. 3).

53. Macpherson, *Democratic Theory*, p. 234.

54. Just in terms of thinkers, here is a history that weaves its way through the thought of Hobbes, Locke, Hume, Rousseau, Jefferson, Bentham, James Mill, John Stuart Mill, Hobhouse, Schumpter, Dahl, Schmitt, Strauss, Larmore, Oakshott, Rawls, Rorty and others.

55. Carl Schmitt, *The Crisis of Parliamentary Democracy* (trans. Ellen Kennedy), Cambridge, 1923.

56. War has become a 'fuzzy' category, no longer spatially confined or restricted to clearly identified combatants; casualties of non-combatants continually exceed numbers who fight.
57. See Schmitt, *The Concept of the Political*, pp. 73–6.
58. Francis Fukuyama, *The End of History and the Last Man*, New York: The Free Press, 1992.
59. G.W.F. Hegel, *Phenomenology of Spirit* (trans. A. V. Miller), Oxford: Oxford University Press, 1977, para. 255, p. 155.
60. Ibid., para. 292, p. 176–7. Hegel was well aware of the implication of recurrence, if not of change: 'The universal is thus, to begin with, only what remains identical with itself; its movement is only the uniform recurrence of the same action' (para 245, p. 147).
61. Heinrich Meier, *Carl Schmitt and Leo Strauss: The Hidden Dialogue*, p. 43, n. 40.
62. Ibid., p. 71.
63. A sustainably built building, crammed full of sustainable gizmos, can be the home of a company that markets rubbish foods, makes weapons electronic guidance systems, manages investments in biotech companies, sells mobile phone services or promotes gambling. Sustainable technologies are making no impression on growth-based economic development, consumerism or overall global environmental impacts – they are completely outpaced by the unsustainable.
64. Carl Von Clausewitz, *On War,* London: Penguin Books, 1988, p. 119.
65. Hobbes, *Leviathan,* Introduction, p. 9.

Chapter 10: Design Beyond the Limits

1. This has also been argued at length elsewhere, see: Tony Fry, *A New Design Philosophy,* Sydney: NSW University Press, 1999; Tony Fry, *Design Futuring: Sustainability: Ethics and New Practice,* London: Berg, 2009 and in numerous articles (especially published by *Design Philosophy Papers*).
2. On limit and delimitation see John Sallis, *Delimitation: Phenomenology and the End of Metaphysics*, Bloomington: Indiana University Press, 1995. With reference to the Greeks, see p. xiii.
3. Clearly his thinking overlapped with the German concept of *'bildung'*.

4. Carl Schmitt, 'The Legal World Revolution (trans. G.L. Ulmen) in *Telos* 72 (1987), p. 88.

5. Carl Schmitt, *Concept of the Political* (trans. George Schwab), Chicago: University of Chicago Press, 1996, p. 54.

6. John Dewey, *Liberalism and Social Action,* p. 202 and *Freedom and Culture,* p. 130 and p. 125 as cited by C.B. Macpherson, *The Life and Times of Liberal Democracy,* Oxford: Oxford University Press, 1977, pp. 73–5.

7. For a developed exposition of this view see Larry A. Hickman, *John Dewey's Pragmatic Technology,* Bloomington: Indiana University Press, 1990, pp. 140–205.

8. Schmitt, *Concept of the Political,* p. 57.

9. For a full account of this bizarre relation between technology, the past, fantasy and fascism see Jeffrey Herf, *Reactionary Modernism: Technology, Culture, and Politics in Weimar and the Third Reich,* Cambridge: Cambridge University Press, 1984.

10. We can view the face of ethnocentricity with the instruments of logocentrism!

11. John Rawls, *A Theory of Justice,* Cambridge, MA: Harvard University Press, 1971. This work was directly bonded to a political philosophy of liberalism in presented in his 1993 *Political Liberalism,* New York: Columbia University Press.

12. Martin Heidegger, *Nietzsche* (ed. David Farrell Krell., trans. Joan Stambaugh, David Farrell Krell, Frank A. Capuzzi), New York: Harper Collins, 1991, vol. 3, pp. 141–7 and pp. 35–51.

13. Ibid., p. 142.

14. The mode of the 'thinging' of the designed thing as it does 'good'/sustains.

15. Fred Dallmayr, *The Other Heidegger,* Ithaca: Cornell University Press, 1993, p. 41.

16. Martin Heidegger, *The Question Concerning Technology and Other Essays* (trans. William Lovitt), New York: Harper & Row, 1977, pp. 115–54.

17. Ibid., pp. 153–4.

18. Friedrich Nietzsche, *Thus Spoke Zarathustra* (trans. R.J. Hollingdale), Harmondsworth: Penguin Books, 1969, p. 85.

19. Such a disruption was powerfully voiced by Maurice Merleau-Ponty in his chapter 'The Thing and the Natural World' in *Phenomenology of Perception* published in France in 1945 and translated into English in 1962 (London: RKP).

20. A continuum of these concerns is graphically illustrated by Marshall McLuhan's seminal essay 'The Medium is the Message' in *Understanding Media,* London: Abacus, 1964, pp. 15–30, through to its reworking and extension by Jean

Baudrillard in essays like his title essay in *In the Shadow of the Silent Majority*, New York: Semiotext(e), 1983, pp. 1–64.

21. Jacques Derrida, *Spectres of Marx* (trans. Peggy Kamuf), London: Verso, 1994, p 79.

22. Ibid., pp. 79–84. Derrida's remarks here are usefully supplemented by his essay 'Call it a Day for Democracy'. See Jacques Derrida, *The Other Heading* (trans. Pascale-Anne Brault and Michael Naas), Bloomington: Indiana University Press, 1992, pp. 84–109.

Select Bibliography

Adorno, Theodor and Max Horkheimer,
Dialectic of Enlightenment (trans.
John Cumming), London: Verso,
1969.

Adorno, Theodor, *Negative Dialectics*
(trans. E.B. Aston), London:
Routledge, 1973.

Agamben, Giorgio, *Homo Sacer* (trans.
Daniel Heller-Roazen), Stanford:
Stanford University Press, 1998.

Agamben, Giorgio, *State of Exception*
(trans. Kevin Attell), Chicago:
Chicago University Press, 2005.

Amin, Samir, *Unequal Development*
(trans. Brian Pearce), Hassocks:
Harvester, 1976.

Arendt, Hannah, *On Violence*, New York:
Harcourt Brace & Co., 1969.

Arendt, Hannah, *The Life of the Mind*,
New York: Harcourt, Brace & Co.,
1978.

Baudrillard, Jean, *For a Critique of the
Political Economy of the Sign* (trans.
Charles Levin), St Louis: Telos Press,
1981.

Baudrillard, Jean, *In the Shadow of the
Silent Majority* (trans. Paul Foss, Paul
Patton and John Johnson), New York:
Semiotext(e), 1983.

Benhabib, Seyla (ed.), *Democracy
and Difference: Contesting the
Boundaries of the Political*,
Princeton: Princeton University
Press, 1996.

Benhabib, Seyla, *The Reluctant
Modernism of Hannah Arendt*,
London: Sage Publications,
1996.

Calarco, Matthew and Steven DeCaroli
(eds), *Giorgio Agamben: Sovereignty
A Life*, Stanford: Stanford University
Press, 2007.

Calhoun, Craig and John McGowan
(eds), *Hannah Arendt and the
Meaning of Politics*, Minneapolis:
University of Minnesota Press, 1997.

Cassirer, Ernst, *The Philosophy of the
Enlightenment* (trans. Fritz C. A.
Koelln and James P. Pettegrove),
Princeton: Princeton University Press,
2009 (revised edition).

Clastres, Pierre, 'Of Ethnocide' in
Archaeology of Violence (trans.
Jeanine Herman), New York:
Semiotext(e), 1994.

Critchley, Simon, *The Ethics of
Deconstruction,* Oxford: Blackwell,
1992.

Dallmayr, Fred, *The Other Heidegger,*
Ithaca: Cornell University Press,
1993.

Davis, Mike, *Planet of Slums,* London:
Verso, 2006.

Deleuze, Gilles, *Spinoza: Practical
Philosophy* (trans. Robert Hurley),
San Francisco: City Lights, 1988.

Derrida, Jacques, *Writing and Difference*
(trans. Alan Bass), Chicago:
University of Chicago Press, 1978.

Derrida, Jacques, *The Other Heading*
(trans. Pascale-Anne Brault and
Michael Naas), Bloomington: Indiana
University Press, 1992.

Derrida, Jacques, *Spectres of Marx:
The State of the Debt, the Work of
Mourning and the New International*
(trans. Peggy Kamuf), London:
Routledge, 1994.

Diamond, Larry and Marc Plattner (eds),
Democracy: A Reader, Baltimore:
John Hopkins University Press, 2009.

Dyer, Gwynne, *Climate Wars,*
Melbourne: Scribe, 2009.

Edgerton, Robert, *Mau Mau: An African
Crucible,* London: I. B. Tauris & Co.,
1990.

Esposito, John L., *The Islamic Threat,*
Oxford: University of Oxford Press,
1999.

Ferry, Luc, *The New Ecological
Order* (trans. Carol Volk), Chicago:
University of Chicago Press, 1995.

Foucault, Michel, *Madness and
Civilization* (trans. Richard Howard),
London: Tavistock Publications, 1967.

Foucault, Michel, *Discipline and Punish*
(trans. Alan Sheridan), London: Allen
Lane, 1977.

Foucault, Michel, *History of Sexuality*
vol. 1 (trans. Robert Hurley), New
York: Penguin Books, 1981.

Fry, Tony (ed.), *RUATV? Heidegger
and the Televisual,* Sydney: Power
Publications, 1993.

Fry, Tony, *A New Design Philosophy: An
Introduction to Defuturing,* Sydney:
UNSW Press, 1999.

Fry, Tony, *Design Futuring:
Sustainability, Ethics and New
Practice,* Oxford: Berg, 2009.

Fry, Tony, Nora Kinnunen, Petra
Perolini and Will Odom, *Metrofitting:
Adaptation, the City and Impacts
of the Coming Climate*, Brisbane:

Griffith University, Queensland College of Art, 2009.

Fukuyama, Francis *The End of History and the Last Man*, New York: The Free Press, 1992.

Gadamer, Hans-Georg, *Truth and Method* (trans. Joel Weinsheimer and Donald G. Marshall), New York: Continuum/Crossroads Publishing, 1990.

Gramsci, Antonio, *Selections from Prison Notebooks* (trans. Quintin Hoare and Geoffrey Nowell Smith), London: Lawrence & Wishart, 1971.

Habermas, Jürgen, *The Theory of Communicative Action* (trans. Thomas McCarthy), Boston: Beacon Press, 1984, vol. 1.

Hall, David L. and Roger T. Ames, *Thinking Through Confucius*, New York: SUNY Press, 1987.

Hall, David and Roger Ames, *Anticipating China*, New York: SUNY Press, 1995.

Hardt, Michael and Antonio Negre, *Empire*, Cambridge, MA: Harvard University Press, 2000.

Haar, Michael, *Heidegger and the Essence of Man* (trans. William McNeill), New York: SUNY Press, 1993.

Hawken, Paul, Amory Lovins and L. Hunter Lovins, *Natural Capitalism: Creating the Next Industrial Revolution*, New York: Little Brown & Co., 1999.

Hegel, G.W.F., *(Hegel's) Philosophy of Nature* (ed. and trans. M.J. Petry), London: George Allen & Unwin, 1970.

Hegel, G.W.F., *Phenomenology of Spirit* (trans. A.V. Miller), Oxford: Oxford University Press, 1977.

Martin Heidegger, *Being and Time* (trans. John Macquarrie and Edward Robinson), London: Blackwell, 1962.

Heidegger, Martin, *What is Called Thinking?* (trans. J.Glenn Gray), New York: Harper & Row, 1968.

Heidegger, Martin, *Poetry, Language, Thought* (trans. Albert Hofstadter), New York: Harper & Row, 1975.

Heidegger, Martin, *Early Greek Thinking* (trans. David Farrell Krell and Frank A. Capuzzi), San Francisco: Harper & Row, 1975.

Heidegger, Martin, *The Question Concerning Technology and Other Essays* (trans. William Lovitt), New York: Harper Torchbooks, 1977.

Heidegger, Martin, *Schelling's Treatise on the Essence of Human Freedom* (trans. Joan Stambaugh), Athens: Ohio University Press, 1985.

Heidegger, Martin, *Kant and the Problem of Metaphysics* (trans. Richard Taft), Bloomington: University of Indiana Press, 1990.

Heidegger, Martin, *Nietzsche Vol. 2* (trans. David Farrell Krell), New York: HarperCollins, 1991.

Heidegger, Martin, *Nietzsche* Vol. 3 (ed. David Farrell Krell., trans. Joan Stambaugh, David Farrell Krell, Frank.A Capuzzi), New York: HarperCollins, 1991.

Heidegger, Martin, *Aristotle's Metaphysics Θ 1–3 On the Essence of Force* (trans. Walter Brogan and Peter Warnek), Bloomington: Indiana University Press, 1995.

Heidegger, Martin, *The Fundamental Concepts of Metaphysics: World, Finitude, Solitude* (trans: William McNeill and Nicholas Walker), Bloomington: Indiana University Press, 1995.

Heidegger, Martin, *Contributions to Philosophy (From Enowning)* (translation of the *Beiträge* by Parvis Emad and Kenneth Maly), Bloomington: Indiana University Press, 1999.

Heraclitus, *Fragments* (trans. T.M. Robinson), Toronto: University of Toronto Press, 1987.

Herf, Jeffrey, *Reactionary Modernism: Technology, Culture and Politics in Weimer and the Third Reich*, Cambridge: Cambridge University Press, 1984.

Hickman, Larry A., *John Dewey's Pragmatic Technology*, Bloomington: Indiana University Press, 1990.

Hill, Christopher, *The World Turned Upside Down*, Harmondsworth: Penguin Books, 1975.

Hobbes, Thomas, *Leviathan*, Richard Tuck (ed.), Cambridge: Cambridge University Press, 1996.

Jullien, François, *The Propensity of Things* (trans. Janet Lloyd), New York: Zone Books, 1995.

Jullien, François, *A Treatise on Efficacy* (trans. Janet Lloyd), Honolulu: University of Hawaii, 2004.

Kaufmann, Walter, *Hegel*, London: Weidenfeld & Nicolson, 1966.

Laclau, Ernesto, *Emancipation(s)*, London: Verso, 1996.

Laclau, Ernesto and Chantel Mouffe, *Hegemony and Social Strategy: Towards a Radical Democratic Politics*, London: Verso, 1985.

Lapping, Brian, *End of Empire*, London: Granada Publishing Ltd, 1985.

Latour, Bruno, *Politics of Nature* (trans. Catherine Porter), Cambridge: Harvard University Press, 2004.

Lefort, Claude, *Democracy and Political Theory* (trans. David Macey), Cambridge: Polity Press, 1988.

Levinas, Emmanuel, *Totality and Infinity* (trans. Alphonso Lingis), Pittsburgh: Duquesne University Press, 1969.

Levinas, Emmanuel, *Collected Philosophical Papers* (trans. Alphonso Lingis), Dordrecht: Martinus Nijhoff Publishers, 1987.

Levinas, Emmanuel, *Otherwise than Being or Beyond Essence* (trans. Alphonso Lingis), Dordrecht: Kluwer Academic, 1991.

Lotringer, S. *Foucault Live (Interviews 1966–84)* (trans. J. Johnson), New York: Semiotext(e), 1989.

Luhmann, Niklas, *Social Systems* (trans. John Bednarz Jr. with Dirk Baecker), Stanford: Stanford University Press, 1995.

Lyotard, Jean-François, *The Inhuman* (trans. Geoffery Bennington and Rachael Bowlby), Stanford: Stanford University Press, 1988.

Macpherson, C.B., *Democracy Theory: Essays in Retrieval*, Oxford: Clarendon University Press, 1973.

Macpherson, C.B., *The Life and Times of Liberal Democracy*, Oxford: Oxford University Press, 1977.

McCormick, John, *Carl Schmitt's Critique of Liberalism*, Cambridge: Cambridge University Press, 1997.

McLuhan, Marshall, *Understanding Media*, London: Abacus, 1964.

Meier, Heinrich, *Carl Schmitt and Leo Strauss: The Hidden Dialogue*, Chicago: University of Chicago Press, 1995.

Medearis, John, *Joseph Schumpeter's Two Theories of Democracy*, Cambridge: Harvard University Press, 2001.

Merleau-Ponty, Maurice, *Phenomenology of Perception* (trans. Colin Smith), London: Routledge: 1962.

Mouffe, Chantal, (ed.), *Dimensions of Radical Democracy*, London: Verso, 1992.

Mouffe, Chantal, (ed.), *The Challenge of Carl Schmitt*, London: Verso, 1999.

Müller, Jan-Werner, *A Dangerous Mind*, New Haven: Yale University Press, 2003.

Nancy, Jean-Luc, *The Inoperative Community* (trans. Peter Conner et al.), Minneapolis: University of Minnesota Press, 1992.

Nancy, Jean-Luc, *The Experience of Freedom* (trans. Bridget McDonald), Stanford: Stanford University Press, 1993.

Nietzsche, Friedrich, *Thus Spoke Zarathustra* (trans. R.J. Hollingdale), Harmondsworth: Penguin Books, 1969.

Peperzak, Adriaan, *To The Other: An Introduction to the Philosophy of Emmanuel Levinas*, West Lafayette: Purdue University Press, 1993.

Rawls, John, *A Theory of Justice,* Cambridge: Harvard University Press, 1971.

Rawls, John, *Political Liberalism,* New York: Columbia University Press, 1993.

Readings, Bill, *The University in Ruins*, Cambridge: Harvard University Press, 1999.

Sallis, John, *Delimitation: Phenomenology and the End of Metaphysics*, Bloomington: Indiana University Press, 1995.

Scalapino, Robert A. and George T. Yu, *Modern China and Its Revolutionary*

Process, Berkeley: University of California Press, 1985.

Sartre, Jean-Paul, *Existentialism and Humanism* (trans. Philip Mairet), London: Eyre Methuen, 1948.

Schmitt, Carl, *Political Theology* (trans. George Schwab), Chicago: University of Chicago Press, 1985.

Schmitt, Carl, *Political Romanticism* (trans. Guy Oaks), Cambridge: MIT Press, 1986.

Schmitt, Carl (1923), *The Crisis of Parliamentary Democracy* (trans. Ellen Kennedy), Cambridge: MIT Press, 1988.

Stiegler, Bernard, *Technics and Time 1* (trans. Richard Beardsworth and George Collins), Stanford: Stanford University Press, 1998.

Stiegler Bernard, *Technics and Time 2* (trans. Stephen Barker), Stanford: Stanford University Press, 2009.

Stambaugh, Joan, *The Finitude of Being*, New York: SUNY Press, 1992.

Svensson, Brigitta and Ola Wetterberg (eds), *Malmberget: Structural Change and Cultural Heritage Processes – A Case Study*, Stockholm: The Swedish National Heritage Board, 2009.

Terchek, Robert and Thomas Conte (eds), *Democratic Political Theory: A Reader*, Lanham: Rowman & Littlefield, 2001.

Tzu, Sun, *The Art of War* (trans. Thomas Cleary), Boston: Shambhala, 1988.

Williams, Raymond, *Keywords*, London: Penguin, 1976.

Viljoen, Andfe (ed.), *CPULS Continuous Productive Urban Landscapes*, Oxford: Architectural Press, 2005.

Von Clausewitz, Carl, *On War*, London: Penguin Books, 1988.

Index

Adorno, Theodor, 83, 128, 157, 215–17, 275, 278

aesthetic, 37, 161

Africa, 24, 210

Agamben, Giorgio, 10, 30–2, 43, 106, 107, 256, 263, 264

Akkach, Samer, 274

America (see United States of America)

Ames, Roger, 84, 149, 153, 154, 160, 161, 162, 255, 262, 269, 270

Amin, Samir, 255

Anaxagoras, 152, 153

animal rationale, 119

anthropocentrism/anthropocentricity, 1, 12, 15, 43, 45, 46, 51, 54, 59, 82, 117–9, 121, 123, 146, 147, 157, 159, 169, 170, 176, 185, 190, 199, 203, 211, 216, 221, 225, 226, 228, 232, 239, 243– 46, 248, 250, 253

anthropological, 157, 158

Arctic Circle, 67, 69

Arendt, Hannah, 30, 145, 147, 159, 268, 269

Aristotle, 49, 81, 84, 85, 86, 153, 197, 212, 274

artificial, naturalized 54, 60

Atomists, 152, 153

Asia, 210
    South East, 24, 102

Austin, John L., 155

Australia, 10, 49, 73, 272
    AusAID, 93
    Government, 262, 263
    White Paper on Defence, 91, 92

Australian Broadcasting Corporation, 74

autonomic technology/technocentrism, 146, 190, 199, 200, 202, 203, 244

Bangladesh, 26, 64

bare life, ix, x, 10, 29, 106, 199

Bataille, Georges, 43, 258, 271

Bateson, Gregory, 259
Baudrillard, Jean, 128, 217, 245, 281
Benhabib, Seyla, 257, 266, 268
belief, system of, 19
Benjamin, Walter, 128
de Benoist, Alain, 106, 256, 257, 263, 264
Bentham, Jeremy, 36, 278
Bentley, Arthur F., 155
Berlin, 78
  University, 117
bild, 192
bildung, 192–8, 200–2, 204, 273, 274, 279
  neu (see *neu bildung*)
biodiversity, 3
biocentrism, 45, 231
bio-diesel, 32
bio-fuels, 113
biological engineering, 55
biopolitics, 10, 12, 29, 30, 32, 43, 224, 235
bios, 29, 32
body politic, 29
border security, 26
bricolage, 90, 129, 165
Brogan, Walter, 262
Bunyan, John, 35

Calhoun, Craig, 269
capital, 78
capitalism, 15, 50, 52, 99, 161, 267
  corporate, 159
  culture of, 240
  liberal, 39, 40

capitalist
  order, 40
  system, 40
care, 206–8, 233, 236
  structure, 120, 207
Cassirer, Ernst, 265
Catholic Church, 212
change
  agents, 79
  climate (see climate change)
  community, 42, 46, 67, 175
  platforms, 42, 67
  redirective, 170
  techno-political, 58
China, 24, 52, 84
  ancient, 87
  cultural revolution, 87
Chinese culture (classical), 84, 85, 87, 154, 162, 163
  thought, 85
  tradition, 86
chorismos, 79, 83
CIA (Central Intelligence Agency), 10
City Move, 67, 68, 72
Clastres, Pierre, 159, 269
Clausewitz, Carl von, 135, 233, 279
Cleary, Thomas, 85
climate change, 12, 27, 74, 101, 123, 180, 185
climate/climatic, 110
  impacts, 111
  modelling, 22
civil society, 221
Cold War, 230
common good, 103, 130, 146, 214, 215

commonality in difference, 45, 46, 110, 146

Commonwealth, 35

communism
communalist, 37

community, 206, 210, 236

Confucianism (neo), 87

Confucius, 84

Constructivism, 99

consumer/consumerism 123
democracy, 8
desires, 122
sovereignty, 8, 102, 122, 130

consumption, 64, 65, 66, 82

Conte, Thomas, 257

Copenhagen, 72

Copenhagen Climate Change Congress, 26

Copenhagen Climate Change Summit, 102

cosmologies, 44

craft, 65, 92, 139, 140, 208, 235, 236
industries, 94
practice, 94
skills, 93

creative
communities, 103
industry, 92, 93, 94

Critchley, Simon, 271

Cromwell, Oliver, 35

crisis, xi, 12, 120, 123, 124, 250
of crisis, 3, 110, 123, 190

Crusades, 254

Cuba, 10, 107

cultural
capital, 70

production, 65, 252
studies, 122, 194, 266

culture 19, 21
commodity, 28
consumer, 51
of consumption, 240
industrial, 22
material, 82
of learning, 203
politics, 192
popular, 128
production, 90
postmodern, 243
Western, 80
of Sustainment, 192

cultus, 273

cyborg, 163, 202

Dahl, Robert, 155

Dallmayr Fred, 59, 247, 256, 259, 280

Darwin (city), 91

dasein, 117, 163

Davis, Mike, 255

Declaration of Independence (American), 36

Declaration of Rights of Man (French), 36

Deconstruction, 116, 165, 192

defuture(d)/defuturing, 4, 7, 11, 13, 14, 21–5, 27, 28, 32, 43, 63, 103, 107, 123, 124, 130, 136, 146, 147, 152, 166, 167, 170, 176, 185, 189, 191, 198, 199, 202, 209, 216, 218, 222, 227, 228, 239, 246

democracy/democratic, x, 5, 7–9, 12, 14, 15, 27, 33–5, 37, 39, 50, 52, 103,

131, 143, 148, 150, 157, 159, 161, 164, 165, 175, 202, 210–12, 219, 220, 247, 248
capitalist, 9, 38, 115
communicative, 38
deliberative, 38
government, social and liberal, 34
ideal (Greek), 37
interest-based, 38
liberal, 11, 35, 38, 40, 150, 157, 159, 218, 230
liberal parliamentary, 41
parliamentary, 52, 125, 218, 221
pluralism, 149
politics, 39, 40
power, 37
process, 34, 36, 88
radical(s), 38, 247
rationalism, 38
regimes, 10
representative, 102, 250
socialist/socialism, 34, 39, 40
societies, 10, 244
subsidiary, 38
theory, 46, 155
Western, 11, 126
Deleuze, Gilles, 276
Democritus, 152, 153
demos, 34
Derrida, Jacques, 116, 117, 119, 131, 132, 165, 250, 257, 265, 267, 271, 281
design vii, viii, x, 2, 3, 5–7, 11–13, 15, 19, 45, 47, 62, 73, 75–7, 103, 105, 110-12, 121, 151, 164, 166, 167, 170, 171, 173, 178, 181, 189, 192,

198, 203, 204, 206, 215, 216, 227, 234, 235, 237, 238
adaptive, 114
chronal, 138
education, 203
elimination, 134, 138
emotional, 82
green, 191
industrial, 81
ontological, 46, 54, 56, 59, 84, 86, 90, 111, 123, 134, 166, 170, 178, 180, 188–90, 193, 197, 203, 206, 208, 211, 242, 246
as politics, 12, 94, 101, 115, 116, 134, 141, 146, 186, 203, 207, 238, 246, 252
practice(s), viii, 28
radical, 267
redirective, 174
world, 11
Design Futures Program, 73
Design Futuring, viii, 11, 12, 14
desire(s)/desired, 25, 42
Dessauer, Friedrich, 259
Destruktion, 165
development, 19
Dewey, John, 40, 62, 240–2, 244, 280
Diamond, Larry, 257
Diggers, 35
Dili, 263
Dilnot, Clive, xi
dioxis, 79
Dubai, 24
Dutch East Indies, 91
Dwelling, 2, 7, 198
Dyer, Gwynne, 255, 268

English Revolution, 34, 35
ecology, 133, 162
  change, 27
  economic(s), 31
  exchange, 23
  of the image, 176, 190, 217
  and liberalism, 149
  of mind, 227
  production, 252
  semiotic, 138
  systems, 22
economy, 19, 21, 23, 65, 125, 166
  command, 113, 114
  of ecology, 162
  general, 203
  quality, 95, 208, 235
  restrictive, 230
  sign, 173
  of Sustainment, 66
Edgerton, Robert, 264
Elkins, Jenny, 43, 258
Elimination, 250
Empedocles, 152, 153
enframing (*Gestell*), 55, 59
England, 35
Enlightenment (the), xi, 4, 53, 61, 80,
    193, 212, 213, 216, 218, 220, 221,
    240, 245
  post-, 4, 80
  rationalism, 195
entertainment, 249, 250
  industry, 129
environmental
  commons, 215
  impacts, 23
  refugees, 26, 64, 102, 114, 180, 229

technologies, 102
environments
  artificial, 109
epistemological monism, 153
Esposito, John L., 258
essentialism, 160
ethanol, 32
ethics/ethical, 103, 119, 171, 206, 212,
    215, 232, 247
ethnic cleansing, 241
ethnocentrism, x, 125, 149, 150, 200,
    231, 245
Europe, 34, 35
Existentialism, 188, 189

Fairfax, Duncan, xi
Ferry, Luc, 267, 268
Freyer, Hans, 259
finite/finitude, 12, 16, 19, 151, 160, 185
First World War (*see* war),
Ford, Henry, 112
Foucault, Michel, 6, 30, 37, 99, 253,
    256
fossil fuel, 22, 23
free trade, 126
free world (*see* world)
freedom(s), 15, 38, 45, 46, 59, 107, 112,
    113, 121, 124, 144, 150, 151, 155,
    156, 157, 159, 209–15, 217–20, 222,
    223, 230, 233–5, 243, 250, 252
  human, 39
  sacrifice, 41
'friend and enemy' distinction, 118, 121,
    135, 164
Fry, Tony, 254, 257, 260–3, 265, 266,
    268, 272–4, 279

Fukuyama, Frances, 177, 230, 272, 279
fundamentalism, 9
Funnell, Antony, 260
futural, x, 42, 120, 121, 174, 205
future(s), x, 19, 22, 39, 239
  with a future, xi
futuring 9, 45, 77, 124, 204, 218, 235,
  236, 252

Gall & Medek, 73
Gadamer, Hans-Georg, 195–7, 201, 274
Gellivare, 67, 71
Geist, 196
genetic
  engineering, 244
  inheritance, 56
Germany/German, 117, 125, 192
  culture, 194
gestalt, 160
Ge-stell, 189
global
  financial crisis, 24
  population, 51, 102
  warming, 22, 185
globalization, x, 9, 24, 25, 33, 39, 44, 50,
  102, 149–51, 221, 228, 243
God, 44, 99, 104, 106, 172, 174, 195,
  214, 223, 225, 226, 233, 254
Gold Coast
  Archipelago, 74
  City Council, 73
  Two, 73, 74
Goethe, 157
Gottfried, Paul, 276
Gramsci, Antonio, 48, 258

Greek(s)
  ancient, 34, 52, 80, 84, 86, 153, 154,
    196, 238, 242, 249, 256, 261, 273
  system, 34
  tradition, 87
greenhouse
  gases, 24
  emissions, 22, 51, 107, 185
Griffith University, Queensland College
  of Art, 73, 93
Guantanamo Bay, 10, 30, 107

Haar, Michael, 275
Habermas, Jürgen, 257
habitus, 56, 120
Haekle, Ernst Heinrich, 133
Hall, David, 84, 149, 153, 154, 160, 161,
  162, 255, 262, 269, 270
Haraway, Donna, 202, 274
Hardt, Michael, 266
Hawkin, P., 255
Hegel, G.W.F., 43, 80, 121, 132, 133,
  177, 195–8, 213, 216, 221, 226, 230,
  231, 267, 270, 279
Heidegger, Martin, vii, 1, 2, 54, 55, 59,
  60, 85, 121, 128, 129, 153, 163, 213,
  216, 227, 245–8, 253, 258–62, 267,
  268, 269, 271, 275, 276, 280
Heraclitus, 84, 144, 268
Herder, Johann Gottfried, 195
Herf, Jeffery, 259, 280
Hickman, Larry H., 280
Hill, Christopher, 256
Hirst, Paul, 119, 265
historical materialism, 189

history, end of, 230
Hitler, Adolf, 117
Hobbes, Thomas, 35, 58, 61, 105, 126,
    173, 201, 219, 221–7, 229, 232–4,
    277–9
Hong Xiuguan, 87
Horkheimer, Max, 83, 128, 158, 217, 278
human (the), 99, 106, 109, 111, 112,
    120, 149, 154, 157, 158, 163, 192,
    202, 225, 227, 235, 238, 243
  centred(ness), 123, 189, 199
  form of, 200
  nature, 123, 222
  rights (*see* rights)
humanism, 59, 99, 116, 123, 158,
    199–201, 218, 225, 240–3, 245
  liberal, 201
  socialist, 165
  Western, 158
humanity, x, 16, 21, 29, 39, 52, 99, 101,
    107, 119, 198, 223, 237, 243
Humboldt, Wilhelm von, 194, 195
Hurricane Katrina, 24

impact population ratio, 51
imperialism, 9, 126
India, 24
Indonesia, 91
  Forces, 89
Industrial Revolution, 3, 28
Ingram, David, 275
inhuman (the), 158
inoperative community, 90
instrumental/instrumentalism, 54, 80,
    83, 147, 169, 176, 191, 199, 206
  reason, 127

Intergovernmental Panel on Climate
    Change (IPCC), 26, 254
International Red Cross, 26
Islamic culture, 108

Jacquard loom, 53
Jacquard, Joseph Marie, 258
James, William, 155
Jena, University, 133
Jefferson, Thomas, 35
joyance, 139
Jullien, François, 85, 86, 262, 269
Jünger, Ernst, 258
justice, 103, 171

Kant, Immanuel, 80, 195, 213, 214, 226,
    245, 276
Kaufmann, Walter, 267
Kenya, 107
kinesis, 85
King John of England, 34
Kinnunen, Nora, 260
kulture, 192, 273

Laclau, Ernesto, 164, 165, 257, 267, 271
Lapping, Brian, 264
Latin America, 24
Latour, Bruno, 29, 202, 223, 274
law, 106, 108, 109, 171, 173, 229, 246
  divine, 225
  (of) nature, 226
  rule of, 233
League of Nations, 173
Lefort, Claude, 6, 37, 253, 257
Leibniz, Gottfried Wilhelm, 53
Leipzig, 154

Leonard, Stephan, 269
Leroi-Gourhan, André, 258
Leucippus, 152, 153
Levellers, 35
Levi, Neil, 257
Levinas, Emmanuel, 145, 214–16, 275, 276
liberal, 5, 157, 226
  democracies, 169
  democratic popularism, 110
liberalism, 14, 15, 100, 143, 164, 203, 209, 214, 216, 218–20, 222, 223, 227, 228–30
  economic, 221
  political, 221
  technocratic, 126
LKAB, 68, 69, 71, 260
Locke, John, 35, 221, 226, 227, 245, 278
logocentrism, 162, 231
Lopes, Abby, xi
Lotze, Herman, 154, 269
Lovins A., 255
Lovins, H., 255
Löwith, Karl, 10
Luhmann, Niklas, 193, 194, 273
Luther, Martin, 35
Lyotard, Jean- François, 99, 155, 263

Macpherson, C.B., 9, 36, 130, 227, 254, 256, 257, 267, 277, 278
Magna Carta, 34
Malmberget, 67, 72
Malthusian, theory, 32
Mandela, Nelson, 214
Marcil-Lacoste, Louise, 150, 151, 269, 271

Marx, Karl, 36, 121, 131, 132, 161, 219, 224, 245
Marxism, 188, 189, 266
masses, the 46
Mau Mau, 107, 263, 264
McCarty, Thomas, 257
McClure, Kirstie, 155, 269
McCormick, John, 58, 127, 228, 258, 259, 266, 270, 271
McGowan, John, 269
McLuhan, Marshall, 217, 280
McNeill, William, 261
Medearis, John, 39, 257
media, the, 249, 250
Meier, Heinrich, 126, 223, 232, 260, 261, 265, 266, 277, 279
memory, 200, 204, 205, 236
Merleau-Ponty, Maurice, 45, 145, 209, 268, 275, 280
metrofitting, 63, 77, 111, 136, 137, 167
micro-finance, 95
Middle East, 102, 210
Mill, James, 36
Mill, John Stuart, 36
modern, the, 19
  university, 221
modernism, 162
modernity, x, 15, 127, 150, 162, 199, 221, 223, 231, 243
  neo-, 243
modernization, 28
modes of production, 189
monoculture(s), x
morality, 44
Mouffe, Chantel, 160, 164, 165, 267, 269, 270, 271

Müller, Jan-Werner, 257
Muslim, 9, 44
Mussolini, Benito, 48
mythologies, 44

Nancy, Jean-Luc, 212, 213, 216, 275, 276
nanotechnology, 244
national identity, 174
national interest, 37
national security 37, 38, 131, 229
  state, 11
National Socialist (Party)/Nazi(s), 2, 117, 242, 267, 272
nations, liberal democratic, 125
natura, 273, 278
nature, 15, 23, 29, 43, 57, 105, 132, 151, 194, 199, 201, 214, 224, 231, 234
  human, 29, 40
  laws of, 31
  second, 224
naturalized artificial, 146, 239
Needham, Joseph, 87, 264
Negri, Antonio, 266
Ndecha, Joseph, 264
non-Western,148
neo-conservative, 9
neu bildung, 14, 15, 175, 187, 192, 193, 198, 200–4, 206–8, 235, 246, 252
New Model Army, 35
New Orleans, 24
New York Times, 255
newly industrialized nations, 25, 28
Nietzsche, Friedrich, 1, 33, 59, 146, 158, 163, 171, 177, 213, 234, 239, 246, 248, 280

Norton, Lisa, xi
nomos, 105, 162, 173, 175, 199
  of the earth 179
nous, 4
nuclear weapons, 102

Obama, Barack, 130
Odom, William, 260
oikos, 162, 174
oiko-nomia, 162
Olivi, Petrus Johannia, 145
ontic, 148, 231
ontological, 29, 33, 44, 55, 86, 118, 119, 215
  design (*see* design)
  transformation, 234
ontologies, 22, 55, 120
ontology, 23, 24, 82, 19, 155, 211, 216
  fundamental, 198
  instrumentalized, 233
Oscusse, 91
Overman, 1

Pacific Island, 26
Palvers, Wolfgang, 203, 274
Patton, Paul, 256
'people', the, 35, 106, 125, 232
Peperzak, Adriaan, 270
Perolini, Petra, 260
phenomenology, 133, 187, 248
phrönesis, 79
phusis, 29, 52, 85, 105, 195, 196, 201, 224, 273, 278
Piccone, Paul, 276
platforming, 134
Plattner, Marc, 257

Plato, 153, 212, 223

pluralism/pluralist, 13, 39, 52, 99, 143, 144, 148 151–65, 194, 216, 220, 228, 247, 250, 267

plurality, 144, 145, 148, 151–3, 156, 165, 228, 238

polis, the, 34, 249

political (the), x, 3, 5, 6, 13, 115
  act, 105
  activists, 104
  agent, x
  commentary, 4
  culture, 164
  history, 124
  parties, 52
  philosophy, 4
  practice, 4, 11
  science, 4
  theory, 105
  things, 105
  thought, 104

politics, viii, x, 3, 5, 6, 8, 9, 10, 21, 22, 29, 43, 47, 62, 143, 149, 156, 167, 174, 200, 201, 203, 224, 227, 246
  of agricultural production, 32
  design, 79
  end of, 115
  environmental, 45
  finitudinal, 160
  of freedom, 228
  identity, 131
  last, 230
  liberal democratic, 232
  of nature, 223
  postmodern, 122

  of the redesign of politics, 227
  representational, 99, 125
  of Sustainment, 108, 166, 228
  televisual, 217, 249
  without danger, 127

popularism, 52, 127

Portuguese, 89

post-democratic /post-democracy, 166, 179

practice
  redirective (*see* redirective practice)

postmodern culture (*see* culture)

post-nation, 179

pragmatism, 23, 32, 40, 148, 151, 161

pre-Socratic, 81, 84

producer services, 65

productivism, 52, 53, 54

psychology, 44

Queensland Conservatorium of Music, 272

Ramos Horta, José, 91

Ranters, 35

Rawls, John, 221, 245, 277, 280

Readings, Bill, 194–6, 273, 274

reason, 53, 221, 229
  faith in, 31, 213

recoding, 134, 248

Red Army, 117

redirective practice, viii, 11, 42, 77, 78, 80, 103, 166, 167, 175, 179, 181, 189, 190, 208

redistributive justice, 27

refugees, environmental, 50

Reformation (the), 35, 220

relationality, 116, 132, 156
religion
  of technicity, 61
  Western secular, 44
representatives, elected, 36
resources, renewable, 45
retrofitting, 23, 63, 134, 136, 137
rights, 15, 34, 232
  of citizens, 221
  civil, 220
  human, 174, 220, 225, 227, 243
  intrinsic, 231
  natural, 225–7
riots, food, 32
ritual, 19
Rorty, Richard, 155
Rousseau, Jean-Jacques, 35
Russian Revolution, 181

sacred, the, 19
sacrifice, 22
St Augustine, 158
Sallis, John, 279
Sartre, Jean-Paul, 189, 272
Scalapino, Robert A., 262
Schelling, Friedrich, 213, 216, 275
Schmitt, Carl, 13, 14, 37–9, 41, 54,
  56–62, 88, 100, 105, 106, 108,
  115–23, 125–9, 131, 134, 136, 141,
  147, 159, 163, 172, 173, 209, 218,
  219, 221–3, 229, 232, 234, 241, 242,
  254, 257, 258–61, 263, 265–7, 270–2,
  276–80
Schoenichen, Walter, 267
Schumpeter, Joseph, 39–41, 156, 161
science, 43, 154, 227, 246

Self-Strengthening Movement, 87
serious entertainment, 122
settlement, 2, 237
Shakespeare, William, 158
slag, 71
social
  ecology, 64, 109, 156
  relations, 13
socialism, 39, 161
socialist
  states, 8
socialization, 56
Sombart, Werner, 259
Soteriological, 79
sovereign/sovereignty, x, 13, 14, 34, 100,
  105–10, 112, 169, 171–4, 178, 192,
  217, 223
species being, 145
Spengler, Oswald, 259
Spinoza, Benedict de, 212, 213, 215
Stambaugh, Joan, 254
standing reserve, 54, 227
state of exception (the), 10, 30, 37, 38,
  106, 123, 171, 210, 229
state of emergency, 127
Stiegler, Bernard, 202, 258, 274
Stockholm, 68
strategic military planners, 26
Strauss, Leo, 61, 218, 261, 266
streamlining, 112
Strong, Tracy, 218, 276
subjects
  Islamic, 44
Sumerian civilization, 105
Sun Tzu, 85, 262
superman, 1, 2, 171

sustainability, 51, 110, 176, 202
sustain-able, x, 93
sustainable development, 51, 239
Sustainment, viii, ix, x, xi, 4, 11, 13–15,
    23, 25, 27, 32, 39, 41, 42, 45, 46,
    63, 64–6, 76–82, 88–90, 100, 104,
    105, 107–10, 112–19, 121, 123,
    124, 127, 131, 133, 134, 137, 140,
    141, 143–6, 157–64, 167, 169, 170,
    173–9, 186, 192, 193, 198, 201,
    202–9, 218, 220, 227, 229–31, 239,
    240, 243, 244–8, 252
  culture of, 52, 61, 95
  dialectic of, 118, 120
  dictatorship of, 211
  economy of, 52
  World Council of (proposed), 178
Sweden, 67, 68
Swedish Industrial Design Foundation,
    72

Taiping Rebellion, 87
Taoist, 88
  philosophy (Chinese), 89
tais, 92
techne, 4
technocentrism, 169
techno-culture, 56, 59
techno-futures, 104
technology, 12, 19, 22, 24, 30, 52–60,
    63, 66, 99, 115, 120, 125, 127, 129,
    146, 163, 176, 190, 194, 199, 200,
    203, 206, 222, 227–9, 233, 242–4,
    247, 248
  green, 42, 176
  salvation, 127

sustainable, 32, 89, 233
technosphere, 12, 55
techno-structure, 59
televisual, 129, 217, 224, 244
telos, 146, 196
Terchek, Robert, 257
'things', 28
  ethical, 104
  political, 88, 104
Third Reich, 117
time, 14, 22, 31, 116, 122, 139, 174,
    198
  the being of, 21
  as change, 49
  make/making, 39, 170
Timor-Leste (East Timor), 89, 91, 92,
    262
Timor Sea, 92
Tokyo, 24
tonus, 140
tradition, 19
transcendence, 160

Ulmen, G. L., 278
underdevelopment, 50
undevelopment, 50
unfreedom(s), 15, 157, 210, 215, 216,
    233, 234
United Nations (UN), 50, 91, 108, 123,
    173, 179
  Development Program (UNDP), 24,
    255
  UNHCR, 180, 255
United States of America (US/USA), 25,
    150, 161–3, 219, 277
  Patriot Act (2001), 10

unsettlement, 2, 12, 13, 22, 43, 63, 101, 112, 127, 198, 201, 209, 216, 237
unsustainable (the)/unsustainabilty, viii, x, 7, 13, 16, 19, 50, 61, 109, 120, 123, 169
structural, 7, 12, 16, 21, 23, 25, 29, 33, 38, 39, 42, 63, 88–90, 103, 110, 111, 113, 120, 121, 124, 134, 137, 157, 170, 173, 176–8, 185, 189–91, 193, 198, 200, 202, 210, 211, 218, 219, 226, 228, 230, 238, 239, 246, 250
urbanization, 7
USSR, 114
utilitarianism, 36
utopia/utopian(ism), 12, 35, 37, 103, 121, 206, 217

Victoria, State of, 177
violence, 9, 15, 22, 89, 147, 220, 225, 229, 232
colonial, 44
ethnocidal, 157

Walker, Nicholas, 261
war, 19, 32, 58, 109, 135, 136, 217, 222, 233
art of, 86
First World War, 155
by technology, 234
on terror, 10, 38, 126
Warnek, Peter, 262
Weber, Max, 125, 126, 212
Weile, Carl, 259
West, the, 27, 28, 50, 52, 83, 85, 126, 128, 144, 148, 210, 225, 256

Western, 99, 108
metaphysics, 81, 83
mind, 154
rationalism, 89
society, 83
thought, 153
traditon, 80
will to power, 146
Williams, Raymond, 273
Willis, Anne-Marie, xi, 263
Wolin, Sheldon, 266
world, ix, x, 11, 22, 24, 38, 42, 61, 239
democratic, 8
denaturalized, 119
design (see design),
developing, 30
of entertainment, 128
free, 50, 219
human-centred, 189
making, 52
natural, 57
new, 14
order, 10, 107, 108
population, 32
rational, 120
of things, 116
trade, 32
within the world, 224
World Bank, 26
worlding, 206

Yu, George T., 262

zoe, 29